IT Disaster Recovery Planning

Planning

FOR

DUMMIES®

IT Disaster Recovery Planning
FOR
DUMMIES®

by Peter Gregory, CISA, CISSP

Foreword by Philip Jan Rothstein, FBCI

Wiley Publishing, Inc.

IT Disaster Recovery Planning For Dummies®

Published by
Wiley Publishing, Inc.
111 River Street
Hoboken, NJ 07030-5774

www.wiley.com

For general information on our other products and services, please contact our Customer Care Department within the U.S. at 800-762-2974, outside the U.S. at 317-572-3993, or fax 317-572-4002.

For technical support, please visit www.wiley.com/techsupport.

Wiley also publishes its books in a variety of electronic formats. Some content that appears in print may not be available in electronic books.

Library of Congress Control Number: 2006923952

ISBN: 978-0-470-03973-1

Manufactured in the United States of America

10 9 8 7 6 5 4 3 2 1

WILEY

About the Author

Peter H. Gregory, CISA, CISSP, is the author of fifteen books on security and technology, including *Solaris Security* (Prentice Hall), *Computer Viruses For Dummies* (Wiley), *Blocking Spam and Spyware For Dummies* (Wiley), and *Securing the Vista Environment* (O'Reilly).

Peter is a security strategist at a publicly-traded financial management software company located in Redmond, Washington. Prior to taking this position, he held tactical and strategic security positions in large wireless telecommunications organizations. He has also held development and operations positions in casino management systems, banking, government, non-profit organizations, and academia since the late 1970s.

He's on the board of advisors for the NSA-certified Certificate program in Information Assurance & Cybersecurity at the University of Washington, and he's a member of the board of directors of the Evergreen State Chapter of InfraGard.

You can find Peter's Web site and blog at www.isecbooks.com, and you can reach him at petergregory@yahoo.com.

Dedication

This book is dedicated to Rebekah Gregory, Iris Finsilver, Jacqueline McMahon, and Lisa Galoia, my personal disaster recovery team, and also to professionals everywhere who are trying to do the right thing to protect their organizations' assets.

Author's Acknowledgments

I would like to thank Greg Croy, Executive Editor at Wiley, for his leadership, perseverance, and patience throughout this project. Thank you to Christopher Morris, Senior Project Editor at Wiley, for your help. Also, thanks to Philip Rothstein for technical review and expert guidance — and for writing the Forward to this book at the last minute. And thank you, Laura Miller, for your thoughtful and effective copy editing.

And finally, heartfelt thanks go to Liz Suto, wherever you are, for getting me into this business over twelve years ago when you asked me to do a tech review on your book, *Informix Online Performance Tuning* (Prentice Hall).

Publisher's Acknowledgments

We're proud of this book; please send us your comments through our online registration form located at www.dummies.com/register.

Some of the people who helped bring this book to market include the following:

Acquisitions, Editorial, and Media Development

Sr. Project Editor: Christopher Morris

Acquisitions Editor: Gregory Croy

Copy Editor: Laura Miller

Technical Editor: Philip Jan Rothstein

Editorial Manager: Kevin Kirschner

Media Development and Quality Assurance: Angela Denny, Kate Jenkins, Steven Kudirka, Kit Malone

Media Development Coordinator: Jenny Swisher

Media Project Supervisor: Laura Moss-Hollister

Editorial Assistant: Amanda Foxworth

Sr. Editorial Assistant: Cherie Case

Cartoons: Rich Tennant (www.the5thwave.com)

Composition Services

Project Coordinator: Patrick Redmond

Layout and Graphics: Stacie Brooks, Jonelle Burns, Reuben W. Davis, Melissa K. Jester, Stephanie D. Jumper, Alissa Walker, Christine Williams

Proofreader: Linda Morris

Indexer: Rebecca Salerno

Anniversary Logo Design: Richard Pacifico

Publishing and Editorial for Technology Dummies

    Richard Swadley, Vice President and Executive Group Publisher

    Andy Cummings, Vice President and Publisher

Mary Bednarek, Executive Acquisitions Director

    Mary C. Corder, Editorial Director

Publishing for Consumer Dummies

    Diane Graves Steele, Vice President and Publisher

    Joyce Pepple, Acquisitions Director

Composition Services

    Gerry Fahey, Vice President of Production Services

    Debbie Stailey, Director of Composition Services

Contents at a Glance

Table of Contents

Part II: Building Technology Recovery Plans *75*

Foreword

*I*n the late 1960s, I was first exposed to what would later become known as disaster recovery. I was responsible for the systems software environment for a major university computer center at the time. It was at the height of the Vietnam War protests, and one of those protests spilled over to the building housing the computer room. A number of the protesters were running through the building and randomly damaging whatever was in their path. When they got to the computer room, they found a locked, heavy steel door and moved on.

It suddenly dawned on me that we had no clue — let alone plan — to deal with damage or destruction, should the protesters have gained entry to the computer room. As I thought about it and discussed this with others on the computer operations team, I realized there were many other threats and vulnerabilities that had never been discussed, let alone addressed.

Fast forward forty years. The single-mainframe data center has given way to clusters of dozens, if not hundreds, of servers and decentralized data centers; networking is often more critical than processors; dozens of computer room operators have been replaced by lights-out data centers; a week-long recovery from a data center disruption is now more likely to be an almost instantaneous failover to a backup; and disaster recovery has become a fact of life.

The bad news is that too many data center managers still have not been able to effectively address disaster recovery, whether because of lack of management commitment or lack of knowledge or lack of resources. By effectively, I mean

- A comprehensive disaster recovery plan, based on objective assessment of threats, vulnerabilities and exposure to loss

- Integration with comprehensive enterprise business continuity programs so that IT disaster recovery is consistent with overall business needs and priorities

- A meaningful exercise program, combined with training and plan maintenance, to ensure that the plan is current, realistic, and likely to work when called upon

The good news is that with Peter Gregory's new book, even a team without prior experience in disaster recovery planning can address these issues — " . . . those frustrated and hard-working souls who know they're not dumb, but find that the technical complexities of computers and the myriad of personal and business issues — and all the accompanying horror stories — make them feel helpless," as www.dummies.com points out.

Disaster recovery is not simply about Katrinas nor earthquakes nor 9/11 catastrophes. Sometimes, the focus on these monumental events could intimidate even the most committed IT manager from tackling disaster recovery planning. Disaster recovery is really about the ability to maintain business as usual — or as close to "as usual" as is feasible and justifiable — whatever gets thrown at IT. Peter's book helps to establish this perspective and provides a non-nonsense yet manageable foundation. I actually found, despite my long involvement with business continuity and disaster recovery, that he has identified many issues, techniques, and tips which I found quite useful.

While I confess I enjoyed *Italian Wines For Dummies* more, Peter Gregory's new book succeeds in taking the intimidation factor out of IT disaster recovery and offers a common-sense, practical, yet comprehensive process for analyzing, developing, implementing, exercising, and maintaining a successful IT disaster recovery program — even if he has, regrettably, failed miserably to enlighten me about Super-Tuscan wines.

*Philip Jan Rothstein, FBCI, is President of Rothstein Associates Inc. (*www. rothstein.com*, Brookfield, Connecticut USA), a management consultancy focused on business continuity and disaster recovery since 1984. He has edited or written close to 100 books and more than 200 articles, and is publisher of* The Rothstein Catalog on Disaster Recovery.

Introduction

● ●

Disasters of many kinds strike organizations around the world on an almost daily basis. But most of these disasters never make the news headlines because they occur at the local level. You probably hear about disastrous events that occur in or near your community — fires, floods, landslides, civil unrest, and so on — that affect local businesses, sometimes in devastating ways. Larger disasters affect wide areas and result in widespread damage, evacuations, and loss of life, and can make you feel numb at times because of the sheer scale of their effects.

This book is about the survival of business IT systems in the face of these disasters through preparation and response. You're largely powerless to stop the disasters themselves, and even if you can get out of their way, you can rarely escape their effects altogether. Disasters, by their very nature, disrupt *everything* within their reach.

Your organization can plan for these disasters and take steps to assure your critical IT systems survive. This book shows you how to prepare.

About This Book

IT Disaster Recovery Planning For Dummies contains a common and time-proven methodology that can help you prepare your organization for disaster.

My goals are simple — to help you plan for and prepare your systems, processes, and people for an organized response to a disaster when it strikes. You can make your systems more resilient, meaning you'll need less effort to recover them after a disaster. By using this book as a guide, you can journey through the steps of a disaster recovery (DR) project, as thousands of organizations have done before you.

This book progresses in roughly the same sequence that you must follow if your organization hasn't developed a disaster recovery plan before or if you're about to do a major refresh of outdated or inadequate plans.

How This Book Is Organized

This book is organized into four parts that you can use to quickly find the information you need.

Part I: Getting Started with Disaster Recovery

In Part I, I describe the nature of disasters and their effects on businesses. In Chapter 1, I take you on an end-to-end tour of the entire disaster recovery planning process.

I start Chapter 2 with a discussion of the various ways that a disaster can affect an organization and the role of prevention. I also include how to begin planning your disaster recovery project and emergency operations planning. Then, I show how you can quickly develop an interim disaster recovery plan that can provide some basic protection from a disaster if one occurs before you finish your full disaster recovery plan.

In Chapter 3, I take you on a deep dive into the vital first phase of a DR project — creating the Business Impact Analysis, during which you discover which business processes require the most effort in terms of prevention and the development of recovery procedures.

Part II: Building Technology Recovery Plans

Part II contains the core components of the disaster recovery plan. Chapter 4 describes how you determine which systems and underlying infrastructure support critical business processes that you identify in the Business Impact Analysis. Chapter 5 through Chapter 8 go through the work of preventing disaster and recovering from disaster in distinct groups — end users, facilities, systems and networks, and data. Chapter 9 discusses details about the actual disaster recovery plan documents — what those documents should contain and how to manage their development.

Part III: Managing Recovery Plans

Part III focuses on what happens after you write your disaster recovery plans. Chapter 10 discusses DR plan testing and the five types of tests organizations often perform. Chapter 11 describes what activities you need to do to ensure that your DR plans stay current. Disaster prevention is the topic of Chapter 12. If you can prevent disasters, your organization is better off. Chapter 13 discusses many disaster scenarios and what each one brings to a disaster recovery plan.

Part IV: The Part of Tens

The much loved and revered Part of Tens contains four chapters that are more than mere lists. These chapters contain references to external sources of information, more reasons to develop business recovery plans, and the benefits your organization can gain from having a well-developed recovery plan.

What This Book Is — and What It Isn't

Every business needs to complete disaster recovery (DR) planning and business continuity (BC) planning.

The terms *DR planning* and *BC planning* are often confused with each other, and many people use them interchangeably. And ultimately, they're complementary activities that you have to do before a disaster occurs (in terms of planning), and during and after a disaster (in terms of response and business resumption).

IT Disaster Recovery Planning For Dummies focuses on DR planning as it relates to IT systems and IT users. In this book, I discuss the necessary steps to develop response, assessment, and recovery plans to get IT systems and IT users back online after a disaster.

This book doesn't cover business continuity planning, which focuses on generic business process resumption, as well as continuity and communications with customers and shareholders.

Assumptions about Disasters

When you think about disasters, you may think about horrific natural events, rescue helicopters, hospital ships, airlifts, the International Red Cross or World Vision, looting and mayhem, large numbers of human casualties, and up-to-the-minute coverage from CNN. You may also think of wars, terrorist attacks, or nuclear power plant explosions, and the fallout (no pun intended) that ensues. Yes, these events certainly qualify as disasters, and this book discusses the preparations that businesses can and should take to survive them.

But you also have to think about the less sensational disasters that play out almost every day in businesses everywhere — not only fires, floods, strikes, explosions, and many other types of accidents, but also security incidents, vandalism, and sabotage — not to mention IT system hardware and software failures, data corruption, and errors. All of these problems can become disastrous events that can threaten a business's survival.

Icons Used in This Book

Throughout this book, you may notice little icons in the left margin that act as road signs to help you quickly pull out the information that's most important to you. Here's what they look like and what they represent.

Information tagged with a Remember icon identifies general information and core concepts that you may already know but should certainly understand and review.

Tip icons include short suggestions and tidbits of useful information.

Look for Warning icons to identify potential pitfalls, including easily confused or difficult-to-understand terms and concepts.

Technical Stuff icons highlight technical details that you can skip unless you want to bring out the tech geek in you.

Where to Go from Here

If you want to understand the big picture about disaster recovery planning, go straight to Chapter 1. If your organization has no plan of any kind, Chapter 2 can help you get something started right away that you can have in place next week. (No kidding!) If you want to dive straight into a full-blown DR project, begin at Chapter 3.

If your organization already has a disaster recovery plan, you can turn to Chapters 11, 12, and 13, in which I discuss the activities that you need to perform on an ongoing basis.

You can also just open the book to any chapter you want and dive right into the art and science of protecting the technology that supports your organization from disasters.

Write to Us!

Have a question? Comment? Complaint? Please let me know. Write to me at petergregory@yahoo.com or phg@isecbooks.com.

You can also find me online at www.isecbooks.com.

I try to answer every question personally.

For information on other *For Dummies* books, please visit www.dummies.com.

Part I

Getting Started with Disaster Recovery

In this part . . .

This part introduces the technical side of disaster recovery (DR) planning. Chapter 1 provides an overview of the entire DR process.

Chapter 2 is for organizations that have no disaster recovery plan at all. It shows you how you can make a quick start with an interim plan that provides some protection against disaster while you develop a more formal plan.

Chapter 3 covers the Business Impact Analysis (BIA) — the vital first part of the formal, long-term development of a disaster recovery plan. You use the BIA to identify the most critical business processes — those that need disaster recovery plans the most!

Chapter 1

Understanding Disaster Recovery

Disaster recovery (DR) planning is concerned with preparation for and response when disaster hits. The objective of DR planning is the survival of an organization. Because DR planning is such a wide topic, this book focuses only on the IT systems and users who support critical business processes. Getting this topic alone to fit into a 400-page book is quite a challenge.

In this chapter, I describe why you need disaster recovery planning and what benefits you can gain from going through this planning. You may be pleasantly surprised to find out that the benefits go far beyond just planning for disaster.

I also take you through the entire disaster recovery planning process — from analysis, to plan development and testing, to periodic plan revisions based on business events. If you've never done any work in disaster recovery planning before, this chapter's a good place to start — you can get the entire story in 20 pages. Then, you can branch out and go to the specific topics of interest to you elsewhere in this book.

Disaster Recovery Needs and Benefits

Stuff happens. Bad stuff.

Disasters of every sort happen, and you may find getting out of their way and escaping their consequences very difficult. If you're lucky enough to avoid the direct impact of a disaster, dodging its secondary effects is harder still.

Here are some of the disasters that can assail an organization:

- Fires
- Floods
- Tornadoes
- Hurricanes
- Wind and ice storms
- Severe storms
- Wildfires
- Landslides
- Avalanches
- Tsunamis
- Earthquakes
- Volcanoes

- Security incidents
- Equipment failures
- Power failures
- Utility failures
- Arson
- Pandemics
- Sabotage
- Strikes and work stoppages
- Shortages
- Civil disturbances
- Terrorism
- War

Each of the scenarios in the preceding list has unique primary and secondary effects that you need to take into consideration when developing a disaster recovery plan.

The effects of disasters

The events that I list in the preceding section have the potential to inflict damage to buildings, equipment, and IT systems. They affect people, as well — killing, injuring, and displacing them, not to mention preventing them from reporting to work. Disasters can have the following effects on organizations:

- **Direct damage:** Many of these events can directly damage buildings, equipment, and IT systems, rendering buildings uninhabitable and systems unusable.

- **Inaccessibility:** Often, an event damages a building to such an extent that it's unsafe to enter. Civil authorities may prohibit personnel from entering a building, even to retrieve articles or equipment.

- **Utility outage:** Even in incidents that cause no direct damage, electric power, water, and natural gas are often interrupted to wide areas for hours or days. Without public utilities, buildings are often uninhabitable and systems unable to function.

- **Transportation disruption:** Widespread incidents often have a profound effect on regional transportation, including major highways, roads, bridges, railroads, and airports. Disruptions in transportation systems can prevent workers from reporting to work (or going home), prevent the receipt of supplies, and stop the shipment of products.

✔ **Communication disruption:** Most organizations depend on voice and data communications for daily operational needs. Disasters often cause widespread outages in communications, either because of direct damage to infrastructure or sudden spikes in usage related to the disaster. In many organizations, taking away communications — especially data communications — is as devastating as shutting down their IT systems.

✔ **Evacuations:** Many types of disasters pose a direct threat to people, resulting in mandatory evacuations from certain areas or entire regions.

✔ **Worker absenteeism:** When a disaster occurs, workers often can't or won't report to work for many reasons. Workers with families often need to care for those families if the disaster affects them. Only after they take care of their families do workers consider reporting to work. Also, transportation and utility outages may prevent them from traveling to work. Workers may also not know whether the organization expects them to report to work if the disaster damages or closes the work premises.

These effects can devastate businesses by causing them to cease operations for hours, days, or longer. In most cases, businesses simply can't survive after experiencing such an outage. Businesses supply goods and services to customers who, for the most part, just want those goods and services; if the customers can't obtain those goods or services from one business, they often simply go to another that can provide them. Many businesses don't recover from such an exodus of customers.

Minor disasters occur more frequently

Don't make the mistake of justifying your lack of a DR plan by thinking, "Hurricanes rarely visit my neck of the woods," or "Earthquakes occur only every one hundred years," or "No country has ever invaded our country," or "Mt. Rainier hasn't erupted in recorded history." All of these statements may be true. However, disasters on smaller scales happen far more frequently, often hundreds of times more frequently, than the big ones.

Smaller disasters — such as building fires, burst pipes that flood office space, server crashes that result in corrupted data, extended power outages, severe winter storms, and so on — occur with much greater regularity than big disasters. Any of these small events can potentially interrupt critical business processes for days. In time-critical, service-oriented businesses, this interruption can be a fatal blow. *Contingency Planning and Management Magazine* indicated that 40 percent of companies that shut down for three days or more failed within 36 months. An unplanned outage may be the beginning of the end for an organization — everything starts to go downhill from that point forward. That sobering thought should instill fear in you. You might even put that chilling thought on a sticky-note and attach it to your monitor as a reminder.

Recovery isn't accidental

From a DR perspective, the world is divided into two types of businesses — those that have DR plans and those that don't. If a disaster strikes businesses in each category, which ones will survive?

When disaster strikes, businesses without DR plans have an extremely difficult road ahead. If the business has any highly time-sensitive critical business processes, that business is almost certain to fail. If a disaster hits a business without a DR plan, that business has very little chance of recovery. And it's certainly too late to begin planning.

Businesses that *do* have DR plans may still have a difficult time when a disaster strikes. You may have to put in considerable effort to recover time-sensitive critical business functions. But if you have DR plan, you have a fighting chance at survival.

Recovery required by regulation

Developing disaster recovery plans used to be simply a good idea. These plans are still a good idea, but they're also beginning to appear in standards and regulations, including

- ✔ **PCI DSS (Payment Card Industry Data Security Standard):** Although not really government legislation, it's required for virtually every merchant and financial services firm. PCI is a great example of what I call *private legislation* — laws made by corporations instead of governments. All the major banks and credit card companies impose PCI.

- ✔ **ISO27001:** This international standard for security management is gaining considerable recognition. Many larger organizations require their IT service providers to be ISO27001 compliant.

- ✔ **BS25999:** The emerging international standard for business continuity management.

- ✔ **NFPA 1620:** The National Fire Protection Association standard for pre-incident planning. It's a recommended practice that addresses the protection, construction, and operational features of specific occupancies to develop pre-incident plans that responders can use to manage fires and other emergencies by using available resources.

✔ **HIPAA Security Rule:** This U.S. law requires the protection of patient medical records and a disaster recovery plan for those records.

Over time, more data security laws are certain to include disaster recovery planning.

The benefits of disaster recovery planning

Besides the obvious readiness to survive a disaster, organizations can enjoy several other benefits from DR planning:

✔ **Improved business processes:** Because business processes undergo such analysis and scrutiny, analysts almost can't help but find areas for improvement.

✔ **Improved technology:** Often, you need to improve IT systems to support recovery objectives that you develop in the disaster recovery plan. The attention you pay to recoverability also often leads to making your IT systems more consistent with each other and, hence, more easily and predictably managed.

✔ **Fewer disruptions:** As a result of improved technology, IT systems tend to be more stable than in the past. Also, when you make changes to system architecture to meet recovery objectives, events that used to cause outages don't do so anymore.

✔ **Higher quality services:** Because of improved processes and technologies, you improve services, both internally and to customers and supply-chain partners.

✔ **Competitive advantages:** Having a good DR plan gives a company bragging rights that may outshine competitors. Price isn't necessarily the only point on which companies compete for business. A DR plan allows a company to also claim higher availability and reliability of services.

A business often doesn't expect these benefits, unless it knows to anticipate them through its development of disaster recovery plans.

Beginning a Disaster Recovery Plan

Does your organization have a disaster recovery plan today? If not, how many critical, time-sensitive business processes does your organization have?

If your organization has no DR plan at all, you might be thinking that even if you start now, you can't finish your DR plan for one or two years, leaving your business exposed. Although that may be true, you can start with a lightweight interim plan that provides some DR value to the organization while you complete your full-feature DR plan.

Starting with an interim plan

You can develop an interim DR plan, which you design as a stopgap plan, rather quickly. It leverages current capabilities and doesn't address any technology changes that you may need over the long haul.

An interim plan is an emergency response plan that answers the question, "If a disaster occurs tomorrow, what steps can we follow to recover our systems?"

Although a full DR plan takes many months or even years to complete, developing an interim DR plan takes just two to four days from start to finish. The procedure for developing an interim DR plan is simple: Take two or three of the most seasoned subject matter experts and lock them in a room for a single day. Usually, these experts are line managers or middle managers who are highly familiar with both the critical business processes and the supporting IT systems. Using existing capabilities, the team develops the interim DR plan by following these procedures:

- ✔ **Build the emergency response team.** Identify key subject matter experts who can build the environment from the ground up if the business has such a need.

- ✔ **Procedure for declaring a disaster.** A simple procedure that the emergency response team can use to decide if events warrant declaring a disaster.

- ✔ **Invoke the DR plan.** The procedure for getting the disaster response effort under way.

- ✔ **Communicate during a disaster.** Whom the disaster response team needs to communicate with and what to say. This list of personnel might include other employees, customers, and the news media.

- ✔ **Identify basic recovery plans.** Roughed-in procedures that can get critical systems running again.

- ✔ **Develop processing alternatives.** Ideas on how and where to get critical systems going, in case the building in which you now house them becomes unavailable.

- ✔ **Enact preventive measures.** Steps the organization can take quickly, in advance, to make recovery easier, as well as measures to prevent a disaster in the first place.

- ✔ **Document the interim DR plan.** Write down all the procedures, contact lists, and other vital information that the team develops during the planning process.

- ✔ **Train the emergency response team members.** Train the emergency response team members that the team chooses.

The two or three subject matter experts/managers should develop all the points in the preceding list in one day, and then one of those people should spend the next day typing it up. The other people review the plan to make sure it's correct, and then the experts take half a day to train the emergency response team.

Don't let the organization rely on this lightweight plan as *the* DR plan. It's a poor substitute for a full DR plan, but it can provide some disaster response capability in the short term. The interim DR plan isn't a full DR plan, and it doesn't deliver the value or confidence of a real plan. Have the experts who create the interim DR plan review that plan every three or four months until you complete the full DR plan. Then, you can put the interim plan in a display case in the lobby so passers-by can see it and think, "Gee, that's the first DR plan the company had . . ."

Beginning the full DR project

As soon as possible after you develop the interim DR plan, you need to get the *real* DR project started. The time you need to develop a full DR plan varies considerably, based on the size of your organization, the number of critical business functions, and the level of commitment your business is willing to make.

I estimate that developing a DR project takes three months for the very smallest organization (less than 100 employees and only one or two critical applications) and two years for a large organization (thousands of employees and several critical applications). But you have many other variables besides company size to consider. I don't have a formula to give you because I don't think one exists. My advice: Don't get hung up on timeframes — at least, not yet.

You need to take care of a number of steps before you can begin a DR project, as I discuss in the following sections.

Gaining executive support

DR projects are disruptive. They require the best and brightest minds in the business, taking those minds away from other projects. From a strictly financial perspective, disaster recovery planning doesn't provide profitability, nor should you expect the organization to become any more efficient or effective (although both can happen).

You may find selling the idea of a DR project to management difficult. A DR project doesn't have a ROI (return on investment), any more than data security does. Both disaster recovery planning and security deal with preparing for and avoiding events that you hope never happen (and if you do your job correctly, the fact that the events don't happen *is* your return on investment!). Still, you may need to convince management that DR planning is a worthwhile investment for any (or all) of the following reasons:

- **Disaster preparation and survival:** The most obvious benefit of a completed DR plan is the organization's survival from a disaster — survival that comes as a result of planning and preparation.

✔ **Disaster avoidance:** Disaster recovery planning often leads to the improvement of processes and IT systems that makes those processes and systems more resilient. Events that would result in a severe business interruption before you had the DR plan in place become, in many cases, just a minor event after you enact the plan. Table 1-1 includes many examples of events and their impact on organizations with and without DR plans.

✔ **Due diligence and due care:** Few organizations have never experienced an accident or event that resulted in the loss of data. Neglecting the need for disaster recovery planning can be as serious an offense as neglecting to properly secure information. DR planning protects data against loss. If your organization fails to exercise this due care, it could face civil or criminal lawsuits if a preventable disaster destroys important information.

Table 1-1	Examples of Events without and with a DR Plan	
Event	*Without a DR Plan*	*With a DR Plan*
Server crash and data corruption	Several days to rebuild data from backup media	Recovery from backup server or disc-based backup media
Hurricane, volcano, or tsunami	Several days' outage	Transfer to servers in alternate processing center
Earthquake	Damaged servers, outage of more than a week	Little to no outage because of preventive measures and backup power
Fire	Servers damaged from smoke or extinguishment materials; several days to rebuild data from backup media	Early suppression of fire, resulting in minimal damage and downtime
Severe weather, resulting in extended power outages	Insufficient backup power capability, resulting in several days' downtime	Sufficient backup power or transfer to servers in alternate processing center
Sabotage	Several days' outage to repair corrupted data	Recovery from recent backup media
Wildfire or flood	Evacuation of personnel; servers shut down due to lack of on-site management	Transfer to servers in alternate processing center

Understanding the frequency of disaster-related events

Getting an accurate idea of how frequently certain disaster-related events can occur may be difficult. Some events, such as volcanoes and tsunamis, happen so rarely that you may find quantifying the probability, not to mention estimating the impact, next to impossible. You can statistically predict other events, such as floods, a little more easily (primarily because they occur somewhat more frequently and predictably), but even then these events vary in intensity and effect.

If your organization has any sort of insurance policy that covers disasters, the insurance company might have some useful information about coverage for disasters. Also, insurance companies may offer a premium discount for organizations that have a disaster recovery plan in place, so you should ask your provider whether it offers such a discount.

Civil disaster preparedness authorities in your area may have some helpful information about the frequency and effect of disasters that occur with any regularity in your region. Where I live, many rivers flood in the fall and winter; earthquakes occur fairly regularly; and Mt. Rainier, an active volcano, sits a scant 20 miles away from my residence. Perhaps your location is blessed with hurricanes, tornadoes, or ice storms; regardless, local authorities should have some clues as to the frequency and severity of natural disasters in your area and how businesses can prepare for them.

Completing important first steps in a DR project

After you gain executive support, you probably just want to get started on your DR plan. But you need to take some important first steps before you launch your DR project:

- **Create a project charter.** A *charter* is a formal document that defines an important project. A typical project charter includes these sections:
  - Project definition
  - Names of executive sponsors
  - Project objectives
  - Project scope
  - Key milestones
  - Key responsibilities
  - Sources of funding
  - Signatures

  Chapter 16 contains a more detailed description of a DR project charter.

- **Select a project manager.** An individual with project management experience and skills — someone who can develop and track the plan, work with project team members, create status reports, run project meetings, and (most importantly) keep people on task, on time, and within budget.

✔ **Create a project plan.** A highly detailed description of all of the steps necessary to complete the DR project — the required sequence of steps, who'll perform those steps, which steps are dependent on which other steps, and what costs (if any) are associated with each step.

✔ **Form a steering committee.** The executives or senior managers who are sponsoring and supporting the project should select members for a formal steering committee. The DR steering committee has executive supervision over the DR project team. While you develop the DR project, the DR steering committee may need to meet as often as one or two times each month, but after you complete the DR project, they probably need to meet only two to four times each year.

After you put these initial pieces in place, you can launch the formal DR project, which I talk about in the following section.

Managing the DR Project

Begin your DR project with a kickoff meeting that can last from one and a half to three hours. The entire DR project team, the members of the DR steering committee, all executive sponsors, and any other involved parties should attend. The steering committee should state their support for the DR project.

After the initial kickoff meeting, the DR project team should probably meet every week to discuss progress, issues, and any adjustments you need to make to the project plan. The project manager should publish a short status report every week that you can review in the meeting. You can send the status report to the steering committee members to keep them up to date on how the project is progressing.

You need to identify and manage many more details to manage a project that spans many departments, which a DR project usually does. If you need more details on project management, I recommend you pick up a copy of *Project Management Planning For Dummies* (Wiley), by Stanley E. Portny.

The following sections discuss the sequence of events for an effective disaster recovery planning project.

Conducting a Business Impact Analysis

The first major task in any disaster recovery project involves identifying the business functions in the organization that require DR planning. But you also need to conduct risk analysis of each critical business function to quantify the effect on the organization if something interrupts each of these functions for a long time. This activity is known as the Business Impact Analysis (BIA) because it analyzes the impact that each critical process has on the business.

Setting the Maximum Tolerable Downtime

For each critical process, the team needs to determine an important measure — the longest amount of time the process can be unavailable before that unavailability threatens the very survival of the business. This figure is known as the *Maximum Tolerable Downtime (MTD)*. You may measure an MTD in hours or days.

On the surface, setting the MTD for a given process may appear arbitrary — and, to be honest, it might be at first. Get members from the DR steering committee involved in setting the figures for each MTD. Committee members' somewhat arbitrary estimates may be more educated than estimates you could get from other sources, such as senior management and outside experts.

You may run into some problems setting an MTD:

✔ Strictly speaking, an MTD is hypothetical. If a given business process in the organization *had* been unavailable for that long, you wouldn't be sitting around talking about it because the business would have failed.

✔ You may have trouble finding valid examples of peer organizations that failed because of a critical outage.

✔ You're dealing with degrees of failure. A business could suffer a lengthy outage, resulting in a big loss of market share that leaves the organization a shadow of its former self. Do you consider that failure?

Setting the MTD for each critical process is at least somewhat arbitrary. But the team has to establish *some* figure for each process. And don't worry — you can always adjust the figure if later analysis shows it's too high or too low.

Setting recovery objectives

After you set the MTD for each critical process, you need to set some specific recovery objectives for each process. Like the Maximum Tolerable Downtime (which I talk about in the preceding section), recovery objectives are somewhat arbitrary. The two primary recovery objectives that you usually set in a BIA are

✔ **Recovery Time Objective (RTO):** The maximum period of time that a business process will be unavailable before you can restart it. For instance, you set an RTO to 24 hours. A disaster strikes at 3 p.m., interrupting a business process. An RTO of 24 hours means you'll restart the business process by 3 p.m. the following day.

The RTO must be less than the MTD. For example, if you set the MTD for a given process for two days, you need to make the RTO less than two days, or your business may have failed (or put failure in its destiny) before you get the process running again! In other words, if you think that the business will fail if a particular business process is unavailable for two days, you must make the target time in which you plan to recover that process far less than two days.

✔ **Recovery Point Objective (RPO):** The maximum amount of data loss that your organization can tolerate if a disaster interrupts a critical business process. For example, say you set the RPO for a process to one hour. When you restart the business process, users lose no more than one hour of work.

In the final analysis, arriving at an MTD (as well as an RTO, RPO, and so on) is a business decision that senior management needs to make.

Developing the risk analysis

After you set recovery objectives (see the preceding section), you need to complete a risk analysis. For each critical business process, you need to determine the following:

✔ **Likely disaster scenarios:** List the disasters that can possibly strike. Include both natural disasters and man-made disasters. You might end up with quite a long list, but you don't need to go overboard. Don't get too detailed or list highly unlikely scenarios, such as a tsunami in Oklahoma City or an alien spaceship crash landing.

✔ **Probability of occurrence:** The probability of each scenario actually happening. You can use a high-medium-low scale, or you can get more detailed if you want.

✔ **Vulnerabilities:** Identify all reasonable vulnerabilities within each business process. *Vulnerabilities* are weaknesses that contribute to the likelihood that an event such as a flood or earthquake will result in a significant outage.

✔ **Mitigating steps:** For each vulnerability you list, cite any measures that you can take to reduce that vulnerability.

The risk analysis takes quite some time to complete, even for a smaller-organization that has only a handful of critical business processes.

You may be able to take a shortcut in the risk analysis: Instead of developing a list of all disaster scenarios for *every* business process, you may want to list all scenarios for each business location.

Seeing the big picture

After you complete the MTD, RTO, RPO, and risk analysis for each business process, you need to condense the detailed information down to a simple spreadsheet so you can see all the business processes on one page, along with their respective MTD, RTO, RPO, and risk figures.

If you sort the list by RTO, you can see which processes you need to recover first after a disaster. If you sort by RPO, you can see which processes are the most sensitive to data loss.

You can add a column on your big-picture spreadsheet that expresses the cost or effort you need to upgrade each process so that you can recover it in the timeframe set by its RTO and RPO. You can express these needs roughly by using symbols such as $, $$, $$$, and $$$$, where each $ represents thousands of dollars. A $ represents thousands of dollars, $$ means tens of thousands, and so on.

With this high-quality spreadsheet, you can easily see all critical business processes and the key measures for each. When you rank the processes, you can instantaneously see which processes are the most critical in the organization. Those critical processes — of course — require the most work in terms of disaster recovery planning.

Time for decisions: In or out

Sometimes, a DR team can become overwhelmed by the number of critical processes and the cumulative estimated cost of getting each process to a point at which the organization can recover it within the targeted timeframes. And if the team isn't intimidated by the cost, they may be daunted by the sheer number of IT applications that require work. In this situation, I suggest several remedies:

- **Revise recovery objectives.** When you see the recovery objective and the estimated investment side by side, senior managers can make some decisions about a reasonable amount of investment for a given process. Early estimates can place the cost of upgrading recoverability at a higher figure than the value of the process itself. Senior managers or executives can help to place limits on what you can reasonably spend.

- **Combine recovery capabilities.** You can probably combine the investment for improving the recovery time for several applications, which can reduce costs. For instance, investment in a single large storage system costs far less than separate storage systems.

- **Sharpen those estimates.** The project team can do more detailed work on the investments required to improve recovery times for applications by drawing up actual architectures and plans and then obtain actual estimates for investment. If you proceed with those investments, you need those more detailed numbers, so you can prepare these more accurate figures now and save yourself time later in the DR planning process.

- **Make a multi-year investment in recovery.** After obtaining accurate estimates for improving application recovery, you may reasonably plan for a multi-year investment that improves the most critical applications in the first year and less-critical applications in subsequent years. Or you can use staged investments to incrementally improve recoverability.

> For example, if critical applications' RTO is 24 hours, investment can improve applications' RTO to 48 hours in the first year and to 24 hours in the second year.
>
> ✔ **Do the most critical now and the rest later.** The team can draw a line on the chart, handling processes above the line (those that are most critical) in the current project and processes below the line (those that are less critical) in future DR projects.

DR teams often find that their first set of RTO and RPO figures are just too ambitious, perhaps even unrealistic. You may need to revise the objectives and the investment requirements up or down until you reach reasonable figures.

Chapter 3 describes the end-to-end development of a Business Impact Analysis in detail.

Developing recovery procedures

After the DR planning team agrees on recovery objectives (primarily RTOs and RPOs) and chooses the list of in-scope processes, you need to develop disaster recovery procedures for each process.

Mapping in-scope processes to infrastructure

Before you can start preparing actual recovery procedures for applications, you need to know precisely *which* applications and underlying infrastructure support those processes. Although you probably did some of that work when you made cost estimates for recovery in the BIA (which I talk about in the section "Conducting a Business Impact Analysis," earlier in this chapter), you need to go into more detail now.

Many organizations have equipment and component inventories, so you can use those inventories as a good place to begin. Getting an accurate inventory of all equipment and then mapping that inventory to individual business processes definitely takes some time. But without this information, how can you approach the task of developing a viable recovery plan for a business process?

You can find inventory information and get a better understanding of applications' system support from technical architectures, especially drawings and specifications. Technical architectures give you an invaluable look at how systems and infrastructure actually support a business process. If these architectures don't exist for your organization, consider developing them from scratch.

When you know all the parts and pieces that support an application, you can begin developing plans for recovering that application when disaster strikes.

Developing recovery plans

When you think about it, you have to do an amazing amount of up-front work and planning before you can take pen to paper (or fingers to keyboard) and begin drafting actual recovery plans. But you do eventually get to the plan-writing point.

Disaster recovery has many aspects because you may need to recover different portions of your environment, depending on the scope and magnitude of the disaster that strikes. Your worst case scenario (an earthquake, tornado, flood, strike, or whatever sort of disaster happens in your part of the world) can probably render your work facility completely damaged or destroyed, requiring the business to continue elsewhere. So, you can logically approach DR planning by considering recovery for various aspects of the business and infrastructure:

✔ **End users:** Most business processes depend on employees who perform their work functions. Those employees' workstations may need recovery after a disaster. In the worst case scenario, all those workstations are damaged or destroyed (by water, volcanic ash, or whatever), and you have to get new ones somehow. Chapter 5 discusses user recovery in detail. Employees also need a place to work, but because this book primarily focuses on IT and systems recovery, *where* you put the employees' replacement workstations is beyond the scope of this book.

   When you develop contingency plans for locating critical servers, include work accommodations for your critical employees, also.

✔ **Facilities:** You need to recover the building(s) in which your organization houses its IT systems. If those buildings are damaged, you need to repair them. But if they're beyond repair, you need to identify alternate facilities. No, don't go shopping for space during a disaster — you have to work it all out in advance. Do you need a cold, warm, or hot site? You need to consider that and may more details. I cover all these considerations in exquisite detail in Chapter 6.

✔ **Systems and networks:** The core of IT system recovery is the servers that applications use to do whatever they do. In worst case scenarios, servers are damaged beyond repair, so you need to build them from scratch. And no server is an island, so you also need to recover a server's ability to communicate with other servers and end-user workstations. Chapter 7 goes into these tasks in detail.

✔ **Data:** Data is the heart of most business applications. Without data, most applications are practically worthless. You may find recovering data tricky because data changes all the time, right up until the moment a disaster occurs. You can recover data in many different ways, depending on how much data you need to recover, how quickly that data changes, and how much data you can stand to lose when a disaster strikes. I cover data recovery in its entirety in Chapter 8.

✔ **Preventive measures:** Within the context of developing recovery plans, you have many opportunities to improve applications, systems, networks, and data to make them more resilient and recoverable. An ounce of prevention is worth a pound of cure, and this saying really does apply to disaster recovery planning. You can prevent or minimize the effects of a disaster by taking certain measures, and you should identify those measures. I cover the topic of prevention in Chapter 5 through Chapter 8, as well as in Chapter 12.

Writing the plan

As you prepare to actually develop and document the recovery plans for the components that support critical business processes, you should know what exactly goes into a plan, how to structure it, and how to manage the contents of the plan.

A disaster recovery plan should include the following sections:

✔ Disaster declaration procedure

✔ Emergency contact lists and trees

✔ Emergency leadership team members

✔ Damage assessment procedures

✔ System recovery and restart procedures

✔ Transition to normal operations

✔ Recovery team members

After you write the plan, you need to publish it in forms that make it available to recovery personnel. You can't just put the DR documents on your organization's intranet or the file server because the intranet may be down and the file server unreachable when the disaster strikes. In order to make DR plans available and usable, you need to distribute them in multiple forms (including hard copy, CD-ROM, USB drive, and so on) so emergency response personnel can actually access those plans from wherever they are, without having to depend on the same IT systems that they may be expected to recover.

I cover the details on writing DR plans and more in Chapter 9.

Testing the plan

After you develop the DR plan, you need to put it through progressively intense cycles of testing. If an organization needs to trust its very survival to the quality and accuracy of a disaster recovery plan, you need to test that plan to be sure that it actually works. In disasters, you rarely get second chances.

You need to do several types of tests:

- ✔ **Paper tests:** Staff members review and annotate written procedures on their own.

- ✔ **Walkthrough tests:** A group of experts walks and talks through a recovery procedure, discussing issues along the way.

- ✔ **Simulations:** A group of experts goes through a scripted disaster scenario to see how well the procedures work.

- ✔ **Parallel testing:** The recovery team builds or sets up recovery servers and runs test transactions through those servers to see if they actually can.

- ✔ **Cutover testing:** The ultimate test of preparedness. The recovery team builds or sets up recovery servers and puts the actual business process workload on those systems.

These tests move from simple reviews of DR procedures to simulations to the real thing.

Chapter 10 covers DR plan testing in detail.

Understanding the Entire DR Lifecycle

After you write and fully test the DR plan, you're still not done. Business processes and IT systems change with regularity, almost as often as the sun rises and sets. In even a short period of time, disaster recovery plans can get out of sync with the systems they're supposed to protect, and after enough time, the DR plans have little value.

The time spent on the original DR plan will be a waste if you don't update that plan!

Disaster recovery planning is a lifecycle proposition: After you establish a DR plan, you need to regularly review, revise, and test that plan.

I discuss all the topics outlined in the following sections in Chapter 11.

Changes should include DR reviews

To protect and preserve the value and relevance of your DR plan, you need to modify the plan's coverage of several business processes when changes occur to these processes:

- Technology changes
- Business changes
- Personnel changes
- Market changes
- External changes

When any of the events in the preceding list occur in your organization, you need to review and revise your DR plan so that the plan stays up to date and can continue to protect the business.

Periodic review and testing

Establish a calendar of review and testing to ensure that your DR plans are up to date. For instance, set up a calendar for your disaster recovery procedures like this list:

- Review monthly
- Walkthrough test quarterly
- Parallel or cutover test annually or semi-annually

How often you perform these reviews and tests depends on many factors, including the value and risk associated with supported business processes and the rate of change that occurs.

Training response teams

The stakes are high in disaster recovery planning: The survival of the business may hang in the balance if disaster strikes. Periodically train the likely disaster response team members on recovery procedures. In fact, you should train even staff members who aren't likely to end up on the disaster response team — you never know who'll be available when a disaster hits.

Training, if you do it right, doesn't overburden personnel. Because you should perform testing regularly, that testing can serve as the bulk of the training effort. By including the right personnel in paper tests, walkthrough tests, simulations, parallel tests, and cutover tests, you train them simply by exposing them to the recovery plans in these levels of testing.

Chapter 2

Bootstrapping the DR Plan Effort

*P*utting a full disaster recovery (DR) effort into place for your organization can take a year or two, from inception, to Business Impact Analysis, to plan development and testing. A proper DR project must wrap its arms around the entire business (or, at any rate, around those parts of the business you choose to place in-scope for the project because they're important enough to warrant DR planning); perform a deep analysis of business processes; untangle and analyze dependencies among processes, information systems, assets, and suppliers; and begin building the DR plans themselves.

A DR project is a considerable effort for you to start — and complete. You can take some different approaches to get started. You might think of these approaches as differences in styles, or as ways of addressing operational gaps or risks:

✔ **Conduct a full DR project.** You can just jump into the big DR project, starting with the Business Impact Analysis (BIA), criticality analysis, risk analysis, and specific recovery plans for IT systems.

✔ **Start with a short-term project.** Then again, you might decide to build an emergency operations plan first, just in case a disaster occurs before you complete the main DR plan. Creating an *emergency operations plan* — basically, an established command-and-control structure and a communications plan without any actual recovery procedures — can help you identify and document top-down management structures and communications that need to take place during a disaster.

> ✔ **Develop an interim plan.** You might build an interim DR plan that addresses specific steps you can take to get the IT systems that support critical business processes up and running as soon as possible. An interim DR plan isn't a full plan, and it's not a substitute for one, but it does provide you with some protection in case a disaster strikes before you finish the full DR plan.

In this chapter, I give you things to consider about how to approach DR planning for your organization. Then, I describe the critical resources that you need for DR planning and how to conduct emergency operations planning and interim DR planning.

Starting at Square One

Before beginning a DR planning effort, you need to imagine what effects a disaster would have on your organization. DR planning is about preventing and responding to disasters, and to properly plan, you need to know what to plan for. The following sections take a look at the effects of disasters, and how you can use prevention and planning to reduce the effects of those disasters.

How disaster may affect your organization

Think about disasters that have occurred in your region of the world. Consider the immediate effects that the disaster had: Perhaps the disaster damaged communications facilities; interrupted public utilities, such as electricity or natural gas, for hours or days; or damaged transportation systems, such as roads, railways, and airports.

Now, consider secondary effects of the disaster. When a disaster interrupts major infrastructure facilities, such as communications, transportation, and energy, your business's ability to function is greatly impaired. Workers can't travel and report to work. Customers can't travel to company premises or visit those companies online.

If a disaster's effects are relatively short-lived (meaning only hours or a few days), most businesses can recover. The organization can satisfy pent-up demand for services when it resumes its most critical business processes, usually those processes directly associated with revenue generation or customer service.

If a disaster's effects are more persistent, customers may temporarily divert their demand for goods and services to other suppliers (if other suppliers are available). The nature of the goods or services that an organization provides helps determine whether that organization can recover from a disaster that lasts for more than a few days.

Understanding the role of prevention

You can't prevent either natural disasters or man-made disasters. However, you can *somewhat* control the impact that a disaster has on your organization's operations by reducing the disaster's impact on the business.

In disaster recovery planning, *prevention* means enacting measures in advance that lessen or eliminate the effects that a disaster can have on critical business processes. Here are some examples:

- ✓ **Emergency power:** An organization may be able to mitigate the effects of a disaster by investing in emergency power generation equipment that can produce electricity, even when public utilities are unavailable for several days or longer.

- ✓ **Multiple communications paths:** If you recognize that disasters often cause communications disruptions, you may be able to mitigate this risk by investing in secondary and tertiary communications capabilities that may continue functioning, even if primary facilities are damaged.

- ✓ **Backup computers in another city:** A business that services customers over the Internet may be able to provide those services from virtually anywhere, if those capabilities were designed-in from the beginning.

Although none of the measures in the preceding list *prevent* disasters, those measures can help an organization continue operating after a disaster takes place. All of these measures require advance planning and investment. The time to equip an ocean liner with life jackets is before it leaves port, not after the ship starts sinking.

Understanding the role of planning

The preceding section talks about measures that you can take to lessen the effects of disasters. These measures are the essence of disaster recovery planning. Planning for scenarios in advance, and preparing for them through investment in equipment and training, constitute the bulk of DR planning.

The planning part of DR planning involves figuring out what personnel should do when a disaster strikes. When the earthquake, tsunami, hurricane, landslide, or labor strike hits, what do people need to do to keep critical systems running? If a processing center floods, destroying equipment, how can the organization continue to keep its critical IT systems running? These and many other scenarios require advance planning so emergency operations personnel know how to keep those systems going.

Advance planning is the key to survival when disaster strikes.

Resources to Begin Planning

To get your disaster recovery project going, you need resources from many different parts of the business. The project requires people with a wide variety of skills, as well as a lot of information — and to get that information, you need to involve even more people.

Starting a DR project is no small task. Disaster recovery planning is complicated and multi-disciplinary. It's likely to be one of the larger projects that most organizations undertake, and it brings together many people who don't normally associate with each other. For these and other reasons, you need many important resources before you start a DR project:

- **Executive sponsorship:** A senior manager or executive who's willing to go on record to say, "Disaster recovery planning is so important that we need to complete it by this date." In other words, you need to find someone who's willing to put their money where their mouth is!

- **Budget:** In the early stages of a DR project, you need money for a project manager, technology experts, process experts, or supplemental help for departments as they divert resources away from their usual business to the DR project. In the later stages of the project, you spend money on technology improvements that you need to support recovery objectives.

- **Project manager:** You need a strong project manager for a multi-disciplinary project that can involve dozens of people or more, such as disaster recovery planning. You can have a part-time or full-time project manager, depending on the number of people and activities involved.

- **Subject matter experts:** You need experts in the business processes that the organization has in play, particularly those processes that earn revenue or service customers. You also need technology experts who understand the IT applications and infrastructure that support those processes.

✔ **People with writing skills:** Later phases of DR projects require people who can write processes and procedures in a way that anyone can understand. You never know who might end up on a disaster response team.

A typical DR project can take anywhere from three months (for the smallest organization) to well over a year to complete. How quickly you get a DR plan in place depends on how high a priority you need to make it and how much extra money you have available for outside help.

If you really don't have a good handle on the amount of resources that you may need for your project, here are a couple of suggestions:

✔ **Hire a consultant.** Bring in an experienced DR consultant, just for a short term engagement (no more than a few days), to have a look around and give you some thumbnail estimates on project sizing.

A consultant who says he or she needs a month to give you these estimates either doesn't understand that you want only rough estimates or just wants the billable hours.

✔ **Develop an interim DR plan.** You should develop an interim DR plan, anyway, but by writing this plan, you can get additional exposure on the number of critical processes, systems, suppliers, and so on in your business. That information can help you estimate the size and scope of the real DR plan.

If you're thinking about starting with the full-blown DR plan, turn to Chapter 3 and begin putting together your Business Impact Analysis. If you're considering an interim DR plan, start with the following section.

Emergency Operations Planning

After a disaster strikes, the disaster response team begins to perform its various tasks that relate to the assessment, restart, and recovery of the critical IT systems that support critical business processes. Disaster response involves more than just those people who are recovering systems, however. Other disaster response personnel have to perform a variety of activities, including communicating with customers, company management, suppliers, and partners. As the disaster response unfolds, a lot of people are working, communicating, and making decisions. Controlling all of these activities requires considerable management, leadership, and planning. *Emergency operations planning* is the portion of disaster recovery planning associated with the setup and operations of emergency operations during and immediately after a disaster.

You often undertake emergency operations planning in the early stages of disaster recovery planning. The primary purpose of emergency operations planning is to ensure that company management can continue managing day-to-day business operations, including disaster response efforts, during and immediately after a disaster.

An emergency operations plan may include

- ✔ **Emergency contact lists:** Key personnel need to know how to contact one another when a disaster strikes.
- ✔ **Disaster declaration procedure:** Key personnel need to know how to recognize when an event has disrupted key business activities enough to initiate disaster response.
- ✔ **Emergency communications:** Communications procedures, contact information for additional staff and resources, and perhaps scripted communications to customers or shareholders.

Your emergency operations plan may also include establishing an Emergency Operations Center (EOC). Larger organizations often set up such an emergency command and control center as the nerve center for their emergency operations during a disaster.

Preparing an Interim DR Plan

Most organizations can immediately recognize the risks associated with the absence of a disaster recovery plan. If you know that you can't have a full DR plan in place and tested for more than a year, you may want to have *something* in place while you complete the full DR plan.

Often, an interim DR plan can fill this gap. You can create this plan quickly and with minimal effort. It isn't, of course, as comprehensive as a full DR plan. It's like tossing a tow rope in the back of a car, knowing that you need major engine work — the rope can't fix the engine, but it can help you out of a bad situation if the engine goes belly-up.

The following sections describe one way to build an interim DR plan. Here are the general characteristics of an interim plan:

- ✔ It's built quickly, usually in less than 15 to 20 man-hours.
- ✔ It's built with a relatively low amount of effort.

✔ It provides your business with some limited capabilities if a disaster strikes before you complete the full DR plan.

✔ It's no substitute for the full DR plan that your organization is (or should be) working on.

Why should you build an interim plan? Well, statistically speaking, disasters strike infrequently — but they *do* strike. For example, if your organization is located in a 50-year flood plain (such plains invariably seem to flood every ten years or so — why is that?), the chances are 1 in 25 that a flood will strike in the next two years, before you complete your DR plan for dealing with the flood. Your interim plan addresses what to do if the flood happens in the next two years. It helps keep your business afloat (no pun intended) — but it's not a replacement for a real DR plan.

When you make an interim DR plan, you're developing only a lightweight DR plan.

Staffing your interim DR plan team

The members of senior or executive management who are sponsoring the full DR effort should select two or three experienced and knowledgeable managers to build the interim DR plan. These managers must have pragmatic and hands-on knowledge of the business operations and processes currently in place.

I call this group the *interim DR planners.*

Find the interim DR planners an office or a conference room, and provide them whiteboard space, a couple of notebook computers, and about a day's worth of food.

Looking at an interim DR plan overview

The interim DR planners' objective is to put together an interim DR plan that consists of the following:

✔ An Emergency Response Team (ERT), a group of individuals who are called into action if a disaster strikes

✔ A procedure for declaring a disaster, during or outside normal working hours

✔ A procedure for invoking the interim DR plan

- ✔ A plan for maintaining communications during a disaster
- ✔ Identifying some basic recovery requirements for the business premises
- ✔ Determining alternative ways to continue critical business operations during a disaster
- ✔ Identifying preventive measures to protect business information, records, and critical assets in a disaster
- ✔ Documenting the interim DR plan and making sure that all of the team members have copies of it readily available, regardless of where they are
- ✔ Identifying an off-site location where you can store the interim DR plan
- ✔ Ensuring that the Emergency Response Team is familiar with the interim DR plan and can implement it in a disaster

Creating the interim DR plan should take no more than one or two days of dedicated time from the two or three people on the interim DR planning team. The team may, however, need to spend a few hours a day over a period of a week or two to put this plan together.

Building the Interim Plan

Your interim DR planning team is assembled, and they have ample food and caffeine to support their development of the interim DR plan. Now what do you do? The following sections describe the steps that the interim DR planners need to do to get the interim DR plan built. The steps are as follows:

1. Build the Emergency Response Team.
2. Define the procedure for declaring a disaster.
3. Invoke the DR plan.
4. Maintain communications during a disaster.
5. Identify basic recovery plans.
6. Develop processing alternatives.
7. Enact preventative measures.
8. Document the interim DR plan.
9. Train ERT members.

Step 1 — Build the Emergency Response Team

The interim DR planners first identify a team of individuals within the organization who can be called into action, any time of the day or night, when a disaster strikes. This team is called the Emergency Response Team (ERT). The interim DR planners choose the ERT members from among the general staff population, taking the following into consideration when making their choices:

- ✔ ERT members have management authority.

- ✔ ERT members (for the most part) reside close enough to the business premises that they can most likely get themselves there if a disaster strikes.

- ✔ ERT members are reachable in the event of a disaster. They have more than one means of communication available (for instance, a home phone and a cellphone).

- ✔ ERT members are familiar with present business processes and the technology that supports those processes.

- ✔ ERT members need to know how individual employees get their jobs done from day to day, in grisly detail.

A disaster can disrupt transportation and communications infrastructure, kill or injure staff members or their family members, and damage staff members' property. For any of these (and other) reasons, staff members may be unavailable for short or long periods of time after a disaster. So you should select at least one alternate staff member for each member on the Emergency Response Team. Treat these alternate team members as full team members because you might have to call them into action when a disaster occurs.

Step 2 — Define the procedure for declaring a disaster

The interim DR planners need to figure out how the ERT members will declare a disaster. When they declare a disaster, they launch the interim DR plan into action.

What is a disaster declaration?

Declaration of a disaster is *not* the simple recognition that a destructive man-made or natural event has occurred. For example, a tornado tearing through town, a terrorist attack, or a severe wind storm doesn't equal a disaster. These events may be related to a disaster, but they aren't the disaster by themselves.

A disaster occurs when a natural or man-made event causes a significant disruption to, or completely stops, business operations. More than that, even, a disaster occurs when the ERT says so.

Determine the Maximum Acceptable Outage Time (MAOT) in advance of a disaster — the MAOT may be a period ranging from a few hours to several days or more. The *MAOT* is the longest period of time between the onset of a disaster and the resumption of a critical business process. The ERT should assess the disaster and determine whether your business's critical processes will likely exceed the MAOT. If the ERT (Emergency Response Team) thinks you'll exceed the MAOT, the ERT should declare a disaster.

Knowing when to declare a disaster isn't really difficult, but it isn't obvious, either. Say that a region has experienced a severe wind storm. This sort of natural event usually takes place over a period of several hours. In such an event, storm damage may be highly localized: Buildings may be damaged, power may be disrupted by trees falling into power lines, and some roads may be closed. But you may not immediately know whether the wind storm has caused direct damage to the business premises to such an extent that your business can't perform its normal functions. The business premises themselves may not be damaged at all, but a wind-caused prolonged power outage may prevent the business from operating. Or road closures may prevent employees from being able to report to work, which can also precipitate a disaster.

If you face this sort of situation, allow the ERT to decide whether to declare a disaster. When a man-made or natural event occurs that may disrupt or impair business operations, the ERT members should communicate with one another, perform a quick assessment (for example, determine whether the building is damaged, electric power is still running, employees will be able to report to work, and so on), and make a judgment call as to whether the business should initiate the interim DR plan.

Empowering two or more ERT members with the ability to declare a disaster is a simple and reasonable approach.

Step 3 — Invoke the interim DR plan

After the ERT decides that the MAOT (Maximum Acceptable Outage Time) has been exceeded for critical processes, it invokes the interim DR plan. Here's what you need to do to get your DR plan up and running:

1. **Appoint one of the ERT members to make entries in a logbook.**

   Make sure that member takes note of the following:

   - Overall description of the event that has occurred

   - Damage to premises, assets, systems, and communications facilities

   - Personnel available, and personnel missing, injured, or deceased

2. **Arrange an initial emergency meeting.**

   The team needs to do the following:

   - Appoint an ERT leader.

   - Assign other roles, such as damage assessment and communications.

   - Establish an Emergency Operations Center (EOC).

3. **Make decisions.**

   The ERT needs to determine whether sufficient personnel remain to relocate to another site, for instance.

4. **Initiate recovery plans.**

   The ERT needs to begin performing the recovery plans that the interim DR plan outlines.

Depending on the type of business and the nature of the disaster, the ERT may operate continuously, or in shifts.

Step 4 — Maintain communications during a disaster

At this point, two or more ERT members have determined that business-disrupting events have taken place, signaling the start of DR activities. In this section, I describe some things that can help an ERT during a disaster situation.

When the ERT first convenes to discuss and declare the disaster (which I talk about in the preceding section), the team members have already overcome a number of potential challenges, including dealing with communications outages (which can make it difficult for the ERT members to reach one another). In many disaster scenarios, communications networks are damaged and/or usage spikes create congestion, making it difficult for ERT members to reach one another.

The likelihood that communications will be congested calls for some communications contingencies:

✔ Have at least two different phone numbers for each ERT member.

✔ Make sure ERT members are on several different phone networks so that an outage in any one network won't affect communications to all ERT members.

✔ Avoid depending on only one wireless communications provider.

✔ Avoid putting the organization's phone system (PBX), voice mail, e-mail, and conferencing capabilities on the critical path. (In other words, try to avoid communications bottlenecks brought about by the disaster.)

✔ Use non-company e-mail as an alternative to company e-mail, in the event that company e-mail servers are unavailable.

✔ Use Instant Messaging (IM) as a supplemental means of communication.

✔ Use cellphone text messaging as a supplemental means for transmitting status updates.

✔ Set up emergency teleconference bridges in advance of a disaster.

A *teleconference bridge* is a phone service that permits several people to participate in a group phone call. Include a second teleconference bridge that uses a different provider in case the primary teleconference bridge provider is unreachable. You can find many teleconference bridge providers online.

Some of these contingencies take a bit of time to set up. During the development of the interim DR plan, the team should agree on which communications contingencies are appropriate for their organization.

Also, print at least a portion of each ERT member's contact info on small, laminated cards and give one to each ERT member. With this card, each ERT member has this contact information close at hand when a disaster strikes. I discuss contact-information cards in more detail in the section "Emergency contact information," later in this chapter.

Step 5 — Identify basic recovery plans

This step takes you closer to the meat in the sandwich — identifying basic recovery plans that the interim DR planners need to write. In the preceding sections, you create the Emergency Response Team (ERT), work on the procedure for declaring a disaster, and discuss issues related to communications during a disaster.

The approach I suggest in this section is a little more methodical than those in preceding sections. Follow these steps:

1. **Identify all business functions in the organization.**

   Start at a high level by listing the basic functions (products/services, invoice customers, customer support, process payments, and so on).

2. **Develop a list of business processes that make up the business functions you identify in Step 1.**

3. **Rank this list, placing the most critical processes at the top of the list.**

You probably need to spend at least half an hour on the preceding steps. You don't need to hurry — take your time and consider all of the functions performed in your organization. A typical organization's high-level list might look something like this:

- ✔ Marketing
- ✔ Sales
- ✔ Support
- ✔ Operations
- ✔ Shipping and Receiving
- ✔ Legal
- ✔ Facilities
- ✔ Information Technology (IT)
- ✔ Engineering
- ✔ Human Resources (HR)

Use a copy of the company organization chart (if you have one) to help identify all of the major functions in your organization. You can also use the organization directory, brochures, e-mail distribution lists, and so on in this identification process.

After you create your list of business processes, follow these steps:

1. **Identify which processes you need to restart as soon as possible after a disaster occurs.**

2. **For each process, identify how soon you need to restart the process after a disaster.**

3. **For each process, identify what resources you need to restart the process.**

Here are some issues to consider when you go through the preceding numbered list:

✔ Depending on the type of disaster, only a small fraction of the normal staff may be available.

✔ Suppliers and other supply chain partners may have difficulty maintaining service levels that your organization's critical processes require.

✔ Avoid listing too many critical processes that you must start at the same time. Pace your plans to restart critical processes because many kinds of resources may be limited.

✔ Depending on the nature of your organization's business activities, demand for your business's goods and services could dramatically rise or fall (or it may not be affected at all). For instance, a store selling bottled water is in high demand after almost any kind of natural disaster, whereas a business that manufactures party supplies may see a drop in business.

✔ Communications will be impaired, impacting the ability to restart critical processes, as well as communications with customers and supply chain partners.

Your final list of processes that you need to restart soon after a disaster should take into account the issues in the preceding list. Don't develop an overly-ambitious list of processes to start immediately after a disaster — you probably won't be able to actually get them up and running because of a lack of personnel and other resources.

In interim DR planning, you're developing only lightweight DR plans.

Step 6 — Develop processing alternatives

In many disaster scenarios, you may not be able to restart critical processes. If the systems or assets you need to support a critical process are damaged or destroyed, or if critical personnel are simply unavailable, starting the critical process in the location affected by the disaster just may not be possible — at least, not right away.

Is your business location-sensitive?

In the universe of individual businesses and business models, some businesses are location-sensitive, and others aren't. Knowing where your business fits makes a difference, even for your interim DR planning. Here are some examples to help explain why:

✔ An online Software-as-a-Service (SaaS) isn't location-sensitive. Its customers use its services over the Web from any location. The service provider can host its online presence from anywhere. The logistics of locating employees is relatively minor in comparison to the following two examples because most employees can perform their duties from any location that has Internet connectivity.

✔ An online merchandiser has some location-sensitivity. Its customers shop via the Web from wherever they happen to be. The merchandiser can host its online presence from anywhere in the world. However, the merchandiser probably has to package and ship goods from a warehouse. If this warehouse location is damaged, the business needs to operate from a different location and work with its suppliers to route incoming goods to this new location.

✔ A large retail electronics store is highly location-sensitive. Its customers must travel to its business location to purchase goods and services. If a disaster damages a business such as this store, the business must resume operations in the original site (or close by) so that customers will still be willing to travel there. A business such as this one can't consider changing to a different city, unless the disaster is so severe that it will affect business in the long-term.

These examples illustrate the factors that you must take into consideration when developing processing alternatives.

The interim DR planners need to identify nearby locations where critical business operations can resume in the event of a highly-localized disaster such as a fire, in which buildings even a short distance away remain unaffected.

In a regional disaster, such as a flood or hurricane, locations a short distance away may also be damaged. In this situation, you need to identify locations a greater distance from the main business location.

When considering any alternate location, the team needs to prepare for the possibility that you need to put in place any necessary assets or systems in the alternate location so you can continue business operations. Assets or systems located in the main business location may be damaged by the disaster event, and you may not be able to use them in the alternate location.

Consider these factors when you're searching for alternative locations:

✔ Can it house the assets, systems, and personnel required to continue critical business processes?

> ✔ If the location is a significant distance away from the original business location, is temporary housing available for staff who need to report to work at the alternate location?
>
> ✔ Can customers and supply chain partners adjust their routes and schedules to utilize the alternate location?

Your organization may also have other issues to consider when seeking alternate locations.

You develop an interim DR plan in one to two days. The effort required to make formal business arrangements with an alternate site falls outside of the scope of an interim DR plan.

After a disaster, an organization may need to make compromises in order to continue its critical business processes. The interim DR planners need to take into account these other factors when they consider possible processing alternatives:

> ✔ Reducing service levels or output temporarily
>
> ✔ Substituting components
>
> ✔ Using temporary staff
>
> ✔ Sharing premises with other businesses
>
> ✔ Using more manual processes and relying less on information systems
>
> ✔ Utilizing alternate suppliers and service providers

You know your organization far better than I do. Let your business model and the disaster scenarios you're planning for dictate what alternatives you can consider in your interim DR plan.

You can apply some of what you figure out during the development of your interim DR plan when you develop your formal DR plan.

Step 7 — Enact preventive measures

The loss of key information and assets can be devastating if a disaster strikes. The interim DR plan needs to identify critical information, records, and assets, and come up with prevention measures that can be quickly and easily implemented in order to reduce the likelihood and impact of losing those records and assets.

The following list contains tips on preventive measures that may be appropriate for your organization:

✔ IT preventive measures, such as

- **Confirm working backups.** Make sure that backups are actually backing up critical data. Confirm what systems, directories, and files are being backed up and whether they can actually be restored.

- **Store backup tapes off-site.** Develop a backup media storage plan that includes off-site storage. What good are backups if the backup media are damaged by the same fire, flood, or earthquake that damaged the systems?

- **Practice safe racking.** Make sure that systems in racks are fastened securely, so that an event such as an earthquake won't cause damage. Also, make sure that racks are cross-braced for stability. These measures can also ensure the safety of personnel who work in these areas by preventing injuries from falling equipment.

✔ Recordkeeping preventive measures, such as

- **Centralize records storage.** A logical first step to protecting vital records is to get them out of workers' desk drawers and into a central location.

- **Scan hardcopy records onto file servers.** Consider enacting a project to electronically scan hard-to-replace hardcopy records, such as personnel files and contracts.

- **Photocopy hardcopy records.** Have vital records photocopied and store the copies at a secure off-site location, far enough away that a regional disaster doesn't damage both the originals and the copies.

- **Use fire-resistant file cabinets.** Consider using fire-resistant file cabinets for vital records. In the event of a fire, records stored in these cabinets suffer less damage than records stored in more traditional file cabinets.

✔ Facility preventive measures, such as

- **Use fire-resistant cabinets.** Consider upgrading storage cabinets for critical assets in order to protect those assets from fire.

- **Inspect fire detection and suppression systems.** Make sure that fire extinguishers, smoke detectors, sprinkler systems, and other measures for fire detection and suppression are up to date and working properly. In many locales, local authorities enforce these inspections. In areas where local authorities don't enforce fire-protection inspections, local businesses need to take the burden of these inspections upon themselves.

- **Set up emergency aid and evacuation plans.** Establish and periodically test personnel safety measures — such as first aid supplies, emergency lighting, and evacuation plans. An organization's most important assets are its personnel, and DR planners sometimes overlook them in an overall risk management plan.

Your organization's interim DR planners may come up with other preventive measures, as well.

Step 8 — Document the interim DR plan

After you develop the interim DR plan, you must clearly document it. The DR plans that the interim DR planners develop must be written down and managed. The structure of the interim DR plan might include any or all of the following features:

✔ **Background:** Who promoted and sponsored the development of the interim DR plan, who actually wrote it, and who worked as the interim DR planners.

✔ **Emergency Response Team (ERT):** The members of the ERT and what departments they represent. Include full contact information.

✔ **Disaster declaration procedure:** Describes how your business declares a disaster. This procedure should include the MAOT (Maximum Allowable Outage Time), as well as a justification for the MAOT value.

✔ **Communications procedures:** Describes how the ERT and other business personnel are to communicate, both with one another and with the outside world.

✔ **Recovery plan procedures:** These procedures are the meat of the interim DR plan. They describe recovery procedures, alternate locations, and other contingency information for each business process that you included in the interim DR plan.

✔ **Preventive measures:** Okay, these measures aren't really a part of the interim DR plan itself, but you still need to document the preventive measures in the form of action items so that people and departments actually carry out these measures.

Storage and distribution

When you complete the documentation of the interim DR plan, you need to store and distribute it in such a way that it's adequately protected in the event a disaster strikes. At a minimum, have these copies in place:

✔ **Hardcopy:** Each ERT member should have at least two hardcopies of the plan: one to keep at work and another at home.

✔ **Off-site hard copy:** Have a copy of the interim DR plan available at an off-site location, far enough away that it won't be at risk in a regional disaster.

✔ **Soft copy:** Each ERT member should also have soft copies of the interim DR plan. An ERT member might find a copy on a USB stick useful in case he or she can't get his or her laptop running but can find someone else who does have a laptop that works.

✔ **Online:** Place the interim DR plan in a secure online location, accessible by all ERT members. The online location shouldn't be hosted by the organization itself: If the building that hosts the online copy of the interim DR plan is damaged in a disaster, what good is that copy?

Emergency contact information

In the event a disaster strikes during off-work hours, I suggest the interim DR planners produce small emergency contact cards that can fit into a wallet or purse. Such a card should contain the names and contact info for everyone on the ERT, other communication information (such as conference bridges), and the URL where they can obtain an online copy of the interim DR plan.

Figure 2-1 shows an example of an online contact card.

When each ERT member has this card in his or her wallet or purse, he or she can more easily reach other ERT members if a disaster occurs after business hours, even when he or she is away from home.

JRM Corporation Emergency Response Team

Jim Benson, Dir Ops	w: 972.457.6523	m: 809.334.5928	r: 809.544.6590
Hal Johnson, Facilities	w: 972.457.6999	m: 972.990.4529	r: 809.239.5421
Geoff Beane, IT	w: 972.457.6980	m: 809.366.3860	r: 972.899.3882
Michael Bridge, Legal	w: 972.457.6490	m: 809.335.0988	r: (none)
Jeanne Murphy, Support	w: 972.457.6981	m: 972.834.7239	r: 809.525.9384

Conf Bridge: 1.877.236.5488 or 1.408.539.5600 x488399#
Conf Bridge alt: 1.509.972.5400 x93847392#
Interim DR plan: http://briefcase.yahoo.com/bc/jrmcorp/

Confidential   Updated 8/24/07

Figure 2-1:
A sample
emergency
contact
card.

Step 9 — Train ERT members

Almost done! You've developed and documented the interim DR plan, but do the ERT members know who they are and what to do when a disaster strikes?

All ERT members, and their alternates, need to go through a formal training session, in which they get all of the basics of the interim DR plan, including

- **What the plan is and isn't:** ERT members need to know that the interim DR plan isn't the long-term DR plan, it's just a stopgap until you can fully develop and implement the long-term DR plan.

- **Disaster declaration:** Probably the most difficult part of a DR plan is getting ERT members to actually declare a disaster. They need to be familiar with the procedure and criteria used to determine whether they should invoke a disaster. Make sure they know that the higher-ups will forgive them if they declare a disaster unnecessarily (unless they do so over and over!).

- **Emergency Operations Center (EOC):** The ERT members need to know how to set up and manage emergency operations in the EOC. Each ERT member needs to understand that he or she may be the EOC leader, depending on who's available and how a disaster situation plays out.

- **Enacting recovery operations:** Each ERT member needs to be familiar with the recovery operations in the interim DR plan.

Be prepared for the possibility that new issues may arise in the training sessions — you may need to make small changes to the interim DR plan. But remember, the interim DR plan isn't the save-the-company-from-all-disasters plan: It's the simpler stopgap plan you use until you fully develop and test that larger and more formal DR plan.

Testing Interim DR Plans

An organization that devotes the resources to the development of an interim DR plan wants to know that the interim DR plan will work in a disaster. Granted, you use a pretty lightweight process to develop the interim DR plan, so you can do your testing on the light side, too.

Here's a list of the types of DR tests:

- **Checklist (paper test):** Staff members individually review the plan for accuracy and completeness.

- **Walkthrough:** Staff members gather together to walk through the DR plan as a group, discussing each step along the way.

✔ **Simulation:** Staff members perform a walkthrough in the context of a pretend disaster that includes periodic announcements of events as they occur in the region. The ERT members don't actually perform any recovery steps, however.

✔ **Parallel:** The ERT performs actual recovery steps to move business processes to alternate locations. The ERT builds or starts recovery servers and runs some actual business transactions through the recovery servers while primary servers are also still working. Primary everyday business processes should continue uninterrupted.

✔ **Interruption (cutover test):** The business stops performing critical business processes, as though an actual disaster has occurred. The ERT and other staff members carry out business operations according to the interim DR plan.

Sure, you built the interim DR plan on a shoestring. But it was time well-spent because the interim DR plan is *the* DR plan if a disaster strikes before you finish the full DR plan. Although it's unlikely, your business's long-term future may depend on the quality of the interim plan. A disaster *could* occur tomorrow.

At a minimum, you should checklist test and walkthrough test the interim DR plan. Seriously consider simulation testing, as well. Here's a breakdown of how to run each of these tests:

✔ **Checklist testing:** Every Emergency Response Team (ERT) member, plus selected other staff members in the organization (particularly those who will be assisting with interim business operations during a real disaster), should carefully review the entire interim DR plan. Ask them to make suggestions for changes or improvements in the plan. The authors of the DR plan make the recommended changes and distribute the plan for comments one more time to be sure everyone agrees that the DR plans are accurate and complete.

✔ **Walkthrough testing:** The entire ERT should take as much time as needed (half a day to a full day or longer) to go over the interim DR plan, step by step. They should have plenty of discussions, including question-and-answer sessions.

The people who developed the interim DR plan should be present, even if they themselves aren't ERT members. That way, the plan's authors can answer any questions raised.

✔ **Simulation testing:** If disaster recovery planning is new to your organization (and it probably is if you're developing an interim DR plan), also perform simulation testing on your new plan. A simulation test enables the ERT to more vividly imagine how actual response will take place during a disaster.

The main difference between walkthrough testing and simulation testing is where you do it. In a walkthrough, you're in a conference room with four walls and a whiteboard; in a simulation test, you walk all around your building, DR plan in hand, observing, asking questions, and pointing out issues that you can see only in person.

Chapter 3

Developing and Using a Business Impact Analysis

*O*rganizations have limited resources. You can do only so much with the people, budget, and equipment available. Software companies want to add more features and functionality to their products; financial services organizations want to have additional investment and management plans available for their customers; automobile manufacturers want to have additional models, features, and accessories available for their customers to choose from. But these organizations can't always add what they want to their products and services.

Businesses that want to develop disaster recovery (DR) capabilities are also constrained by limited resources. At first glance, it makes sense that all business processes and information systems should have disaster recovery capabilities. However, an organization just can't have DR plans for all of its processes and systems — it doesn't have enough resources or enough time. So how does an organization decide which processes and systems warrant the expense and effort related to the development of DR plans? Most businesses use a Business Impact Analysis (BIA) to help them make this decision.

You use a structured, top-down approach to create a BIA. In this chapter, I take you through a tour of the ins and outs of BIA development and how it supports long-term DR development.

Understanding the Purpose of a BIA

A *Business Impact Analysis* (BIA) is a detailed inventory of the primary processes, systems, assets, people, and suppliers that are associated with an organization's principle business activities.

The BIA starts out as a list, but it becomes a web. You end up with a connected set of lists in which the entries in one list refer to entries in other lists — dependencies across the spectrum of processes, systems, assets, people, and suppliers. Process A depends on Systems K, L, and M; requires the use of Assets S and T; is operated by key personnel in Department Q; and depends on supplies delivered by Suppliers Y and Z. Think of the BIA as a sort of three-dimensional connect-the-dots, in which entries in various layers have connections to entries in other layers. Like in the organization itself, everything is interconnected.

The core purpose of a Business Impact Analysis is to identify which processes and systems are the most critical to the survival of an organization.

Here's a closer look at two of the terms I use in the preceding paragraph:

✔ **Critical:** This word refers to those processes and systems that your business absolutely needs in order to perform its main functions.

✔ **Survival:** Saving your business from suffering a catastrophic blow that could result in substantial damage to the business, including closing its doors for the last time and shutting down for good. I'm not talking about avoiding a bad financial year or trying not to lose customers or market share.

Here's what the Business Impact Analysis does:

✔ Determines which business processes you need to recover and restart as soon as possible after a disaster

✔ Determines how soon you need to restart business processes

✔ Identifies the resources you need to restart these business processes

Without a BIA, you don't know which processes are *mission critical* (crucial to the ongoing success of the organization) or *time critical* (those processes that negatively affect the organization when they're not performed promptly), and you don't know which ones require attention in the DR planning and testing phases. Without a BIA, you're just guessing, and you're liable to identify processes and systems as critical by some less-than-ideal criteria, including

✔ Your favorites

✔ Those with which you're most familiar

✔ The ones that the executives like best

✔ The shiny, new ones

✔ Pet processes (the favorites of others)

✔ The easy ones

The criteria listed above don't make good business sense. The BIA uses objective criteria to select those processes that are truly the most critical to the organization, instead of relying on subjective criteria.

Scoping the Effort

Early on, you need to clearly establish the scope of the entire project. If the scope of an organization's DR project is unclear, members in the project team may arbitrarily cut out important components or increase the scope beyond what the project's sponsors originally intended.

You need to first establish the boundaries of the DR project by addressing the following questions:

✔ **Project team:** Which staff members will make up the DR project team? How much time per week do you expect each team member to work on the DR project?

Similarly, do you have any staff members on loan for the DR project, and do you need to obtain any contractors for the project?

✔ **Scope:** Which sets of business functions are in the scope of the DR project, and which are out? Have you established a quick analysis of dependencies in order to firmly establish the scope?

✔ **Project plan:** Have you established a high-level project plan that includes important dates?

✔ **Budget:** What budget are you establishing for each phase of the DR project? Have you established the budget in such a way that you can use the results of the BIA to help shape the budget for the DR effort itself, after you know better how much investment you need in order to meet established recovery criteria?

Has management committed to establishing an annual budget that can help maintain the DR plan and keep it relevant and effective?

Should you hire a consultant?

You may want to hire an outside consultant who's an expert at disaster recovery planning and performing a Business Impact Analysis. Hiring an outside consultant for this type of work has its pros and cons. The pros include that the consultant is

✔ An expert at DR planning

✔ An expert at creating Business Impact Analyses

✔ Objective

Consultants do have their downside:

✔ They're not familiar with your business

✔ They have few, if any, relationships with staff

✔ Their services are costly

You need to weigh these factors and decide how much you want a consultant to do for you. You can have him or her give you a little up-front advice, or you can let him or her manage the entire process.

✔ **Executive support:** What level of executive support do you have for the DR project? Are company executives firmly behind the DR project, or are they only lukewarm about it?

 You need a formal, written charter that answers all the questions in the preceding list if you want a truly successful DR project. In all but the smallest organizations, a DR project can easily take a year or longer, from the inception of the BIA all the way to the investment in any necessary systems and equipment, training, and testing.

Conducting a BIA: Taking a Common Approach

The information-gathering stage of the BIA involves a great number of interviews that one or more people carry out. You need to develop a common approach so that every interviewer gathers the same information from every person he or she interviews about every process, system, asset, and supplier.

Instead of steaming headlong into interviews and other information-gathering activities without a plan, spend some time developing procedures and templates so that you can make the interviewing process (probably the most labor-intensive of all BIA activities) as efficient and effective as possible.

Your BIA should focus on identifying and inventorying several key aspects and characteristics of an organization, including

- **Business processes:** This generic term refers to business activities that your business's personnel carry out, often with the help of machinery — including information systems. Processes are made up of one or many procedures. Business processes can be fairly simple, one or two people carrying them out with minimum dependency on other resources; or they can be quite complex, involving people in many parts of the organization, as well as suppliers and other external resources.

- **Information systems:** This generic term means computer systems, applications, databases, and devices. An information system can be as simple as an Excel spreadsheet on a desktop computer or as complex as an application running on dozens of servers in locations throughout the world.

- **Assets:** The equipment needed to facilitate the production of whatever products or services your organization produces. Assets may consist of machinery or tools that are essential to the business. Assets can be servers (although you could argue that computers belong in the information systems category, but don't get too nit-picky); mechanical devices, such as milling machines or lathes; tools, such as forklifts and electric generators; or equipment, such as X-ray machines and CAT scanners.

- **Personnel:** The people who perform the processes or support them in some direct way. These people may be located anywhere, and they can include your employees, contractors, and temps.

- **Suppliers:** The outside organizations that supply your business with goods or services that it needs in order to produce its goods or services. Suppliers include organizations that provide you raw materials, such as steel, lumber, or blank CDs; a public utility supplying electricity, natural gas, or water; and a service organization, such as an Internet colocation facility or a data storage provider.

Gathering information through interviews

The best approach to inventorying all of the items in the preceding section is to schedule discussions with key people in the business. Business processes and information systems can't explain themselves, so you need to talk to the people who are responsible for those processes and systems.

You're not going to be able to create a complete list of people you need to interview initially. When people describe their processes and systems to you, they may point out *more* names that you need to add to your list of interviewees.

Don't look at the incompleteness of your initial list of suspects as a sign of weakness — it's just a simple fact. Few organizations have a single individual who has an exceedingly clear view of every critical process, system, and supplier.

Here are some tips for these interviews:

✔ Arrange the interviews in advance with department or business unit owners, letting them know what to expect so they can be prepared.

✔ Plan the interviews so that they'll be effective and won't waste time. For instance, create a list of standard questions so that you can get more consistent answers, particularly if more than one person does the interviewing.

✔ Conduct the interviews in person when possible.

Using consistent forms and worksheets

You can make the information-gathering stage of the BIA most effective if you ask for the same types of information from each process or system owner. You can (arguably) most easily accomplish this conformity by developing forms that you (or whoever conducts the interview) use when interviewing each process owner. Using forms has several advantages, including

✔ **Completeness:** You can be sure that you ask all the key questions in every interview.

✔ **Conciseness:** You can more easily capture a higher amount of detail in interviews by including details in forms.

✔ **Consistency:** Whether one person or several people are conducting the interviews, they're more likely to ask the same questions every time if you use a form.

You can use simple paper forms that the interviewer fills out in hardcopy, then the interviewer enters that information into spreadsheets or databases later; or you can use soft forms in Microsoft Word or Adobe Acrobat that the interviewer can fill out on-screen. Electronic note-taking may be more efficient because you don't have to transcribe the written notes. Exactly how you conduct your interviews is up to you.

Here are some tips as you develop your information gathering forms and procedures:

✔ **Use one form per process, not one per interview.** Unless an interviewee is responsible for only one process, use a separate form for each process (or system, asset, person, supplier, and so on). You want your information gathering to focus on the processes, not the personnel you're interviewing.

✔ **Cross-reference.** On a process intake form, list critical suppliers, personnel, assets, and systems. Likewise, on a critical supplier's intake form, cross-reference the processes and systems that supplier supports.

✔ **Include metadata.** Be sure that the form includes information such as the name of the interviewee, the interviewee's contact information, who conducted the interview, and when it took place. You want to be able to trace data back to its source in case you come up with more questions later.

To help clarify this whole business of interviews and intake forms, Figure 3-1 shows a part of a sample intake form that you can use as a starting point. You can see the *metadata* (information about the information gathered, such as the names of the people interviewed, who did the interviewing, the date of interviews, and so on) and dependencies in this sample process intake form.

As you develop your forms, keep this in mind: You'll probably want to transfer the data gathered on the forms into a spreadsheet, in which you'll be able to view the data that you gather, as well as sort, filter, and merge that data with other related data that you might have on-hand.

The information-gathering stage of the BIA should help you build a high-level view of critical business processes and the systems that support them that lets you examine the details without getting mired in them.

The bird's eye detailed view of the business

Often, an organization doesn't have personnel who have a comprehensive view of *all* an organization's processes, suppliers, assets, and personnel until the organization undertakes its first Business Impact Analysis. Many in the organization will want to get their hands on your business's completed BIA that describes the entire business in detail, including rank-ordered lists of critical processes, systems, suppliers, assets, and personnel.

No one knows the details of a business as well as DR and security people do. These personnel are responsible for reducing risk across the entire business, and in the process of doing so, they accumulate much knowledge about all aspects of the business.

Interviewee	
Interviewee title	
Interviewee contact info	
Interviewee department	
Interviewer	
Interviewer contact info	
Date	
Process name	
Process owner name and contact info (if not interviewee)	
Process purpose	
Process inputs	
Process outputs	
Customer facing (Y/N)	
Who or what performs this process	
Process dependencies (list process that this process depends upon)	
Supplier dependencies	
Personnel dependencies	
Information system dependencies	
Communications dependencies (phone, Internet, FAX, and so on)	
Asset dependencies	
Facilities dependencies	

Figure 3-1: Use this sample intake form for a critical process to help you create your own.

Capturing Data for the BIA

The BIA is all about gathering information and then analyzing it. Gather information for the BIA methodically, consistently, and in a way you can repeat. In a larger project, in which more than one person gathers information, you should get the same details, regardless of who's doing the gathering.

You gather a lot of information on a variety of topics for the Business Impact Analysis. Even though this book focuses on the IT side of disaster recovery planning, you can't ignore the fact that IT systems support business processes. Ultimately, you need to know about the business processes — which ones are the most critical and how quickly you need to recover them. The BIA helps you figure out your organization's processes.

Business processes

Business processes, or just processes, are the activities that an organization performs in support of its primary purpose(s): the production and delivery of goods and/or services.

All businesses have processes, although they may not be called processes. The following list includes some possible features of a business's processes:

- ✔ **Processes contain one or more procedures.** *Procedures* are (usually) written instructions that people carry out. Simple processes may contain only a single procedure, whereas complex processes may have many procedures (which personnel don't necessarily carry out sequentially). Examples of procedures include *intubate the patient*, *install the operating system*, and *replace the brake pads*.

  Procedures consist of one or more tasks, which are the individual steps that you need to perform in a procedure. Example tasks include log out of the application, turn off the power supply, and fasten the sensor to the bracket.

  A DR project can expose weaknesses in business processes, including when you don't have procedures in writing. In a smaller, newer, or less formal organization, you may be able to get away with maintaining a procedure in more of an oral tradition, rather than in a formal written form. But an organization that wants to establish an effective disaster recovery plan needs to document its procedures, in both disaster and peacetime settings.

- ✔ **Processes are carried out by people.** Examples of people who carry out processes include bank tellers, database administrators, and mechanics. In highly automated processes, such as oil refineries, the machinery does most of the real work, but operators and engineers are in there somewhere, turning equipment off and on, and making adjustments to machinery as it continues operation.

- ✔ **Processes may depend on information systems.** Personnel can carry out some processes without using an information system, but increasingly, business processes require information systems in some direct or indirect manner. Examples of these dependencies include the availability of a patient records system in order to admit a patient, the availability of an inventory system in order to identify the location of a replacement part, and the availability of a directory server to perform backups.

- ✔ **Processes may require assets.** Processes often depend on one or more assets. For instance, a medical office needs a copier or scanner to make copies of insurance benefit cards and scales to weigh patients. A fueling station needs tanks and pumps. A manufacturing company needs its forklifts, packing machines, machine tools, and assembly lines.

Some organizations list their computer systems under assets rather than under information systems. I won't get in the middle of that argument: As long as you document the dependencies, you can label them any way you want that makes sense for your organization.

✔ **Processes may depend on suppliers or service providers.** Most processes require supplies or raw materials, which your business often gets from external suppliers.

The Business Impact Analysis contains all the features in the preceding list about business processes in a high level of detail. Your BIA may contain several worksheets listing the organization's business processes, one per row (or even one per worksheet), with columns containing the individual items in the preceding list.

Bottom line: The BIA contains a detailed list of all the processes (at least, the important ones) that the organization carries out. It's a summary of everything the organization does.

Information systems

The BIA contains an inventory of the organization's information systems. Like the list of processes (which I discuss in the preceding section), the list of information systems probably will be quite detailed.

I deliberately use the rather general term *information system,* as opposed to more specific terms such as application, server, device, or database system. The term *information system* includes some or all the components in an IT environment. To some extent, what falls into your information systems group depends on how your organization thinks about its own information systems.

For example, a large medical clinic has a patient information system that manages all the information about its patients. If you think about the patient information system as an application, the system contains not only the application, but the servers it resides on; (potentially) separate database servers; and other elements, such as directory servers, print servers, and file servers. Without all these other elements, the patient information system wouldn't function. And don't forget the network (at least a part of it), as well as workstations and other equipment.

Your business model, information systems, application architecture, and even the structure of your *org chart* (who works for whom, and how responsibilities align with senior managers and executives) may dictate the ways that you slice and dice your complete collection of information assets. You don't have to worry about a right way or wrong way, as long as the methods for identifying and classifying your information systems work for you.

External or internal: It depends on scope

Many larger organizations perform not only the activities that directly result in the delivery of their primary goods and services, but also many supporting activities. Here are some examples:

✔ An office supply company may have its own fleet of delivery vehicles.

✔ An online travel services provider may operate its own Internet data center.

✔ A fleet of limousines may have its own tow trucks and mechanics.

The scope of a DR project determines whether you consider supporting or adjunct services internal or external. For example, if the scope of the online travel services provider's DR plan includes only its software applications, the company may consider the Internet data center's services external, even though they're performed by the same organization, because the Internet data center isn't a part of the company's DR project.

Structure your inventory of information systems in such a way that you can easily identify dependencies between processes and information systems, as well as assets, personnel, and suppliers.

Assets

A Business Impact Analysis contains a list of important assets that the business uses, particularly those assets that are directly or indirectly related to the production of whatever goods or services the business produces.

Your organization's assets might be any of the following or something entirely different:

✔ Delivery vehicles

✔ Cranes

✔ Printing presses

Regardless of the specific items on your list of assets, a BIA should contain the assets that are related to the organization's primary activities.

Cross-reference your assets with whichever lists are relevant — processes, information systems, suppliers, and personnel.

Personnel

Every organization has its replaceable personnel, as well as those who aren't so easily replaced. The point of a list of personnel (if, indeed, you even need such a list) is to identify those people who are critical to the delivery of the organization's principle goods and services.

To avoid the nearly inevitable political posturing and other unnatural behavior that occurs when personnel try to prove their worth, avoid coming up with a list of critical personnel at all. Instead, identify critical personnel (if and as needed) within the most critical business processes and leave it at that.

You may decide to draw up a list of critical personnel — those people whose unanticipated absence could make the business suffer most. You can use this list to identify any critical paths that you can alleviate by cross-training or redistributing duties. Remember, the purpose of DR planning is to ensure the survival of the organization in a disaster. In serious disasters, key personnel may be killed, injured, or unable to report to work because of transportation disruptions.

Suppliers

Like processes, information systems, assets, and personnel (which you can read about in the preceding sections), you probably have several key suppliers, without which the organization's output of goods and/or services would grind to a halt.

Identify key suppliers within each business process. If the organization is highly dependent on external suppliers (which may include other distant parts of the organization that fall out of scope of the DR project, as the "External or internal: It depends on scope" sidebar, in this chapter, states), the BIA may include a separate list of those suppliers, just so you can see them all in one place.

If you include a separate list of suppliers in the BIA, cross-reference each supplier back to the process(es) that it supports.

Statements of impact

In the preceding sections, I describe lists that you need to add to the BIA: processes, information systems, assets, personnel (optionally), and suppliers. Those lists contain a lot of details about each of the processes, information systems, and so on, including dependencies between processes and suppliers.

You need to add something else to those lists — the impact of nonperformance, or the impact of unavailability. In other words, the impact upon the organization as a whole if the particular process, supplier, or asset is disrupted or unavailable for a period of time.

In your BIA report, add *statements of impact* — words or short phrases that describe the impact if each process (or supplier or asset) is interrupted or unavailable. Examples include inability to process customer deposits, inability to transfer goods from inventory, and inability to access patient medical history.

Each business process is somehow — directly or indirectly — related to the organization's production of goods and services. What if a disrupting event knocks the process offline (literally or figuratively) for an extended period of time?

Your Business Impact Analysis can also show a cost figure associated with each process. This figure represents the cost to the business per unit time, such as dollars per hour, if the process is unavailable.

Calculating cost impact can be quite complicated, and you should do it only for those processes you rank as most critical. You probably need the expertise of one or more financial people in your organization to help you make these calculations. You can get the heady details in *Activity Accounting: An Activity-Based Costing Approach* (Wiley), by James A. Brimson, and *Activity-Based Cost Management: An Executive's Guide* (Wiley), by Gary Cokins.

Criticality assessment

The BIA report contains, in addition to statements of impact (which you can read about in the preceding section), criticality rankings for each process. You probably also want to include criticality rankings in the other lists, such as information systems and suppliers.

You can code criticality on a scale such as L, M, H, C (for low, medium, high, or critical impact) or a numeric scale rated 1 through 4.

Although you can rate or rank each data point fairly simply, criticality has tremendous impact on the results of the BIA. When you collect all the business processes on a spreadsheet and sort them by criticality, you get a rank-ordered list of the organization's most critical processes — one of the primary objectives of the Business Impact Analysis.

The *criticality ranking* is a well-informed estimate of overall impact on continuing business operations if that process is interrupted.

MTD and governments

If the local city or county government can't perform a critical process past its MTD, is it really going to go out of business? You probably find it hard to imagine a government actually ceasing to function altogether, but a lot of people could end up with really big problems if the critical process that's not available involves keeping the water or electricity flowing to that government's citizens.

In businesses such as governments that rarely just stop functioning entirely, the MTD might instead be the point at which the customers (citizens) are likely to revolt and force out the top officials.

Maximum Tolerable Downtime

For each process in the BIA, you need to determine its Maximum Tolerable Downtime (MTD).

Maximum Tolerable Downtime is the time after which the process being unavailable creates irreversible (and often fatal) consequences. Generally, exceeding the MTD leads to severe damage to the viability of the business, including the actual failure of the business. Depending on the process, you can express the MTD in hours, days, or longer.

Arriving at a reasonable MTD for a process is anything but easy. You can't ask yourself, "Last time this process became unavailable to the organization, how long was it before the organization actually failed?" And such occurrences happen so rarely, even among other organizations similar to yours, that you have very little data to reference when you estimate an MTD. You really have to ask yourself, how long *would* it take for this organization to go fins-up if this particular process was down for a long time?

Still, you have to put something in that spot. You may need to turn to the expertise of more seasoned senior or executive management, and even then, you can come up with only a somewhat arbitrary figure. You really need to think out the figures for MTD because those figures contribute to the calculation of other figures discussed in the following sections.

Recovery Time Objective

After you determine MTDs for processes (see the preceding section), you can begin setting targets for recovery. One important target is the Recovery Time Objective (RTO).

The *Recovery Time Objective* is the period of time in which the organization intends to have the interrupted process running again.

Time critical versus mission critical

When you gather information about critical processes, and when you're estimating Maximum Tolerable Downtime (MTD), Recovery Time Objectives (RTO), and Recovery Point Objectives (RPO), you may notice that

✔ You have time-critical processes (those that must be delivered in a timely fashion).

✔ You have mission-critical processes (those that are vital to the organization's viability).

Your time-critical processes and your mission-critical process aren't necessarily the same.

Your organization may have mission-critical processes that aren't time critical, and you may have time-critical processes that aren't mission critical.

The difference between these two kinds of processes becomes important as you begin using the results of your Business Impact Analysis. As you establish Recovery Time Objectives (RTOs) for processes, you need to balance the cost of attaining those RTOs against the value of the processes that they support.

For any given process, the RTO is less than the MTD. By definition, it has to be. If you set a 14-day RTO for a process with a 7-day MTD, your business has failed before you can get the critical process running again. And what's the point of that?

A process's RTO forms the basis for any DR planning that you'll do for that process. For example, if a process has a 30-day RTO, you can get it running again — purchase a new server, install software, and restore backup data — at a leisurely pace. However, a process with a one-hour RTO requires a hot site with a standby server and data replication in near-real time. The costs for these two scenarios vary greatly.

Time is money. Lower RTOs require more investment in standby systems, as well as the possible need for data replication or other potentially costly technologies.

Establishing RTOs and then determining the costs required to reach those objectives can be a repetitive process. As you discover the costs of achieving an ambitious RTO, you may need to compromise and develop a capability that costs less but delivers a longer RTO.

Recovery Point Objective

The Recovery Point Objective (RPO), like the RTO (discussed in the preceding section), is somewhat arbitrary and based on assumptions that people near the top of the org chart (executives and senior managers) make.

The *Recovery Point Objective* is the maximum amount of data that you can lose if a process is interrupted and later recovered.

Say that an organization wants to establish a four-hour RPO for an order entry system. In order to meet this figure, the organization has to implement a mechanism to back up or replicate transaction data so that it loses no more than four hours of transactions in a disaster scenario.

Similar to the RTO, setting the RPO determines what sorts of measures you need to take to ensure that you don't lose information related to any particular business process.

Speed costs. Lower RPOs generally require greater investment in data replication or backup technology.

Introducing Threat Modeling and Risk Analysis

You need to carry out threat modeling and risk analysis for each critical process that you identify in the BIA. Although they're somewhat different activities, threat modeling and risk analysis are similar enough that you can think of them as a single integrated activity.

Threat modeling is the process of identifying a full range of potential threats, the probability that they'll occur, their impact, and mitigation steps.

Risk analysis is the process of identifying and assessing factors that may jeopardize the ongoing operation of a business process.

If you think that threat modeling and risk analysis are similar, you're right. You perform both processes as a single activity, in which you identify threats and vulnerabilities in business processes and the steps that you can take to mitigate the potential impact of those threats and vulnerabilities.

Mitigation is just a fancy word that means the steps or measures that you need to perform to reduce your risk.

You may need to carry out these activities for each process in the BIA, although in many cases, you can carry out threat modeling on groups of similar processes, rather than each process individually. I mean, a flood is a flood — listing it for every process might be going a little overboard (yes, that pun was intended).

Disaster scenarios

Before you can get to the actual threat and risk analysis, you need to create a relatively complete list of the disasters that are reasonably likely to occur. The following list isn't meant to be complete — some disasters not listed here might belong in your threat model. But this list should give you a good starting point:

- **Natural disasters:** You know, acts of nature — events that occur without any direct help from people. Here are some examples:

  - Fires and explosions
  - Earthquakes
  - Volcanoes
  - Storms (snow, ice, hail, wind, or prolonged rain)
  - Floods
  - Hurricanes, cyclones, and typhoons
  - Tornadoes
  - Landslides, mudflows, and avalanches
  - Tsunamis
  - Pandemic

- **Man-made disasters:** Human-caused events. These disasters include

  - War and terrorism
  - Riots and other civil disturbances
  - Work stoppages
  - Cyber attacks

- **Secondary effects:** These effects can result from both man-made and natural disasters. Secondary effects include

  - **Utility outages:** Electric power, natural gas, water, and so on
  - **Communications outages:** Telephone, cable, wireless, television, radio, Internet
  - **Transportation outages:** Roads, highways, airports, railroads, shipping

Your region or locale may be subject to other events that can disrupt business activities to such an extent that you can consider those events disasters.

Identifying potential disasters in your region

Disastrous events are, by their nature, uncommon in many parts of the world. Where disasters occur frequently, usually everyone leaves, or they make long-term investments in infrastructure to lessen the effects of natural events so those events are no longer disastrous when they occur. Still, you should have a good understanding of the types of disasters that can occur in your region. To find information on the types of disaster you may have to face, check out these sources:

- National and local weather bureaus
- Local civil defense authorities
- Local disaster relief agencies, such as the International Red Cross
- Local law enforcement
- Local newspaper archives
- Army Corps of Engineers (for flood plain data in the U.S. only)
- Peers and colleagues in local trade organizations

One or more of these sources may lead you to other local sources of useful information about potential disasters.

Performing Threat Modeling and Risk Analysis

Threat modeling and risk analysis can consume a significant portion of the total BIA effort. Entire books have been written on the topic, but because this book has only so much space, I describe these activities only in procedural form.

For each process or group of processes in your BIA, follow these steps:

1. **Identify every potential natural disaster that could interrupt the process you're dealing with.**

2. **Determine the likelihood of each disaster occurring within a single calendar year.**

3. **Identify every potential man-made disaster that could interrupt your process.**

4. **Determine the likelihood of each man-made disaster occurring in a single calendar year.**

   For both natural and man-made disasters, assign numeric values for low-to-high likelihood something like this: Rare: 1; Infrequent: 10; Possible: 100; Likely: 1,000; Very Likely: 10,000.

5. **For each threat that you identify in Step 1 and Step 3, rank the impact of the event (if it actually occurs) on this scale: Lowest: 1; Medium: 100; Highest: 10,000.**

6. **Determine the risk of each threat.**

   For each threat, multiply the likelihood figure from Step 2 or Step 4 by the threat figure from Step 5. For example, a threat with infrequent probability (value: 10) and a medium impact (value: 100) equals 1,000. Use this equation for each threat.

7. **Sort the threats by risk (the figure you establish in Step 6).**

   Pay the most attention to the threats at the top of the list. Chances are, these events are most likely to occur in your region.

After following the preceding steps, you have a simple threat analysis. You know which threats you need to pay the most attention to, and you have an idea how likely those threats are to actually occur (well, at least as accurate as your estimate based on the preceding list's rather unsophisticated scale).

I made the threat analysis procedure in the preceding list intentionally simplistic. A real threat analysis should use a broader scale and more realistic probabilities. But hopefully you get the idea of what threat analysis is all about. If you want all the details about threat analysis, you can pick up a copy of *Emerging Threat Analysis: From Mischief to Malicious* (Syngress), by Michael Gregg. You can also find a great free online resource about risk analysis at the U.S. National Institute for Standards and Technology's Web site (www.nist.gov): *Risk Management Guide for Information Technology Systems,* special publication 800-30.

You can perform threat modeling and risk analysis at the same time as the information-gathering process. Because threat modeling and risk analysis are so similar, you might consider doing them as a single task.

Identifying Critical Components

You've collected basic information from all of the important business processes for your Business Impact Analysis. You've identified information systems, personnel, assets, and suppliers that these processes depend on, and you may have created separate lists of these if your business has a lot of them. For instance, you can create separate lists of suppliers by category. You get to decide how you want to organize your information.

Processes and systems

In the list of critical processes that you create in the BIA, you have many important fields that describe the processes, their owners, and so on. Here's a list of the fields you should include:

- ✓ Process name
- ✓ Process owner
- ✓ Description of the process
- ✓ Information systems that this process requires
- ✓ Assets that this process requires
- ✓ Any critical personnel without whom this process would fail
- ✓ Suppliers that this process requires
- ✓ Statement of impact if the process fails or is interrupted
- ✓ Maximum Tolerable Downtime (MTD)
- ✓ Recovery Time Objective (RTO)
- ✓ Recovery Point Objective (RPO)
- ✓ Cost of downtime
- ✓ Criticality ranking

Your list will probably have more fields than the preceding list does, but this list gives you the basics.

I want to focus, for now, on the numeric items in the preceding list — the MTD, RTO, RPO, cost of downtime, and criticality. With these fields, you can manipulate your list in various ways to get an eagle-eye view of which processes are truly important in your organization. You can begin to see which process have the shortest MTDs, RTOs, and RPOs by sorting the list based on those columns. While sorting based on these fields, you can keep your eye on the criticality rankings to see if criticality is in line with those objectives. Do you see any correlation between criticality and your RTOs and RPOs? Maybe you do, and maybe you don't.

If you have a lot of processes (more than can fit on a screen — at least, that's how I decide whether I have a lot of processes), you might group them into High, Medium, and Low categories, based on ranking. For instance, you might divide the entire rank-ordered list of processes into thirds. Depending on the nature of your business (which includes a great many things, including regulatory, financial, and market conditions), your organization might invest in DR capabilities for only the High and Medium processes, not the Low.

Suppliers

In a large BIA effort (say, more than 20 business processes), you may identify several suppliers and other supply chain partners within your processes. You might decide to pull these critical suppliers and make a separate worksheet for them, in which you can capture additional information about them, including

- ✔ Company name, address, phone number, Internet URL, and so on
- ✔ Business contact's name, address, phone number, e-mail, and so on
- ✔ Name of business contact in your organization who has the business relationship with the supplier's business contact
- ✔ The processes that the supplier supports
- ✔ The goods and/or services that the supplier provides

You can use this critical supplier information as a jumping-off point when you begin building your DR plans.

Personnel

As you manipulate, slice, and dice your critical processes list (described in the preceding sections), you may begin to notice a few names of personnel who appear frequently in the most critical processes. You may want to take a closer look at those people and consider whether they're truly critical for so many business processes.

Items in your DR plans that relate to critical personnel may include cross-training or staff augmentation of some sort in order to reduce any possible exposures related to too many processes depending on too few individuals.

Determining the Maximum Tolerable Downtime

I discuss Maximum Tolerable Downtime in the section "Maximum Tolerable Downtime," earlier in this chapter; now, I go into this topic a little deeper.

Maximum Tolerable Downtime (MTD) is the maximum length of time a business process can be interrupted or unavailable without causing the business itself to fail. Here are some examples:

- ✔ An exclusively online retailer might go under if its online catalog is unavailable for several days.
- ✔ An airline might go out of business if it can't book flights for more than 48 hours.
- ✔ A delivery business might fail if it can't get dispatch information to its trucks within an hour of loading them.

You can have a really hard time arriving at reasonable MTD figures for your business, or any business. Business failures that occur because of disasters aren't an everyday occurrence. To my knowledge, no sites on the Internet have statistics on the connection between disasters and failed businesses. With so little data to work with, your MTD figure is probably going to be no better than an educated guess.

Calculating the Recovery Time Objective

The *Recovery Time Objective* (RTO) is the time period in which the organization should have the interrupted process running again, at or near the same capacity and conditions as before the disaster.

To determine the RTO, you need an idea of your Maximum Tolerable Downtime (MTD) value. Common sense should dictate that you need your RTO to be less than your MTD. In other words, you want your critical process restored and operating well before the point at which its downtime would threaten the very viability of the business. Otherwise, it's sort of like waiting three and a half minutes to begin administering CPR to a drowning victim.

For example, if the MTD for a critical process is seven days, you might set your RTO to four days.

You need to be as realistic as possible about the RTOs you specify for processes. A lower RTO does cost more than a higher RTO. You can't have it both ways — you either have a fast recovery or a cheap recovery.

If you've been reading ahead, or if you're just a quick study, you might be thinking that you don't want the cost of achieving a given RTO to exceed the value derived from the business process. For example, it doesn't make sense to invest $100,000 in equipment to reduce an RTO from four hours to one hour if the cost of downtime is only $1,000 per hour. Spending $100,000 to save $4,000 doesn't make good sense.

You figure out how much you can reasonably spend to improve the RTO and RPO much in the same way you buy auto insurance: You need to figure out how much the premiums cost, what the deductibles are, and what events the insurance covers.

In your BIA and DR plan development, you estimate the cost required to achieve an RTO. I go through this procedure in Chapter 6 through Chapter 8.

Calculating the Recovery Point Objective

A *Recovery Point Objective* (RPO) is the amount of data that you can lose in a disaster without being able to recover it.

For example, a company uses an online financial management application to manage its finances. Every day, employees enter invoices, payment requests, journal entries, and receipts. A disaster strikes the data center in which the application's servers reside. Backups were performed once per day, and an entire day's work was lost. This application's RPO is one day — in other words, the company can recover the application only to the point one day prior to the disaster.

Thinking ahead, if the organization wanted to shorten the RPO, it could do so by running backups more often or replicating transactions to another server in another location.

Like the RTO (see the preceding section), shortening a process's RPO generally carries a price. Later in the analysis, you can better determine the right balance between the cost of achieving an RPO and the value it provides the organization. Chapter 6 through Chapter 8 can help you strike this balance as you begin to formulate ways to make the various parts of your environment recoverable.

Part II
Building Technology Recovery Plans

The 5th Wave   By Rich Tennant

"It's a solid ID management and tracking system, Ted. Over 15 years on the Kalahari and we never lost a single lion."

In this part . . .

The chapters in this part are all about improving the resilience and recoverability of your entire technology infrastructure, from workstations to networks to servers and applications. Chapter 4 focuses on identifying which technology components support your critical business processes.

Chapter 5 through Chapter 8 delve into all the components in the layers of technology that support an organization's critical business processes — users, facilities, networks and systems, and applications and data.

Chapter 9 talks all about actually writing down your disaster recovery plans.

Chapter 4

Mapping Business Functions to Infrastructure

In This Chapter

▶ Using inventories to discover systems and devices

▶ Developing high-level architectures and schematics

▶ Finding the dependencies between systems

This chapter should help business people better understand technology. On the other hand, technology people can use this chapter to better understand why business people don't know more about technology.

Technology people, I have something to say to you: Disaster recovery planning isn't about the technology. It's about the business.

This chapter explains mapping business functions to the infrastructure and vice versa. You should know the principles and procedures related to this mapping because DR plans are business-process–centric. Align specific DR plans to business processes. IT systems don't make the business run — business processes do! You need to fully understand which information systems support which business processes. When you know which systems support the most critical business processes, you can take the next step — developing specific DR plans for recovering the right IT infrastructure in the right way, so that you can recover those business processes.

In order to develop DR plans for your IT systems, you need to know what your IT systems currently consist of. Makes sense, right? But a large number of organizations don't have a good grip on what actually makes all their systems work. (If you're in this category, you're in the right place — and I won't tell anyone.)

To begin, you first need to find out what inventory information exists for all of your IT hardware and software, and what applications people use in various departments. Hopefully, inventory information does exist in some form — otherwise, you have to start at the beginning. If you have to do this inventory yourself, just think of it as a treasure hunt — you're going to discover what you have and how it's all tied together!

Finding and Using Inventories

Inventories are just lists of the IT equipment and software that you have. You don't need to make them really complicated. Use the items in the following list to discover what you have in your infrastructure, how your business uses it, and what business applications it supports. If you already have one or more of your applications completely mapped out and inventoried, you can skip those applications and concentrate on what you don't have yet:

✔ **Hardware asset inventory:** The parts and pieces of your infrastructure. All of your servers, routers, firewalls, and other hard components. If you know their status or condition, categorize each appropriately — for example, as active or inactive, production or test. Also get the make, model, serial number, and location (room, rack, whatever), as shown in Figure 4-1. And don't forget network components, cables, fibre, and so on.

✔ **Software inventory:** You need to know what programs are running where. As you go through your servers, note what major components are running on each. Indicate make, version, patch level, which server it's running on, and other data points that make sense to you (such as major configuration options, media location, and so on). You can find a sample software inventory in Figure 4-2.

✔ **Business applications:** Talk with department heads (or their delegates) to find out what internal and external applications their departments use. Ask how they access and log in to these applications. With this information, you can begin to map business applications to hardware and software assets. A sample application inventory appears in Figure 4-3.

Truthfully, I hope you have something better than a spreadsheet (such as a small database or an application) for tracking your assets. However, many people use spreadsheets, and they may work for you if you don't have more than several hundred hardware and software components.

If your IT department doesn't have inventories such as those discussed in the preceding bulleted list, your accounting department probably maintains inventories of hardware and software purchases for depreciation purposes.

Larger organizations may have another readymade, reliable inventory available within a problem-management or helpdesk application, such as Remedy.

Figure 4-1: Sample hardware inventory.

	A	B	C	D	E	F	G
1	Hardware Inventory						
2	12-Aug-07						
3							
4	Building	Location	Rack	Make	Model	Serial	Asset Tag
5	Rdmd Willows Rd	DC 2nd fl	1	Sun	Ultra 2	UJEOF885577	1550
6	Rdmd Willows Rd	DC 2nd fl	1	Sun	Sparcstation 20		945
7	Rdmd Willows Rd	DC 2nd fl	1	Sun	Ultra 2	UJEOF729387	1550
8	Rdmd Willows Rd	DC 2nd fl	2	Sun	Ultra 2	UJEOF888273	1550
9	Rdmd Willows Rd	Dmarc		Kentrox	D-SERV II 56/6	44829	139
10	Rdmd Willows Rd	Dmarc		Cisco	4000M Router	4F56834	290

Figure 4-2: Sample software inventory.

	A	B	C	D	E	F
1	Software Inventory					
2	12-Aug-07					
3						
4	Make	Model	Version	System	Other Info	
5	Microsoft	Windows	Server 2003	Exchange		
6	Microsoft	Exchange	2000	email		
7	Red Hat	Linux	7.0	POP		
8	Red Hat	Linux	7.0	SMTP		
9	Red Hat	Linux	6.2	DNS / NTP		
10	Red Hat	Linux	7.1	Apache/WWW		

Figure 4-3: Sample application inventory.

	A	B	C	D	E	F
1	Application Inventory					
2	12-Aug-07					
3						
4	Name	System	Where	Owner	Description	
5	Quickbooks	spendy	internal	Dir Finance	financials	
6	Outlook/Exchange	exchange	internal	IT Mgr	email	
7	Intranet	intranet.company.com	internal	IT Mgr	intranet	
8	Salesforce.com	www.salesforce.com	external	Dir Sales	sales mgmt	
9	Concur	www.concur.com	external	Dir Finance	expense mgmt	
10	Barracuda	spam filter	internal	IT Mgr	spam filtering	

Top-down and bottom-up thinking

Successful DR planners need to see both views of the IT systems world: top-down and bottom-up. A top-down view of applications gives the DR planner an end-to-end view of the environment, or of a single process or application. Comparing top-down views of applications side by side can help the DR planner understand how resources are shared — or can be shared.

A bottom-up view tells the DR planner the details about each component that supports a system or process. This view permits the DR planning to determine precisely what changes you need to make to

✔ Build a recovery plan.

✔ Enact any prevention measures.

Using High-Level Architectures

One of the dirty little secrets in many organizations is the lack of *high-level architecture* — those boxes-and-arrows diagrams that logically depict systems and data in an organization or among multiple organizations. These diagrams, which are often accompanied by lists of components and/or specifications, show the relationship between components and layers of an application environment.

When you're conducting DR planning, you need to have not only an inventory-level view of your systems and applications, but also a high-level view of it.

You need at least these high-level diagrams of your systems environment:

✔ Data flow and storage

✔ Infrastructure

If you don't have these views of your environment, it's worth the time you need to develop them. Often, these diagrams are the only way you can get a complete end-to-end view of a single application or an entire environment.

Data flow and data storage diagrams

Data flow and data storage diagrams give you decidedly data-centric depictions of information flow within applications and between applications. In almost all cases, applications receive, store, send, and report information. Gaining a data-centric view of an application can help you, the DR planner, better understand how the application works and how it supports business processes, as well as providing you with a data-centric starting point for the development of recovery plans.

You find or create these data flow and storage diagrams so you can identify the systems that contain information and how the information moves between systems. If you want to develop plans for recovering vital and critical business processes, you have to know which systems support those processes and how those systems and processes are interconnected. Without this knowledge, you can't develop DR plans that help recover systems that support those processes — and if those processes aren't supported, they remain idle, putting business survival at risk.

Starting with the big picture often provides you with a path to identifying details. In other words, after you see the big picture, you can select parts of the big picture and explore the details about how specific applications work and are supported.

First example: E-mail environment

This section talks about a simple example of data flow in the Outlook e-mail application, which many businesses use.

Figure 4-4 shows the information flow through only principal components. For example, e-mail that flows between the mail server and the Internet goes through the firewall and spam filter that appear in the diagram, but you can most likely find network devices in the path that don't appear in the diagram, including one or more routers, switches, and security appliances. But for the purpose of e-mail, those other network devices are extraneous — they're just the plumbing.

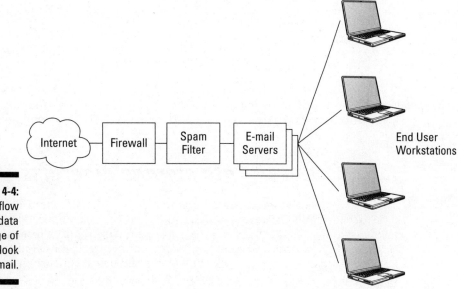

Figure 4-4:
Data flow
and data
storage of
Outlook
e-mail.

Similarly, the flow of e-mail between the mail server and e-mail clients (in other words, end-user workstations that run Outlook) also travels through one or more devices — routers, switches, and so on (devices that don't appear in Figure 4-4).

The purpose of the data flow diagram isn't to identify every component in the application ecosystem, but rather to identify all of the *active* components in the ecosystem — those components that play an actual role in the ecosystem. In an e-mail environment, mail servers, spam filters, and clients count as active components, but pass-through devices, such as routers and switches, don't count. You have ample time to go back and identify individual devices — I cover that in the section "Infrastructure diagrams and schematics," later in this chapter.

Second example: Client/server application

This section discusses a somewhat more complex application, one that has more pieces and parts, to show how you can depict an application environment's components in a data flow diagram. Figure 4-5 shows a financial management application that an organization runs in-house.

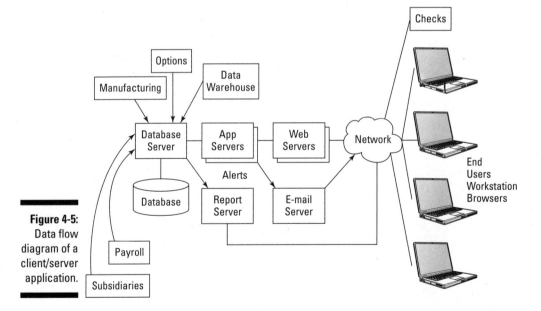

Figure 4-5: Data flow diagram of a client/server application.

This example shows a more complex set of servers, storage, and data flows between the subject application and external applications. The diagram includes a back-end database server, multiple application and Web servers, a reporting server, a data warehouse, an OLAP system (Online Analytical Processing system — another type of data warehouse system), and (of course) end users. The e-mail server also appears in the diagram because the application generates alerts to the end users. The diagram also includes a check-printing workstation — which is also an end-user workstation, but it's a special one because the check printer is directly attached to it.

The diagram also shows *external feeds* — data that flows from external sources (manufacturing, stock options, payroll, and business subsidiaries, in this example) into the financial system. Knowing about these connections to or from the outside world is essential if you want to have complete knowledge about not only the application, but all of the internal and external entities with which the application must communicate on a regular basis in order to work properly.

Don't try to jam all of the components of a complex system onto one piece of paper. Instead, rely on several illustrations that cover all the details, which you can put together to see the big picture.

Third example: External application

Because of the lower operational costs, organizations are flocking to ASP (Application Service Provider) models, now known as SaaS (Software as a Service) application models, in droves. In this section's example, an organization uses an application for internal business use, and the application is hosted by a service provider. Examples of this type of service provider include SalesForce.com, Intaact, and Winweb. Figure 4-6 shows such an environment, including data flows between the organization, service providers, and other internal and external objects.

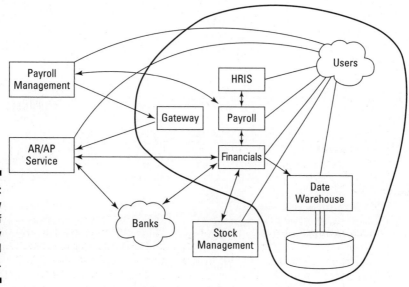

Figure 4-6:
Data-flow diagram of externally hosted applications.

In this example, three service providers — payroll management, an AR/AP (accounts receivable/accounts payable) service, and a stock management service — provide services to the organization, doing so through bi-directional data feeds between the organization and each of the service providers.

Banks are shown as a network cloud, signifying that the organization (and the AR/AP service) have established connections with several banks, presumably for processing electronic payments and receipts.

These external services have data feeds (in batches or real time — at this level of detail, it doesn't matter which) that connect the organization's financial and payroll applications.

The diagram clearly shows which applications and functions are internal to the organization and which are external. You need to distinguish internal versus external because this distinction influences the BIA (Business Impact Analysis), risk assessments, and actual DR plans. Recovering an in-house system is far different from recovering the ability to use an external service. Both internal and external applications may share some infrastructure (the network, for instance), but they require different recovery approaches.

The diagram's connectors between users and many of the system components also implies user interaction with each of the internal and external services. The diagram needs to show where user interaction occurs because user interaction with applications and services is usually essential to the continued operation of critical processes. The node labeled gateway (which connects the external payroll and AR/AP services together) has no user interaction. This lack of interaction, along with the fact that it's called gateway, identifies it as a back-end system that facilitates data transfers between services but otherwise requires no interaction with users. User interaction with specific application components is a subtle detail that matters in the long-run because recovery procedures need to include steps for user connectivity to all critical systems.

Infrastructure diagrams and schematics

Infrastructure diagrams, often referred to as schematics, are bottom-up. *Infrastructure diagrams* are the schematics (or diagrams) that show every piece and part in an environment. If you're a stickler for details, you'll have fun identifying what makes up your environment.

So how do you go about creating these drawings? You can take a number of approaches. You need to do a bit of thinking to figure out what may work best for you. Here are the activities that I discuss in the following sections:

- ✓ Interview subject matter experts.
- ✓ Get information from systems management tools.

✔ Go on walkabouts and have a look at equipment and systems for yourself.

✔ Look at inventory lists to get an idea of the systems and devices that exist (although you still have to figure out the relationships and connectivity between them).

Depending on the size of your environment, a single individual may be able to carry out all of these activities. But in a larger environment, you may need a team of people to get it done.

Interviewing subject matter experts

You can begin putting the overall infrastructure schematic together by interviewing network and systems engineers, and getting from each what information you can in order to figure out how your environment was put together.

In all but the simplest environments, you'll probably encounter one or two anomalies, such as

✔ **Conflicts:** Ted says something is put together this way, but Bill says it's done that way. What really matters is the truth: How does it really work? If you come across such a conflict, someone needs to help the experts decide — or you need to find another expert!

✔ **Gaps:** You may find a part of the network or systems environment that no one knows about. Perhaps the person who built it isn't around any longer, he or she didn't write any documentation about it, and no one else has bothered to figure it out.

Using network and systems management tools

Someone in the IT group may have tools, such as network discovery or mapping tools, that provide some network architecture information that you can use as a starting point.

Here are some examples of the kinds of discover and mapping tools that can give you some indication of the network architecture:

✔ **High-end tools:** High-priced and comprehensive tools that larger organizations use to perform a wide variety of network and device management functions. Here are some examples:

   • **HP OpenView (`www.openview.hp.com/products`):** Expensive enterprise-level tool. If your organization already has it, one of the people using it should be able to get you some network maps.

   • **IBM NetView (`www.ibm.com/software/tivoli/products/netview`):** A high-end full-function network management tool.

- **Sun Solstice Enterprise Manager (www.sun.com/sem):** A high-end environment.

- **LANsurveyor (www.neon.com/LSwin.shtml):** A tool that maps and diagrams a network in real time.

- **netViz (www.netviz.com):** A network visualization tool.

✔ **Less expensive/free tools:** These tools provide some basic functionality for diagramming networks:

- **Network Magic (www.networkmagic.com):** A workstation-based tool that includes diagramming and other functions. Comes in evaluation and fee-based versions.

- **Cheops (www.sourceforge.net/projects/cheops-ng):** Free tool for mapping and monitoring a network. Figure 4-7 shows a screen shot from this tool.

- **FreeMap (www.qualys.com/products/trials):** This free tool is run from a central location, so your network needs to be reachable through the Internet. This tool probably can't map the portion of your network that's behind a firewall. (See Figure 4-8.)

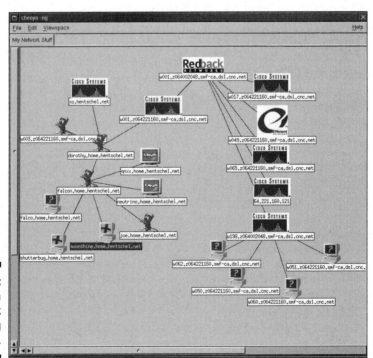

Figure 4-7: Cheops, a network mapping tool.

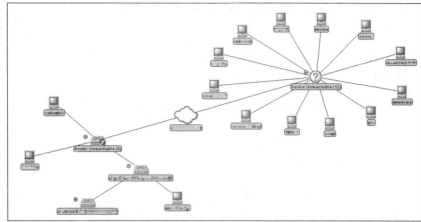

Figure 4-8:
Qualys
FreeMap.

Even good network mapping tools can't identify every device or system in your network — omissions can occur for a variety of technical reasons, including

- **Non-managed and non-networked devices:** A device on the network that doesn't have IP connectivity, such as a dial-in terminal server, modem, CSU/DSU, DACS, and so on.

- **Invisible devices:** Mapping tools probably won't see a non-managed hub that doesn't have an IP address.

- **Bridging firewalls:** Firewalls are like hubs, in that they don't have IP addresses. For that reason, they're invisible. (A separate management port, however, might be visible on the network.)

- **Not powered on:** Of course, mapping or management tools can't see devices that aren't turned on. Those powered-down devices could still be vital, if not critical — for example, cold standby servers and devices that are swapped into service if online components fail.

 Network management and mapping tools may not detect systems and devices on the other side of a firewall, so you may need to use these tools from different logical places on the network to discover everything.

 Even if you have maps that appear to be complete, you still want to interview subject matter experts to validate what the mapping tools have discovered. (The preceding section discusses these interviews.)

Going on walkabouts

A picture paints a thousand words. Whoever creates, verifies, or updates drawings and schematics should get out of his or her chair and have a look at the systems and networks in those drawings.

Bring a subject matter expert (SME) with you. Have him or her point out the servers and devices from your drawing. Be inquisitive: Look around, ask questions, follow cables to see where they go. You might find something that your SME forgot or didn't even know about.

Looking at inventory lists

If you can find them, lists of equipment are another place to start. Granted, inventory lists don't give you much of a clue as to the relationships between devices, but if such a list is all you have, it's a starting point.

Inventory lists can also supplement other data gathering methods, such as interviewing subject matter experts and creating diagrams and schematics.

Here are some potential advantages of inventory lists:

✔ Inventory lists contain devices and systems that you may otherwise miss.

✔ If you can find the person who created the inventory list, that person may be able to help explain how everything works together.

✔ The creation of an inventory list may help you understand the flow or functions of various networks or systems.

Some disadvantages include

✔ Inventory lists may not differentiate systems and devices that are in production use versus development, test, or lab use.

✔ Inventory lists might not indicate that systems and devices are no longer in use. Just because the device is listed doesn't mean it's critical, powered on, or even still present.

Even though inventory lists aren't the best way to determine what components are critical for the performance of an application, *good* inventory lists may add value to the effort.

Even if you have network management systems and mapping tools, still compare what those programs find against your inventory so you can validate the completeness of those programs' results.

Developing the schematics

Describing the steps for drawing a network schematic is a little bit like telling someone how to paint a still-life painting. It's part art and part science. Don't worry about right or wrong methods to depict application environments —

just create a schematic that can help the reader better understand how a system or network is designed and how it works.

You can lay out a schematic in two primary ways:

- ✔ **Location-based:** The arrangement of components on a diagram roughly corresponds to those components' actual locations. For a large network, you could base the diagram's layout geographically. On a smaller scale, you could correspond the diagram's components to the real components' locations on a corporate campus.

- ✔ **Function-based:** Arrange the layout of elements on a diagram according to their function or application.

Figure 4-9 shows a schematic of a portion of a nationwide network. The drawing identifies individual components. However, additional levels of detail can show additional components, with high-level (perhaps national) diagrams illustrating major components, and regional or local diagrams showing individual components in local networks.

The example schematic in Figure 4-9 shows a part of what appears to be a regional or national network. Two ATM switches, FR17 and FR18, connect to what appears to be a fiber ring, one part going towards Vancouver, BC and the other going towards Portland, OR. Full-mesh connections go from these two ATM switches to a pair of routers, SEART01 and SEART02. Behind those routers are more routers and also some switches, each feeding to specific locations and functions.

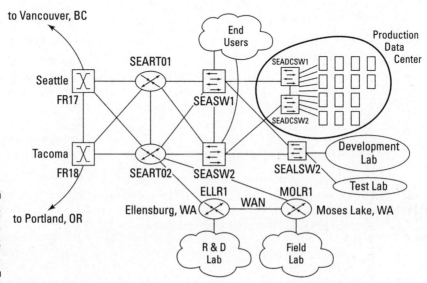

Figure 4-9:
A sample
network
schematic.

This network needs additional drawings, one for each of the functions shown: R&D Lab, Field Lab, Production Data Center, Development Lab, Test Lab, and End Users. This high-level diagram doesn't show individual components for those locations. You can usually show those details much more easily in individual diagrams because the overall network is way too complicated to include all the components in a single drawing.

The example in Figure 4-9 shows network components only, no servers or other components. You need other logical or physical diagrams to depict servers and other devices, including how or where they connect to networks.

Developing and maintaining schematics is a serious undertaking that requires a long-term commitment. However, DR isn't the only function that benefits from such drawings: Network engineering, capacity planning, troubleshooting, and future expansion can all use schematics.

Identifying Dependencies

Creating inventories is practically child's play. Developing data flow diagrams and schematics is a bit more challenging because you have to figure out how and where data comes and goes. But the identification of dependencies between systems, devices, and yet-to-be-discovered components will really bake your noodle. It's the answer to the question, "If I unplug this, what will stop working?"

I don't recommend trying to answer that question by actually unplugging systems or devices. Instead, fall back on these proven methods of gathering information:

- ✔ **Interviews:** Identify subject matter experts and talk with them about systems, networks, and applications. Specifically, ask what internal (to the system), internal (to the organization), and external dependencies exist between devices, systems, and applications.

- ✔ **Configurations:** You or someone with administrative privileges needs to examine system configurations, devices, and applications, and identify external services, systems, devices, and so on.

- ✔ **Management tools and applications:** Perhaps your organization is already using tools and applications to configure and manage systems and devices. For instance, you might have a configuration management database (CMDB) and companion application that you use to manage devices, systems, and/or applications in your organization. If your organization does have a CMDB, you might be using *standard server images* (standard versions and configurations), which probably means that most or all of your servers are configured almost identically. This consistency makes the task of identifying dependencies considerably simpler.

Why identify dependencies? Your mission in this phase of the disaster recovery project is to identify systems that are critical to the support of business processes. The systems that support business processes aren't just the systems with the applications, but also everything else that you need to keep those systems running properly.

The following sections discuss dependencies in greater detail. If you're a propeller-head, you can have a lot of fun in these sections!

Inter-system dependencies

Dependencies may exist within and between systems within your organization. You need to know these dependencies if you want to create high-quality DR plans.

You can find many layers of dependencies in application environments. Even if I had a lot of time on my hands, I'm not sure that I could create a complete list. In this book, I break the layers down by category. But your organization may have more categories than I list in this section. The categories I use are

- System dependencies
- Communications dependencies
- Network service dependencies
- Management service dependencies
- Security dependencies
- Application dependencies

The nature of your business or your applications may necessitate additional categories of dependencies. For instance, you might have dependencies based on security level, organization department, customer, and so on.

System dependencies

System dependencies include features, tools, and other components on a specific system that an application (or other component in the stack) requires to function properly, such as

- **Hardware configuration:** The basics — how much memory, disk space, other components, and also CMOS/BIOS and other hardware-level configurations each system contains.
- **Boot options:** Does each server need any non-default boot configurations or options to work correctly? Does the server boot from an image on a SAN (Storage Area Network) or other external disk storage?

✔ **Clustering and failover:** Organizations often set up clusters of servers with failover or load-balancing capabilities for time-critical applications. I discuss failover and load balancing in detail in Chapter 7 and Chapter 8.

✔ **Inter-Process Communications (IPC):** Sockets, shared memory, messages, and so on. How many do you have, how big are they, what are their security settings, and so on.

✔ **Service configuration:** Does each server have any non-standard services or configurations that it needs to operate properly? Examples include disabled services that are normally enabled (and vice versa), different service restart parameters, and so on.

✔ **Storage configuration:** Minimally, applications or services may depend on disk and file system configuration settings. If the system has on-board or attached RAID (Redundant Array of Independent Disks, which I explain in Chapter 7) or other storage, that storage matters, too.

✔ **User accounts:** Do specific user accounts need to be on the system for each system to function properly, or must certain accounts be configured in particular ways?

✔ **Software tools:** The possibilities are practically endless. A few examples include

 • Disk management tools

 • User authentication tools

 • Management agents

 • Security tools

✔ **Network services on the system:** Network features and tools on the system itself, not elsewhere in the network. These dependencies include incoming/outgoing e-mail (must a service or daemon be running on the system for e-mail communications to work?), domain name service (DNS), Network Time Protocol (NTP), remote console (incoming, outgoing, or both), and potentially many more.

If you have system management tools, they manage most of the dependencies in the preceding list, which makes servers and other devices a little easier for you to manage.

Communications dependencies

Everything is networked (well, almost). Your application servers communicate with users, services, and other applications. This category includes the following communications dependencies:

✔ **Network configuration:** Some of the settings that may matter include the settings for the DHCP server, DNS servers, subnet mask, gateways, routing table entries, and so on.

✔ **Host-to-host communication:** For example, is IPSec or GRE tunneling, or SSH, set up between hosts?

✔ **Fibre Channel to SAN:** The configuration of communications to a Storage Area Network (SAN) may be critical on some systems.

Network service dependencies

This section deals with network services that exist somewhere within the organization. Those services may or may not be hosted on whichever system you're analyzing at the time. Examples of these services include

✔ **Identity management:** Identity management matters if the system authenticates users by using a network-based service. The system must be configured to properly connect to the right service in the right way.

✔ **Two-factor authentication:** Although authentication is technically a part of identity management, it's worth mentioning in its own bullet because you usually have a separate infrastructure involved.

✔ **E-mail:** What organization doesn't have it? Critical applications often depend on e-mail to communicate status to users and sometimes even to transfer data between applications.

✔ **Web services:** Application interfaces based on SOAP (Simple Object Access Protocol, and also Service-Oriented Architecture Protocol) and other technologies.

✔ **PBX (Telephone systems), VoIP:** PBXs, whether the IP kind or older ones, are increasingly digital and networked. VoIP, or Voice over TCP/IP, is totally networked. Although systems themselves may not depend on the VoIP systems, some VoIP systems depend on communications servers or gateways, especially in call centers and other environments in which applications control phone usage to some extent.

✔ **Fax:** Usually human-operated at one or both ends, but often on the critical path for business processes.

✔ **Proxy servers and gateways:** They come in all shapes and sizes; you may think of only Web proxy servers, but you can find proxy servers and gateways that fulfill many other functions, as well.

✔ **Backup:** Organizations generally perform a central back up, using a dedicated backup server.

✔ **Data replication:** May or may not be a part of a server or database cluster. But the data goes to another server or storage system in near-real time.

✔ **Network time:** NTP (Network Time Protocol), the protocol used to synchronize the time-of-day clocks on systems and network devices. System clocks are notorious for *drift* (when clocks stray from the correct time; with enough drift, the strangest malfunctions can occur), and NTP is the standard solution.

Management service dependencies

Services that are specific to the management of systems, devices, applications, and so forth have their own dependencies. Some items you may need include

- ✔ **Agents for patch management:** Agented patch management systems require an agent on each system in order to properly detect the presence of software patches.

- ✔ **Agents for capacity management:** When your system gets low on memory or disk space, does it send alerts or traps (messages) to a management console?

- ✔ **Agents for alert management:** When the system experiences an error (such as service failure or hardware failure), does it send traps to a management console?

Security dependencies

When I talk about security dependencies, I mean security mechanisms or settings that the application or service needs to run, security that organization policy may require, or security that's just a good idea. Some possibilities include

- ✔ **Firewall:** Critical in some environments, a great idea in others. Protects applications from unwanted network traffic, including the kind of traffic that can make an application (or service) malfunction or fail.

- ✔ **Anti-virus:** Maybe your application doesn't require an anti-virus program, but just try and convince others that it's unnecessary.

- ✔ **IDS/IPS (Intrusion Detection System/Intrusion Prevention System):** On-board IDS, which usually runs as some sort of a daemon or service, or shim in the IP stack. It listens to network traffic and alerts on anomalies.

- ✔ **Integrity management:** Tools such as Tripwire may be present and crucial for security and quality management.

- ✔ **PKI (Public Key Infrastructure):** Your application may depend on externally served encryption keys that may be on a key server or an appliance.

Application dependencies

Sometimes, one application depends on another for proper functioning. Hopefully, these examples can help you identify specific dependencies in your environment:

- ✔ **Data feeds:** One application may require a continuous (or batched) feed of transactions from other applications in order to work properly (or to just avoid null results).

- ✔ **Interfaces:** Applications often communicate with each other in real time in order to work properly.

Other dependencies

Heaven forbid, but businesses often have dependencies on end-user workstations. For instance, financial reporting may depend on someone's spreadsheet macros to crunch the numbers in ways that the financial management system just can't do. Having critical processes depend on specific end-user workstations is almost always a bad idea because workstations are nowhere near as robust as servers. Also, because they're in the hands of users, they're subject to changes that the IT department can't control.

External dependencies

Applications and services may require services or functions external to the enterprise in order to function properly, if at all. These services and functions include

- ✔ **E-mail:** The ubiquitous messaging platform used to transport not just messages but also data between entities.

- ✔ **Voice communications:** Oh yeah, people need to be able to communicate with each other via voice. Not always tied directly to applications, but often tied directly to processes.

- ✔ **Fax:** Like voice communications, fax communications can be essential or even critical to the recovery of business processes.

- ✔ **Domain name service (DNS):** Absolutely necessary for any network communications. DNS translates domain names (such as www.avaya.com) into the IP addresses that systems actually use to communicate with each other.

- ✔ **World Wide Web:** Sometimes required by applications, frequently required by people, and sometimes on the critical path of vital business processes.

- ✔ **Federated identity:** Some environments use federated identity for user identity management. You need to understand the data architecture and data flows if your organization uses federated identity.

- ✔ **PKI:** Your applications or supporting infrastructure might depend on an external key services provider for encryption, decryption, or verification of data.

- ✔ **Online language translators:** Some organizations that have constituents in many languages use external online language translators to understand their inbound messages or to translate outbound ones.

- ✔ **External service providers:** The functions that applications use in external service providers, such as Salesforce.com and Winweb, could be on the critical path of internal applications and services.

Generally speaking, you may want to pay attention to the two types of external dependencies:

- **External dependencies for external functions:** Functions that run on external systems may depend on other external systems or services. For example, in order to send an e-mail message from your business to some external addressee, DNS connectivity to the outside world must function so your mail server can get the IP address for the addressee's mail server.

- **External dependencies for internal functions:** Functions that take place inside your network but depend on some external resource. For example, a currency conversion tool runs internally, but it requires a daily refresh of conversion rates which originates from someplace outside the organization. The currency conversion tool may work perfectly today, but if it can't get new rates tonight, it may not work accurately tomorrow.

Chapter 5

Planning User Recovery

· ·

In This Chapter

▶ Making sure end-user workstations keep working

▶ Keeping end users communicating

· ·

*P*eople are an essential part of all critical business processes. Even highly-automated business processes would soon break down without human involvement, guidance, and intervention.

Recovering users means recovering their workstations and their ability to communicate with people inside and outside of their organization. You have to analyze a lot of details to understand the role of end users' workstations and communications needs in critical business processes.

In this chapter, I discuss various aspects of recovering user workstations, including

- ✔ Web terminals (primarily used just as a Web browser)
- ✔ Client-side applications and tools
- ✔ Access to centrally located information

In this chapter, I also discuss recovering users' communication needs, including

- ✔ Voice communications
- ✔ E-mail
- ✔ Fax and instant messaging (IM)

Recovering these capabilities requires recovery plans that quickly restore users' ability to perform their tasks and support critical business processes. This chapter focuses on identifying important issues. When you know these issues, you can help develop the appropriate recovery activities.

In the event that the facilities where your employees work are also damaged in a disaster, those facilities also require recovery efforts. You can read about activities related to recovering facilities and work centers in Chapter 6.

Managing and Recovering End-User Computing

People play a vital role in the operation of business processes. Increasingly, the people portion of business processes involves the use of desktop or notebook computers. End-user computing varies widely, depending on the tasks that each employee performs during his or her workday. Some examples include

✔ Using e-mail to send and receive notifications from applications and other users

✔ Accessing company Web-based applications

✔ Accessing external Web-based applications

✔ Accessing client/server applications

✔ Accessing and working with documents on file servers

✔ Accessing and working with documents on the workstation

For some of the functions in the preceding list, the user's workstation is little more than a terminal. For other functions, the workstation acts as a local processing and/or data resource.

Most users use both the terminal aspects and the local processing aspects of their workstations, but both functions aren't necessarily critical for all people, processes, or tasks.

One of the purposes of the Business Impact Analysis is the careful analysis of business processes. That analysis helps you figure out what functions are critical for any given process or task.

Because employees may use workstations in many different ways, managing and recovering those workstations involves a wide variety of approaches. The following sections discuss these different approaches for managing and recovering workstations, as though they were separate environments:

✔ As terminals

✔ As a means to access centralized information

✔ As application clients

✔ As local computers

Regardless of which of the functions in the preceding list are in play, you also need to figure out how to manage and recover workstation operating systems.

I'm not pretending that employees use end-user workstations exclusively as terminals, or application clients, or local computing resources. Most users utilize their workstations for a combination of tasks. I look at each of these uses separately in the following sections, effectively dissecting users' work patterns.

Although employees frequently use end-user workstations in a variety of modes, you need to consider only the uses that are key to specific business processes.

Workstations as Web terminals

From a disaster recovery point of view, the easiest function to recover on end-user workstations is their use as terminals — especially if those terminal functions use native components, such as Web browser software. But even in this simple case, several factors require consideration:

- ✔ Plug-ins
- ✔ Mashups
- ✔ Web browser configurations

The following sections discuss these factors.

Application plug-ins

Just because you access one or more of your critical applications via Web browsers doesn't mean your DR planning efforts are going to be issue-free. When you're mapping out all the moving parts and pieces of an end-to-end application environment, you need to identify all Web browser plug-ins that your Web applications require to operate properly.

Some examples of Web applications include, but are certainly not limited to, the following:

- ✔ **Adobe Acrobat:** To read PDF files
- ✔ **Apple Quicktime:** To play video and audio clips
- ✔ **Adobe Flash:** To display Web pages' rich Flash content
- ✔ **Shockwave:** To display Web pages' Shockwave content
- ✔ **Windows Media Player and other media players:** To play video and audio clips
- ✔ **Document viewers:** To view documents, spreadsheets, presentations, project plans, technical drawings, and so on

✔ **Java Virtual Machine (JVM):** To run Java applets

✔ **Custom plug-ins:** Developed by your organization or a third party

If your critical Web application(s) use plug-ins, take a closer look at those plug-ins. Some of the issues related to plug-ins and other browser add-ons that may need attention are

✔ **Installation and update:** Where do your required plug-ins come from — are they hosted by your application server or a third party, or do they come from external sources?

✔ **Configuration:** Do any of your plug-ins require configuration, and do those configurations have default or non-default settings?

✔ **Management:** Do the plug-ins require central management via IT infrastructure management tools or by the end users themselves?

✔ **Access control:** Do the plug-ins require access to other resources, such as files on the end-user workstation or elsewhere in the environment?

You usually need to dissect your end-user workstations to answer the questions in the preceding list and identify other issues that may make the difference between easily recovered end-user workstations and those that just won't work despite a lot of troubleshooting.

Managing mashups

Some Web-based applications have code that brings in content and functions from a lot of different applications at the same time. Mashups use APIs (Application Programming Interfaces — ways of getting at information from within another program) from various Web sites, blending code from these different sources to create the result seen in the browser window. Here are examples of some visually interesting mashups:

✔ **HousingMaps.com:** A mashup of Craigslist classified ads and Google Maps. HousingMaps.com shows individual classified ads against a Google Maps backdrop, allowing the user to choose items by their visual location. Clicking a pin brings up an Ajax window with the address and thumbnails. You can see HousingMaps.com in Figure 5-1.

✔ **Chicagocrime.org:** This mashup shows reported crimes of various types against street maps of the city of Chicago.

In some critical environments, such as the sites in the preceding list, mashups aren't small potatoes — they're necessary elements of an application.

Applications that don't have well-documented specifications make you do some sleuthing to discover mashups. You can start by talking with the application's Web developers. Then, you have to do some analysis to determine whether any of the mashups you found are critical to the user experience or are merely nice-to-have features.

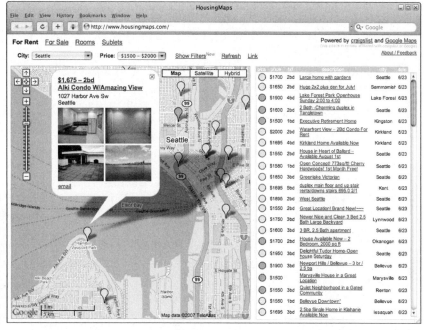

Figure 5-1:
A mashup
that
combines
Craigslist
and Google
Maps.

Mashup Web sites don't necessarily increase application risks with regards to disaster recovery. They *do* make applications more complex, however. You definitely need to identify mashups in business applications so you can develop proper DR plans for those applications.

The casual observer may not easily see mashup code in a Web-based business application. You may need to conduct interviews with system designers to identify any mashups in business applications.

Recovery notes for workstations as Web terminals

In this section, I discuss specific recovery efforts that an organization might take in order to get workstations as Web terminals up and running as quickly as possible during and after a disaster.

Many of the concepts in the following list are proactive in nature — they're things you need to do far in advance before a disaster occurs:

✔ **Use standard configurations for Web terminal workstations.** Developing and sticking to standard configurations has many business benefits, including recoverability. Ensure that standard configurations include all necessary plug-ins, document viewers, network configurations, authentication settings, and other items necessary for the workstations' proper function.

✔ **Use imaging technology for standard configurations.** Using standard images permits your IT department to quickly *build* (meaning install and configure the operating system, applications, and tools for) replacement workstations.

✔ **Build workstation images for a variety of hardware configurations.** Having these images increases the likelihood that IT staff will be able to build workstations by using not only the hardware that your organization uses on a regular basis, but also other hardware that you use less often.

✔ **Consider using a thin-client workstation model for production use, as well as for recovery purposes.** Thin-client technology, such as Citrix, permits workstations to act as terminals, even when the workstation uses programs such as Word and Excel, which are actually run on a central server rather than locally on the workstation. A thin-client environment greatly simplifies centralized management and configuration of client-side software.

✔ **Back up workstation imaging systems so that you can quickly rebuild them in a disaster.** These backups facilitate the rapid recovery of end-user workstations.

Also consider the workstation operating system recovery issues discussed in the section "Managing and recovering workstation operating systems," later in this chapter.

Workstation access to centralized information

I would argue that a sensible organization promotes (if not requires) that documents, spreadsheets, and other files are stored centrally on servers, rather than solely on user workstations.

Workstations that function as Web terminals, distributed application clients, and standalone computing platforms also need access to centralized information, often in similar ways and requiring some common features and services to do so.

The types of server access workstations require include to

✔ File and print servers

✔ Web servers

✔ Application servers

I explore these types of access in more detail in the following sections.

Accessing file and print servers

File servers store information for workgroups, departments, and organizations, often organizing the information into hierarchies of folders. IT departments often set up one or more drive letter mappings, in which they map a PC-like drive letter, such as `M:`, to a file server name, such as `\\server2\depts\ legal`. Linux and Mac systems use different mechanisms than Windows, but the effect is the same.

Print servers operate similarly, except that they facilitate access to network- or direct-attached printers, plotters, and other output devices.

Here are the primary issues related to file and print server access:

- ✔ **Mapping:** Whether through Windows drive mapping, shortcuts and links, Samba, or NFS (Network File System), end-user workstations require some configuration information so they can find the server.
- ✔ **Authentication:** Users need to authenticate to the network, or to servers directly, in order to access files and printers.
- ✔ **Access controls:** File and print servers use access controls that determine which users can access directories, files, and printers.
- ✔ **Directory service:** Applications need domain name service (DNS) or Windows Internet Name Service (WINS) so user workstations can locate systems on the corporate network, such as application servers, file servers, and print servers, as well as systems on the Internet.

Accessing Web servers

Web servers facilitate access to both static content and information in applications. Web-server access issues include

- ✔ **Authentication:** Users often need to be authenticated to networks and/or applications in order to access content on Web servers.
- ✔ **Access controls:** Web servers use access controls to determine which users and groups are permitted to access specific information in the Web server.
- ✔ **Directory service:** Workstations need domain name service (DNS) so they can locate Web servers on the network.

Accessing application servers

Application servers run software programs that are a part of a business application. Client/server and distributed application environments also have separate application components installed on end-user workstations. This client/side software needs to be able to communicate with application servers.

Issues related to application server access include

- ✔ **Authentication:** Applications need to know who's requesting access. Usually, the client-side component collects user credentials and passes them to the application, which then must consult an internal database or a network-based authentication service to validate the user.

- ✔ **Directory service:** Workstations need domain name service (DNS) so end-user workstations can find servers and other resources on the network.

Recovery notes for workstation access to central information

When end-user workstations need to access various types of information on the network, file servers, Web servers, and application servers manage this access. Consider these tips for preparation and recovery:

- ✔ Properly configure DNS and/or WINS so end-user workstations can find these servers on the network.

- ✔ Include a network authentication service so users can identify themselves to servers and other resources.

- ✔ Make the entire set of access control permissions within servers easily recoverable and transferable to replacement servers so the same access controls protect information in a recovery environment.

- ✔ Regularly back up servers — or replicate data to off-site servers — so you can recover data in the event of a disaster.

- ✔ Set up a replacement network that has different IP (Internet Protocol) address numbering and different logical and physical architecture so you can transfer the entire set of workstation-server interaction if you need to.

- ✔ Consider bandwidth-intensive interactions between servers and workstations for optimization. In a recovery environment, servers and workstations may be separated by considerable distance and/or slow networks.

Workstations as application clients

Client/server computing revolutionized computing in the early 1990s by freeing up valuable resources on central computers and moving UI (user interface) logic out to end-user workstations that had relatively ample computing power. Many organizations implemented client/server applications, and many of those applications are still in use today.

One of the issues that was often overlooked in client/server computing was the burden of managing client-side software and related configurations. Network-based workstation management software was still in its infancy, but even in today's more advanced management platforms, managing client/side software is still a major chore for IT shops. So, naturally, you need to make the whole matter of client-side software management a part of your DR plans if you have any client/server software.

Often, client/server software has multiple client-side components, including

- ✓ **Base software:** Software installed on application servers
- ✓ **Client-side application business logic:** Software installed on workstations
- ✓ **Configuration data:** Settings that determine how base software and client-side software communicate with each other
- ✓ **Patches:** Fixes and updates made to the base software and client-side software since initial installation

When I use the term *client/server* in this book, I mostly refer to distributed, two-tier, three-tier, or multi-tier applications with some of the pieces running on your end-user workstations.

The following sections delve into the management and recovery of these components in greater detail.

Client/server base software

Some client/server environments use a standard client-side software package installation, plus separate programs or scripts for each business application.

A number of questions and issues about client/server base software arise:

- ✓ **Installation:** Can you make the base software a part of the workstation image? Can you automatically install it over the network? To install the software, does a human need to enter a license code or configuration data?
- ✓ **Availability:** Is the version you're using still generally available?
- ✓ **Release/installation media:** Do you have portable release or installation media for the software?
- ✓ **Compatibility with newer operating systems:** Does the base software work with newer versions of Windows and other operating systems?

The questions in the preceding list indicate that you're dealing with *old* software. Client/server environments aren't in this season, and they haven't been for quite a while. The main question you need to ask about your client/server software is, "Could I rebuild the client side of my client/server environment if I had to rebuild it from scratch?" The preceding list should help you find the answer.

Client-side business logic

Client/server applications have some of the application code running on the server and some running on the client. On the client side, the software is installed and updated in some manner. You can use some of the following mechanisms to get client-side software onto the workstation:

✔ Written (and, optionally, compiled) by a developer and installed through an updating mechanism within the client/server environment

✔ Written by a developer and installed through a separate updating mechanism, such as Microsoft SMS (Systems Management Server)

✔ Written by a developer and installed manually by IT personnel, either in person or through an Internet (or intranet) connection

The preceding list isn't all-inclusive, but it can jog your memory about the possible means by which client-side software in a client/server environment finds its way to the clients — your end-user workstations. You can find information in the manuals that came with the base software — hopefully, someone has saved those manuals!

Client-side configuration data

Depending on which client/server environment you're using, your end-user workstations may have another dimension to consider — configuration settings in the workstation's client/server software. Configuration settings may be separate from the client-side code itself. Centralized management tools may manage those settings, or you may have to make any adjustments manually on each workstation.

Here are some of the possible configuration settings:

✔ Server name

✔ Port number to use when communicating with the server

✔ Authentication settings

✔ Behavior settings, such as initial views

✔ Usability settings, such as colors and fonts

Some of these settings are critical to the basic function of the application, but others are more for the user's convenience and preferences. All of the settings in the preceding list, except for usability settings, may govern whether the application functions.

Determine whether all the end-user workstations in a given client/server environment require and have the same configuration settings, different classes of workstations have their own settings, or configurations are more chaotic with no rhyme or reason behind the variations in settings.

Client-side patches

Your client/server environment may use patches to get software, application, or configuration updates out to client systems. If your environment uses patches, it may have its own patching mechanism, or it may use a centralized mechanism, such as Microsoft SMS (Systems Management Server), or a third-party tool, such as Blade Logic.

Consider the following client software patching issues:

- ✔ Does the client/server environment use patching at the application level?
- ✔ Can you use a management view to determine which clients have which patches installed?
- ✔ Is the historical record of patching well documented?

The answers to the questions in the preceding list can tell you how to make updates to client-side software, as well as determine what patches are on your client workstations today. I discuss patching in more detail in the section "Managing and recovering workstation operating systems," later in this chapter.

Recovery notes for workstations as application clients

The following list gives you some specific preparation and recovery actions that you can take to get end-user workstations that have client/server software back on the air:

- ✔ **To the greatest extent reasonably possible, use standard configurations for client/server workstations.** Standard configurations also help reduce support costs. Ensure that standard configurations include all necessary components, from base software to application code and configuration, and whatever OS settings are required to support the software.

- ✔ **Use imaging technology and tools that can help you quickly build replacement client/server workstations.** Test your images in a variety of workstation types: In a disaster scenario, you may have to build workstations on hardware platforms that you don't routinely work with.

- ✔ **Consider a thin-client environment, with client/server software installed on servers, reducing workstations to smart terminals.** Thin-client technology, such as Citrix, enables the organization to centralize client-side software installation, configuration, and maintenance.

- ✔ **Back up workstation imaging systems.** If you can recover those imaging systems in a disaster, you can use them to build new client/server workstations, as needed.

The section "Managing and recovering workstation operating systems," later in this chapter, explains how to recover the base operating system on end-user workstations.

Is it any wonder that organizations are trending away from client/server computing to Web-based applications? The responsibility of managing software and configurations on hundreds or thousands of computers is more than most IT departments can shoulder.

Workstations as local computers

Many workers in an organization use their workstations to compose and manage documents, spreadsheets, presentations, technical drawings, and project plans. Workstations may have additional software tools for application development and testing, data analysis and modeling, graphical modeling, statistical analysis, and who knows what else.

Often, users store the data (the actual files or databases that they create and use) locally on the workstation, especially when the workstation is a laptop.

You need to decide whether using these other programs is truly critical to specific business processes or whether end-user workstations are more ancillary to these processes. Are workstations, acting as local computers, really on the critical path for a given process, or do they have a non-critical role?

The management and recovery of workstations as local computers have three important aspects:

- ✔ **Programs:** The application programs that you use to create and manage documents and data.
- ✔ **Data:** The data that users create and work with on their workstations.
- ✔ **Procedure:** Documents about the use of local programs, in terms of its support of critical business processes.

The three classes of information in the preceding list differ greatly in terms of management and recovery. When you determine that workstations fall in the critical path of business processes, both programs and data are vital, but you manage them in different ways.

Workstation software

A successful disaster recovery effort needs to manage the local software for workstations on the critical path of business processes. Consider these factors as you build your DR plans:

- ✔ **Installation:** What method do you use to install programs into the local workstations? Are the programs part of a standard workstation image, or do you install them by using an install image on a server? Did the end user purchase the software directly? How do end users or the IT department manage activation keys? What installation options are chosen? (Now you know why IT departments are averse to a lot of non-standard tools on workstations!)

✔ **Configuration:** Are configuration settings centrally managed, or does each end user control them? If more than one end user performs similar tasks, do they all use identical configurations?

✔ **Versioning:** Does IT control which versions of software tools get installed and maintained on workstations? Do workstations have the latest versions or some older versions? Can these older versions be installed on newly-built workstations? Will the vendor provide license keys for the older versions that you still use?

✔ **Patches:** Do the programs on end-user workstations have patches installed? Are those patches configured to check for and install updates? Do the end-user workstations need access to release media in order to install patches? Do patches alter the behavior of the software, potentially altering the business process (or other systems)? Do you maintain any central management or recordkeeping related to patches?

✔ **Configuration:** Document settings associated with the correct operation of the program, rather than the look-and-feel preferences (although those preferences are important, too, because they help make end-user procedures more consistently match the actual appearance that the workstation software imparts).

The issues in the preceding list should get you thinking about your own environment. You may have more issues to consider as you develop your DR plan.

Business data on workstations

When I encounter a situation in which an employee's workstation is, in fact, on the critical path for a critical business process, the first question I usually ask is, "Why?"

Warnings go off in my head when I hear about an employee's workstation in any process's critical path. Here are my main concerns:

✔ **High integrity storage:** IT can't (and shouldn't) guarantee the integrity of storage on end-user workstations. Hard drives fail — it's a fact of life. You should store business information on systems with commercial-grade storage — maybe RAID (Redundant Array of Independent Disks), mirroring, or another option.

✔ **Backups:** Regularly back up business information, especially when that information is associated with critical business processes. Typically, IT backs up IT servers but rarely backs up end-user workstations.

✔ **Management:** IT servers are generally better managed than end-user workstations. IT servers are more likely to have correct configuration and protection, patches, and so on. IT has absolute control over its servers, both in terms of physical access and everything about configuration and use.

✔ **Environment:** End-user workstations are subjected to abuse: Users drop them, subject them to extreme temperatures, and spill coffee on them. IT servers, on the other hand, are housed in facilities with controlled temperature and humidity, and they don't get knocked around nearly as much as a user's laptop.

✔ **Power:** Cleaner power protects IT servers. An Uninterruptible Power Supply (UPS), line conditioners, or generators can assure the servers' power is never interrupted.

✔ **Physical access:** Businesses usually put IT servers in locked rooms with controlled and limited access. End-user laptops, on the other hand, are out in the open and frequently stolen.

✔ **Availability:** All of the factors in this list make data on IT systems far more available to all users when they need it, when compared to data on an employee's laptop, wherever it might be at a given moment.

Keeping critical business information on end-user workstations involves a lot more risk than centrally storing and managing that same information on IT servers. Still, you may have situations in which end users must process data locally, with very sound business reasons for doing so. Here are a few examples of such practices:

✔ **Field-based operations:** Field workers in many industries (including, but certainly not limited to, workers in insurance claims, building inspection, law enforcement, and disaster relief) must collect information in the field by using computer-based data entry. Even in situations in which workstations are equipped to connect to the Internet, those workstations often can't get a strong enough signal, so the user has to work offline.

✔ **Work in-transit:** Many workers travel extensively, and they often have to work on contracts, presentations, strategies, and so on while they travel. A laptop computer on a trans-oceanic flight is a boon to productivity.

✔ **Document management:** Workers in most any business department are responsible for creating policy documents, legal contracts, procedures, and so on. If workers want to make changes to these kinds of files, they should check out those documents from a server to their workstations, make the appropriate changes, update the server. Editing documents — especially large ones — over the network can be difficult because of the slow response time you experience over a network versus accessing the document stored on the local hard drive.

Businesses can have many legitimate activities that require workstations with their own standalone software tools and business information storage. You may or may not be the one to make judgment calls about the legitimacy of this or that use of standalone workstations.

Using workstations as standalone computers, including using local tools and locally stored business data, is more complicated in many ways than other workstations uses. The issues related to managing business information stored on user workstations include

✔ **Availability:** Whether users can access the data when they need it, not only from the workstation it resides on, but from other workstations. Because of availability issues, don't store critical business information on a lone workstation — instead, locate it on a centralized server so that users can access it from anywhere.

✔ **Capacity:** Workstations are fickle beasts, and their users are unpredictable. If a user fills up his or her workstation with other information, whether business-related or not, how can he or she perform important tasks with what little resources remain?

✔ **Confidentiality:** You need to protect business information from unauthorized disclosure. Control and log who accesses business data on the workstation by using mechanisms such as file or whole-disk encryption, access controls (user IDs and passwords, and possibly also a biometric, smart-card, or other two-factor authentication), and access logging (in which the computer tracks who accesses the data).

✔ **Integrity:** Put controls in place to ensure that business information on the laptop isn't changed by anything other than officially permitted means. Permit only specific users and programs to access and make changes to the data.

You can manage most of these issues more easily on IT servers, but if a workstation is really on the critical path for business processes, you need to address these issues to protect the integrity of the process.

Procedures for using workstations

When business processes include tasks that employees carry out on workstations, you need to establish written procedures for those tasks and for other steps in the process that take place on other workstations and servers. Give all tasks in a business process equal formality, regardless of whether they take place on a formal IT server platform or a user's workstation.

Gap in PC procedure causes corporate crisis

Some years back, while I was working as a consultant, a colleague in another organization came to me for help. In this international organization and U.S. public company, the finance department couldn't close its quarterly financial books in time to meet an S.E.C. (U.S. Securities and Exchange Commission) filing deadline.

The finance department had missed the deadline by several days, and the matter had become a corporate crisis that reached the CEO and the boardroom.

The cause? An overseas subsidiary couldn't close its books. The reason? One of the steps that the overseas subsidiary took to complete its month and quarter-end financials was a procedure in which a financial report was downloaded to a PC's spreadsheet program, where a spreadsheet macro performed some calculations that the subsidiary used in its financial results.

This time, the subsidiary ran into a problem: The macro had become corrupted and wouldn't run.

The contractor who created the macro was nowhere to be found. No one in the finance department knew what the macro did or how it worked. That macro was an undocumented step in this critical business process; the original software was gone, and nothing about it was documented.

Avoid this kind of a scenario in your organization by formally documenting and controlling all software that you use to process business information.

Recovery notes for workstations as local computers

Using workstations as local computing platforms has some operational risks. Nonetheless, it's advantageous and necessary in many circumstances.

Follow these preparation and recovery steps to successfully recover work station-based functionality in the event of a disaster:

- ✔ Use formal change and configuration management capabilities while managing software tool installations and configurations on critical workstations.

- ✔ Ensure that formal process, procedure, and task documentation for business processes includes all of the steps that are performed on workstations.

   Such documentation should cover not only procedural steps, but also the workstation and software tool versions and configurations required to support the tasks.

- ✔ Take steps to ensure that business information on workstations is easy to recover.

   You may need to regularly back up data, or you may need to know how to recover lost data by repeating steps used to obtain information from its external source(s). In fact, you may need to do both, depending on the details surrounding the workstation procedures.

✔ Make sure that you have sufficient controls in place on end-user workstations to prevent unauthorized access to business information on the workstation and the tools used to create and/or manage that information.

Consider both preventive controls and detective controls, depending on implementation details and associated risks. Talk with your internal or external auditors if you're unsure of the role of controls and risks in your organization.

✔ Be sure that workstation operators understand the procedures associated with processing workstation-based information, as well as general security procedures and precautions.

✔ Use imaging procedures or tools that can manage the entire workstation footprint, as well as quickly build or rebuild workstations.

Imaging and workstation build procedures need to cover all aspects of operating system and tool installations and configurations.

✔ Make sure that workstation imaging and provisioning procedures include software licensing and activation steps.

Also, be sure that you can recover business information onto newly built workstations in disaster scenarios.

✔ Consider recovering critical workstation functions in a Citrix-like environment, in which you can house tools and data on IT-managed servers.

Also, consider the workstation operating system recovery issues discussed in the following section.

Workstation operating systems

Operating systems power workstations. Whether Windows, Linux, Mac OS, or something else, operating systems are at the heart of end-user workstations, no matter whether they're used as intelligent Web terminals, distributed computing clients, local computing platforms, or all of the above. Rather than repeat all the OS-centric issues in each of the sections in this chapter, I discuss them in this section.

This list includes the major facets of workstation operating systems that require attention for recovery purposes:

✔ Hardware platform

✔ Operating system version, configuration, and patch levels

✔ Network connectivity

   ✔ Authentication

   ✔ Authentication resets during a disaster

   ✔ Security

In the following sections, I discuss all the elements in the preceding list.

Hardware platforms for workstations

In the context of disaster recovery planning, knowing and tracking hardware platforms for end-user workstations is a critical activity. You need workstations in *some* capacity during and after disasters so you can recover and operate critical processes.

Each hardware platform has its own workstation *image* — the files, directories, and configurations that are installed on that workstation. Often, when a workstation manufacturer updates the hardware, even within a specific model line, the changes require that you update the image to accommodate differences in the hardware. IT departments can end up managing dozens of images at any one time, not to mention the archive of images they need to retain for all of the older workstations still in use.

Recovery of end-user workstations can take on a life of its own in a disaster scenario. In a situation in which business offices have suffered significant destruction, recovery teams may need to build entirely new workstations from the ground up so that essential personnel can get back to the business of recovering and operating critical business processes. But what if you can't get your hands on the standard make and model of workstation hardware?

Recovering mobile platforms

Mobile computing platforms, such as PDAs and smart phones, are becoming more commonplace, and they may increasingly become critical platforms. In fact, during a disaster, they might be the *only* way to get some things done.

The principles of planning for the recovery of mobile platforms are the same as for end-user workstations — but the technologies and the dependencies are a little different.

In your DR planning, you might need to develop recovery or alternative plans for mobile devices, or mobile devices might be viable alternatives to thicker platforms, such as laptops.

The security mechanisms for protecting information on mobile devices is less mature than what you find on laptops. You may need to conduct a risk analysis to understand the risks associated with storing corporate information on mobile platforms.

Time-critical processes demand that you build workstations, often the backbone of computing, on whatever hardware platform you can get — very likely, you have to work with a different brand entirely. You may find your inventory of ready-to-run images useless because those images probably won't work on the replacement workstations.

When you build workstations on unfamiliar hardware platforms — which is what you may have to do to build replacement workstations in a disaster — you need to use some creative thinking to figure out how to provide workstation capabilities for end users. And you need to document workstation images very well so you can build them from the ground up on new hardware platforms.

Operating system version, configuration, and patches for workstations

Managing operating systems (OSs) on a small number of servers is a lot of work. But managing OSs on larger numbers of end-user workstations presents many special challenges that you must meet if you want the organization's DR strategy to succeed. End-user workstations are in the equation of nearly every business process and business application — they're the windows (no pun intended) into applications and data. Without them, businesses are blind, deaf, and dumb.

Managing operating systems has its own set of issues, including these concerns:

- ✔ **Supported versions:** Knowing what OS versions are in common use, and which user workstations they're on at any one time, may be a key component to your DR plan. The ability to recover end-user functions may depend on which versions of operating systems you're using so you can get critical users up and running in a disaster scenario as soon as possible.

- ✔ **Operating system patches and updates:** Know what OS patches and updates are supported and working on user workstations. Depending on your environment, you may need to know which updates and patches are supported, or you might need to go the extra step and actually figure out which specific patches and updates are present on each critical user's workstation. Your application and tools requirements dictate how much detail you need to know.

- ✔ **Operating system configuration:** Modern OSs have more knobs and dials than the Space Shuttle, but you can use only a finite number of known, supported combinations on those OSs. You need to know the configurations for many scenarios, supporting every type of connectivity, every tool and application, and every type of user.

- ✔ **End-user capabilities:** Knowing what each end user can do on a workstation is an important element in DR planning. If your end users are local administrators on your workstations, you'll have a more difficult time managing workstation configurations because end users can make many changes on their own.

✔ **Supporting business applications and functions:** Know the required OS version, patch level, and configurations for each tool and application that runs on the workstation. You can either document those configurations now or figure them out in a disaster scenario when you're frantically trying to get a workstation functioning correctly while the executives are tapping their fingers nervously.

The devil's in the details, and the OS is probably the biggest bucket of details you have to consider and accommodate.

Network connectivity for workstation operating systems

You need to understand the methods of network connectivity in use in your organization, regardless of a workstation's function. Web browsers and applications must be able to communicate with systems inside the business and possibly in the external world.

I discuss several connectivity scenarios in this section, and I may address issues related to your specific environment. Understanding these cases can help you better understand your own environment:

✔ **Network access control:** Do your target applications limit access to specific IP addresses or IP ranges? If so, you may need to reconfigure them so your recovered workstations can still connect, even if they're connected to new, temporary networks.

✔ **Remote Access/VPN (Virtual Private Network):** Are your applications and servers accessible via any existing remote access or VPN service? If not, you may have extremely limited recovery options because you may need to temporarily locate recovered users away from your server environment.

✔ **Access to multiple servers:** Do your applications require concurrent access to multiple application servers? I discuss this concept in the "Managing mashups" section, earlier in this chapter.

The connectivity issues in this section all relate to your applications. Your business probably uses workstations as devices to access business applications, and some of those applications are at the heart of many business processes. If you can't get to the applications (or file servers or whatever resources are critical to the support of business processes), do your workstations have any value?

Authentication for workstation operating systems

Users have to provide credentials to log on to enterprise resources — or do they? Authentication occurs in several different ways, from the very simple to complex and esoteric. You should explore some of these authentication elements:

- ✔ **User ID and password:** Easy enough, in most cases.

- ✔ **Biometric:** Usually requires extra hardware, such as fingerprint scanners. If employees log in to applications that require biometric authentication, how will that work in a disaster scenario?

- ✔ **Smart card:** Similar to the biometric problem, smart-card authentication requires hardware that most workstations don't have.

- ✔ **One-time password:** Often, one-time passwords take the form of tokens and similar devices. Although users may still have their tokens in a disaster scenario, the token-authentication infrastructure may not still be operating.

- ✔ **Single identity and single sign-on:** Some Web-based applications depend on centralized services to manage authentication. I cover this authentication process fully in Chapter 8.

Your temporary workstations (those workstations that you must build during and right after a disaster) need to be able to log in to your applications and resources. If you implement any two-factor authentication, your replacement or rebuilt workstations may need to support your authentication methods, such as smart cards, biometrics, or whatever you use.

Authentication resets during a disaster

Users need an authentication reset if they forget their passwords, fat-finger their logins and lock themselves out, or lose their smart cards and security tokens. With this in mind, you might consider the following methods for managing resets:

- ✔ **Passwords via e-mail:** Often, applications can e-mail the existing password, a new temporary password, or a new permanent password to a user who has lost his or her password. For this password assistance to work, the user has to have access to e-mail.

- ✔ **Passwords via live support:** In many cases, users can call a manned support desk to get their passwords reset. Of course, you need to have a manned helpdesk available in a disaster situation for this approach to work.

For additional information on authentication, check out Chapter 8.

Workstation operating system security

Security is the thread that's woven into most IT fabrics these days. I mention security in several places in this chapter, but these security issues deserve their own list:

- ✔ **Security configuration:** Security configurations in every layer of the workstation stack — from *BIOS passwords* (hardware passwords required to boot the computer) to application authentication, and many places in between — enable recovery if you properly configure them or stop recovery dead in its tracks if you don't.

✔ **Encryption keys:** You can use encryption in many places, including file encryption, e-mail message encryption, session (communications) encryption, encryption of data such as credit cards and passwords, and encryption of entire workstation hard drives. When you work to recover processing capabilities, you often need to recover the original encryption keys to facilitate the continuation of processes. Often, you can't simply create *new* encryption keys because the new keys don't allow access to data that you encrypted with the old, pre-disaster keys.

✔ **Digital certificates:** You use certificates (which are closely akin to encryption keys) for encryption, digital signatures, and authentication. And like encryption keys, you often can't simply create new certificates to access data stored under old certificates.

Security is often an enabler when you design it from the beginning into an application environment. This is evident in effectively designed authentication and data protection mechanisms, as I discuss in this section. But when you omit key components of security from your DR plans, security can be the thing that prevents recovery.

Recovery notes for workstation operating systems

You need to plan for workstation operating system (OS) recovery, regardless of whether your business uses those workstations as Web terminals, clients in distributed environments, or standalone computing platforms. Follow these preparation and recovery steps to recover workstation operating systems:

1. **Install an OS.**

   This broad category covers licensing, installation media, activation, and imaging for workstations. If you have an older version of an OS, be sure that you'll still be able to activate it well into the future. A disaster isn't the time to discover that the OS vendor can no longer activate an OS platform that you need to recover a critical business function!

2. **Configure your OS.**

   Whether you have centralized workstation OS management or you configure OS components manually, you need to identify and document all the salient points of workstation configuration so you can configure workstations to support critical business functions.

3. **Patch and update your OS.**

   Know what versions of OS patches and updates workstations need to support applications, network access, and other functions.

4. **Set up authentication and access control.**

   Make sure you can support both local and network-based authentication so users can access the resources they need to continue critical functions.

You may also need to include any configuration or hardware necessary to support two-factor authentication.

5. **Set up networking and remote access.**

Recovered workstations must be able to access resources across networks, including new, temporary networks that you may need to set up in a disaster. You may need to change server- or network-side configurations to permit new methods of access.

6. **Set up security.**

You may need encryption keys, digital certificates, and other security settings to facilitate access or proper processing.

The items in the preceding steps are broad, high-level preparation needs. You may also need to identify and attend to a lot of details to make sure you have the greatest level of preparedness when disaster strikes. Also, you may need to follow additional steps for your specific organization and business needs.

Managing and Recovering End-User Communications

Although end-user computing is definitely an important aspect of employee support of business processes, communications are arguably even more important. Even in *peacetime* (meaning when you don't anticipate a disaster), communications are a vital ingredient in everyday business. Employees routinely rely on one or more of the following elements in support of business processes:

- ✔ Voice communications or voice mail
- ✔ E-mail
- ✔ Fax
- ✔ Instant messaging

I discuss these elements in the following sections.

Voice communications

Organizations equip their workers with voice communications in a wide variety of ways, including but not limited to

✔ Simple direct-dial telephone service

✔ Telephone company-based PBXs (Private Branch eXchanges, formerly known as Centrex — a fancy word for a telephone system), in which the local telephone company manages direct-dial extensions for a business.

✔ Analog or digital PBXs connected to analog or digital office extensions

✔ IP-based PBXs connected to digital or IP-based phones, or connected to IP-based softphones via wired or wireless networks

Your organization may have more advanced voice communications capabilities, including

✔ Voice communications integrated into contact-center management systems

✔ Inbound 1-800 service, possibly with inbound load balancing and capacity management services that route incoming calls to one or more contact centers

✔ Managed or predictive outbound dialing systems integrated with contact-center management systems

✔ Integration with wireless carriers, either through extension trunking (a way of connecting branch offices to main offices, for instance) or on-premise wireless base stations

✔ Voice mail connected to e-mail gateways

The preceding lists should drive home the point that your voice telecommunications capabilities, in and of themselves, may warrant extensive DR projects! These projects can get especially complicated because you may have extensive types and levels of integration between enterprise applications, telecommunications, and the telephone companies themselves. The complexity of these systems requires detailed planning that's beyond the scope of this book.

I could devote an entire book to DR for voice communications alone. Here are preparation and recovery tips to ensure rapid recovery of voice communications:

✔ Use formal management of voice capabilities, which includes change management, procedure documentation, and configuration management.

✔ Back up all configuration information in PBX and other supporting equipment so you can recover those systems.

✔ Identify all integration points between PBX, other supporting equipment, and other internal networks, systems, and applications.

Formally document all such interfaces and integration points, both in terms of configuration and operations procedures.

✔ Identify all integration points between PBX, other supporting equipment, and external service providers, including telecommunications service providers and other entities.

Formally document all these interfaces and integration points.

✔ Identify integration points between voice communications and other forms of communications, including but not limited to voice mail, e-mail, and wireless.

✔ Identify business continuity planning efforts that support customer contact centers and other business functions that rely heavily on inbound and outbound voice communications.

Make sure that you have ample coordination between business continuity and disaster recovery planning efforts because the two are symbiotic in nature.

✔ Consider alternative carriers, service providers, and other contingencies for emergency voice communications in the event of a disaster.

Remember that much of an organization's voice communications capabilities depend on external suppliers and service providers, whose disaster response may or may not translate into rapid and timely restoration of the services that your organization needs.

✔ Develop emergency contact lists for emergency operations personnel, other responders, and parties who will be involved in disaster operations.

Include several means for contacting these individuals. A regional disaster may result in the widespread failure of several forms of communications.

Because of the wide variety of complexity and integration with other systems, your own needs may vary from the preceding list.

E-mail

Once considered a nice-to-have mode of communication, e-mail is now considered critical in most organizations. People use e-mail not only to communicate routine messages, but also as a file transfer mechanism and a formal alerting mechanism. Increasingly, applications send and receive e-mail as part of their normal function. Take away e-mail, and nearly everything stops dead.

Aspects of e-mail that typical DR projects need to address include

✔ E-mail clients

✔ E-mail servers

✔ E-mail gateways to the outside world

✔ E-mail gateways and interfaces to internal applications

✔ E-mail security

You can look at these areas in more detail in the following sections.

E-mail clients

In most architectures, users who send and receive e-mail do so by using client software that's installed on their workstations. This software provides the user interface with which users read, create, and send e-mail, and often also locally store e-mail messages. Some issues to consider about e-mail clients include

- ✔ **Configuration:** E-mail clients often have several configuration items that deal with a user's identity, the location of mail servers in the organization, where local messages are stored on the workstation, and so on.

- ✔ **Local e-mail storage:** Many e-mail clients locally store e-mail messages, enabling the user to read and compose e-mail messages while offline.

- ✔ **Address lists:** E-mail clients often allow the user to create local lists of recipients, groups, and aliases within his or her own address list. In some environments, these local lists may also be stored on the e-mail server.

- ✔ **Filters and forwarding rules:** Many e-mail clients include the ability to store, delete, or forward messages based on criteria.

You'd be surprised at the number of organizations that depend on these user-centric features on the critical path of important business processes.

E-mail servers

E-mail servers receive, store, and forward e-mail to and from other e-mail servers and users. Larger organizations have several e-mail servers, with a portion of the workforce assigned to each server. One of these e-mail servers may also send and receive mail from external entities and the Internet, or separate servers may be dedicated for this purpose.

You need to address several issues when considering e-mail and servers:

- ✔ **E-mail storage:** E-mail servers store e-mail messages in users' mailboxes, and often they permanently store all sent and received e-mail messages for all users in the organization (except in cases in which a user can archive or remove his or her messages).

- ✔ **Recipient directories:** E-mail users need to be able to locate other e-mail recipients in online address books. These recipients consist of other users in the organization, plus other entries, such as group addresses and external recipients that e-mail administrators put into the directory.

- ✔ **Groups, distribution lists, and aliases:** E-mail servers often contain other e-mail recipients, including groups, distribution lists, and aliases.

- ✔ **Filtering and forwarding rules:** E-mail servers often use rules for forwarding, filing, and deleting incoming messages.

The preceding list gives you just the highlights; your servers may have more features and functions that you need to identify, dissect, and incorporate into your DR plans.

E-mail gateways and Internet connectivity

In addition to transmitting e-mail among users within an organization, users can also send e-mail to recipients outside the organization. And e-mail from outside sources arrives for delivery to local recipients. In some environments, the main mail servers perform all these duties, but in others, separate systems handle these functions. You have plenty of issues to consider regarding your e-mail servers:

- **Configuration:** The gateways and other systems that process e-mail have configurations that permit them to do their work properly. These configurations include information about neighboring mail servers and ways to get e-mail messages to the outside world.

- **Local storage:** Often, these gateways store messages, usually but not always temporarily, while those messages wait to be transmitted to their final destinations.

E-mail gateway configurations are usually custom-built for an organization, and sometimes, no one fully documents the details of these configurations. If your organization doesn't have this configuration documentation anywhere, someone needs to create it now.

E-mail interfaces

Organizations increasingly use e-mail to send messages and data to and from applications, not just people. Many systems and server applications can routinely send e-mail messages for a vast array of reasons, including

- **Status:** Some applications and tools send information about their status to the people who maintain them.

- **Reports:** Some applications send the results of reports and queries via e-mail to people who request or run them.

- **Errors:** Applications can send e-mail messages to specific personnel when errors occur.

You can probably find a half dozen other examples of applications, tools, and systems that originate e-mail messages intended for recipients (or other applications, tools, and systems); the preceding list gives you just a few examples.

E-mail security

It's becoming common practice for IT departments to configure e-mail systems to apply protection of various kinds to e-mail messages. This protection takes on various forms, and both servers and end users use it. The primary means for protecting e-mail messages are

✔ **Encryption:** To scramble the contents of messages so that eavesdroppers can't read them while those messages are in transit, users and systems apply encryption algorithms to the contents of e-mail messages.

✔ **Digital signatures:** E-mail systems can use digital signatures, often known as *hashing,* to protect e-mail. Digital signatures don't hide the contents of e-mail messages like encryption does, but they do tell the recipient whether the contents of the message were altered anywhere along the way between the originator and the recipient. Digital signatures also provide a way to verify the identity of a message's originator.

✔ **Anti-spam:** E-mail systems often employ spam filters that block and remove (or quarantine) incoming e-mail messages that the filters think might be spam. Spam filters can block spam in four ways:

• **Server-based:** Spam-blocking programs can run on the same system as the e-mail server.

• **Appliance:** A separate hardware appliance can block incoming spam so the spam doesn't enter the e-mail server.

• **Client:** Spam blocking software can run on the client workstations, blocking spam messages after they arrive in a user's inbox.

• **Service provider:** All e-mail coming into an organization is sent to a spam-blocking provider's server, which filters the spam and sends the good e-mail to the organization's mail server.

✔ **Anti-virus:** E-mail servers often have anti-virus software that removes viruses and other malware from incoming e-mail messages before they're delivered to end users.

You can read more about blocking spam in *Blocking Spam and Spyware For Dummies* (Wiley), which I wrote with Mike Simon. Also, get the scoop on viruses in *Computer Viruses For Dummies* (Wiley), by yours truly.

Recovery notes for e-mail

E-mail is the message plumbing in organizations, with wider scope and application than you probably know about. As you scrounge around in your e-mail environment and begin building your prevention and recovery plans, keep these tips in mind:

✔ Know how e-mail flows into, around, and out of the organization — including servers, clients, gateways, and so on.

✔ Document all the facts about your organization's Internet domain registrations, which include MX Records that determine where incoming e-mail from the Internet should be delivered. Making the changes your business's domain servers need to be prepared when a disaster strikes can take considerable time.

✔ Trace all uses of e-mail through business processes to determine the e-mail addresses, distribution lists, filtering rules, and other features that those e-mail messages require to make it to their destinations.

✔ Ensure that any replacement spam- and virus-blocking mechanisms that you introduce in temporary recovery scenarios don't inadvertently block critical messages.

✔ Make sure that e-mail servers have ample storage capacity during disaster scenarios. In disasters, e-mail may accumulate more than usual, resulting in far greater storage needs than on a typical sunny day.

 ✔ Consider an e-mail service provider that uses an external service to receive and store all incoming e-mail during a disaster scenario. With this kind of provider, users log in to read e-mail over the Web. Make sure the provider can handle special-purpose messages, such as those that are sent from (or to) applications.

✔ Consider pre-registering critical users (and non-human recipients) with an alternate e-mail server, just in case.

✔ Archive all encryption keys and tools that your business uses to encrypt e-mail so you can still encrypt and decrypt e-mail messages in a disaster scenario.

✔ Back up e-mail folders and systems so you can recover them if you need to. In a disaster scenario, you may need the ability to recover existing messages, not just send and receive new ones.

As you survey and analyze your end-user e-mail environment and identify all the critical-process touch points, you'll probably uncover additional issues critical to your recovery.

Fax machines

Many organizations still rely heavily on facsimile (or fax) to transmit business documents, such as contracts, receipts, invoices, and so on. Although many organizations are making the transition to digital imaging, fax machines are nonetheless critical for many key business processes.

Here are some factors to consider for faxing in a business environment:

✔ **Directories:** People who need to send faxes need to know those destination phone numbers. Capture your business's fax numbers in process documentation, if those numbers aren't already included.

✔ **Incoming fax numbers:** Some organizations use widely advertised or publicized fax numbers. In a disaster scenario, the organization may need to have incoming faxes routed to another fax machine or fax server. You can coordinate this rerouting with a local telecommunications service provider.

add these, and to Miss Service Saver.

✔ **Fax server configuration:** Fax servers are systems that are connected to phone lines or T-1 circuits, and fax servers can accept larger volumes of incoming faxes than fax machines in an office environment can.

Fax server have rules for storing faxes, forwarding them to other faxes, and forwarding them to e-mail recipients in the form of attached image files. You need to know these rules for business processes that rely on faxes for critical tasks so incoming and outgoing faxes can continue to work properly in a disaster scenario.

An organization that relies on faxes for critical business processes needs to consider these tips for disaster preparation and recovery:

✔ Record and document critical incoming and outgoing fax numbers in business processes.

✔ Route critical incoming fax numbers to other locations in the event of a disaster that damages a facility or cripples communications.

✔ Consider online fax for inbound or outbound fax needs. Several commercial services, such as eFax (www.efax.com), offer fax-to-e-mail and e-mail-to-fax services that are performed in remote, hardened data centers.

✔ Record and back up fax server configuration and processing rules so you can recover critical faxes that use fax servers by whatever means you need.

✔ Consider using the scan-and-e-mail approach for processes that currently use fax so you can reduce your business's reliance on fax machines and phone lines.

You need to collect all the fax facts in your organization in order to expedite recovery.

Instant messaging

Instant messaging, or IM, is frequently considered an ad hoc, counterculture, or underground communications tool in many organizations. Still, many organizations use IM, and although it might not be on the critical path for business processes, it's still handy for casual communications, such as

✔ Hey, the conference call has started. Are you joining us or what?

✔ Where are you?

✔ My e-mail program just died. What's the number for today's online meeting?

These kinds of communications might be handy in a disaster scenario, when too few people are doing too many things in an unfamiliar environment.

Although IM might not be on your critical path, being able to use it during a disaster may help hold teams together. Consider these tips for recovering instant messaging:

> ✔ Publish emergency response team members' IM addresses on emergency contact lists.

> ✔ Don't rely on a single IM provider, in case that provider is involved in the same disaster you are.

> ✔ If your organization uses a centrally managed IM server, consider setting up an external service as a backup.

> ✔ If your organization uses only outside IM services, consider internalizing it and making it available in disaster scenarios.

Most IM providers don't encrypt the messaging traffic between parties. A notable exception is Skype. Skype not only encrypts traffic, but its encryption scheme has stood up to expert scrutiny.

Chapter 6

Planning Facilities Protection and Recovery

In This Chapter

▶ Keeping your processing facilities safe

▶ Choosing an alternate processing site

This chapter focuses on the recovery of facilities — information processing facilities, mostly, but also work locations for critical personnel. You can't plan just where the computers will go: You must also plan where people will work. Although this is an IT-centric book, you can't take people completely out of the equation. Even if others in the organization are doing the business- and process-centric business continuity and disaster recovery planning that includes alternate work locations for all categories of personnel, I still give 'em an honorable mention here — this book primarily talks about recovering IT systems, but we all know that *people* need to have a place to work, too.

Protecting facilities can help an organization reduce or eliminate the effects of a disaster, improving the chances that an organization will survive a disaster — the overarching objective of DR planning.

This chapter discusses various strategies for alternate processing sites — places where you can get computers up and running after a disaster strikes so critical business processes that rely on information systems can resume functioning.

Protecting Processing Facilities

Information processing facilities are high concentrations of computers and equipment that support critical business processes. Within a single room, equipment supporting virtually all of an organization's critical processes is usually stacked on special equipment racks placed side by side, with masses of power cables and network cables connecting this equipment to power supplies and networks. A room of very modest size, say 20 feet by 20 feet, can be as critical as 50,000 square feet of office space housing 250 workers who use the information systems contained in that small room.

Not only is the equipment expensive, but the business value derived from the use of the equipment is potentially very high. In many businesses, most operations cease to function if the supporting information systems become unavailable for any reason. Many of the reasons that operations stop have a lot to do with the environmental features (power, cooling, and so on) present in the facility in which these information systems are housed.

The types of mechanisms for protecting IT equipment include

- ✔ Physical access control
- ✔ Electric power
- ✔ Fire detection and suppression
- ✔ Chemical hazards
- ✔ Water/flooding detection

An ounce of prevention is worth a pound of cure.

The following sections discuss the features in the preceding list and how those features protect information processing equipment.

Controlling physical access

The high value of information systems — and both the asset value of those systems and their support of revenue-producing business processes — makes today's information processing facilities akin to Fort Knox. Data centers are often an organization's highest concentration of wealth-producing or wealth-enabling assets. Consequently, access to these places needs to be tightly controlled, so only authorized personnel with a valid business reason for being there are permitted to enter and leave.

Physical access controls prevent man-made disasters brought about by sabotage and other malicious or accidental damage.

Data centers often employ several physical access controls that work together to both detect and prevent unwanted entry by unauthorized personnel. The most common controls are

- ✔ Video surveillance
- ✔ Key-card entry controls
- ✔ Man traps
- ✔ Biometric entry controls

✔ Security guards

✔ Hardened facilities

✔ Locking cabinets

✔ Equipment cages

In the following sections, I describe these controls in more detail.

Even in a disaster situation, you must protect information from unacceptable disclosure and corruption by using the same controls that you use on production systems.

Video surveillance

Surrounding a building, inside and out, with security guards, watching every entrance and room, is prohibitively expensive. The common remedy for watching everything everywhere is an extensive video surveillance system that can record the movements of people in a facility. Such a system consists of several components:

✔ **Fixed-focus cameras:** These cameras are permanently pointed in one direction and can't be easily moved.

✔ **Pan/tilt/zoom cameras:** Personnel viewing this type of camera in real time can remotely control the camera by panning and tilting (changing the direction in which the camera points) and zooming (making an object's apparent distance from the camera closer or further away). Figure 6-1 shows several pan/tilt/zoom cameras housed within protective domes on the exterior of a building.

✔ **Viewing monitors:** Many organizations have staff dedicated to real-time viewing of surveillance camera views. Processing equipment can place one or more images onto a single monitor, and businesses frequently use many monitors so that staff can see many views of the interior and exterior of a building at the same time. Figure 6-2 shows a surveillance center that includes several viewing monitors, as well as equipment used to control pan/tilt/zoom surveillance cameras. You can also see in the figure that several of the monitors show images from four cameras at the same time.

✔ **Recording equipment:** Video surveillance systems can record onto video tape, optical disc, or computer hard drives. Three common recording methods are in use:

  • **Motion activated:** The system records a still photo or a short video sequence when the scene in front of the camera changes, such as when a person walks by.

  • **Regular still photos:** A still image recorded every one to ten seconds.

  • **Continuous video:** Images from each video camera are recorded continuously.

> You should keep records for at least several weeks, and perhaps as long as a year or more.

Video surveillance is considered a detective control. Although this kind of surveillance has some deterrent potential, video cameras primarily detect activities by recording them.

Figure 6-1:
Surveillance cameras on the exterior of a building.

Figure 6-2:
Surveillance monitors and camera control equipment.

Key-card entry controls

Information processing facilities — and many regular working locations — contain key-card entry systems that control who can enter work facilities. Key-card systems can also restrict entry to elevators, specific rooms, or individual building floors.

Key-card controls use a variety of technologies, sometimes in combination, to control access. The common types of key-card controls are

- ✓ **Magnetic stripe reader:** A key card contains a magnetic stripe, or magstripe, that's similar to the technology used on credit cards. An employee swipes the key card through the magnetic stripe reader, which momentarily unlocks a door or opens a turnstile, permitting entry.

- ✓ **Contact-less proximity card reader:** A key card contains an RFID (Radio Frequency Identification) or similar technology that permits the card's owner to hold it close to the reader, thereby unlocking the door or turnstile. Figure 6-3 shows a person using a contact-less proximity card reader.

- ✓ **Smart card reader:** A key card contains a smart card memory chip, and a smart card reader reads that card's contents when the user inserts the card into that reader. A smart card differs from magstripe and proximity cards because it uses small metal contacts to complete an electrical circuit between the reader and the electronics contained within the card. Newer smart card technology is contact-less and works in the same way that contact-less proximity card readers (described in the preceding bullet) do.

Figure 6-3: A contact-less proximity card reader permits users to enter a secure room or facility.

Photo by HID Corporation

✔ **PIN pad:** In order to provide additional security for sensitive locations, businesses sometimes use both card readers and PIN pads. In this situation, the employee has to both use his or her key card and enter a PIN (Personal Identification Number, generally a numeric code) to gain entry. A combination of a proximity card reader and PIN pad is shown in Figure 6-4.

PIN-pad door locks

Doors can utilize a standalone PIN pad entry. Larger businesses often use PIN pad entry on rooms with sensitive records or information processing equipment, and smaller organizations that don't need a centralized system can use these locks for main building access. A typical standalone PIN-pad door lock device is shown in Figure 6-5.

Biometric entry controls

Organizations that want security stronger than key cards and PIN pads turn to biometric entry controls. Biometric controls measure a specific characteristic of a person's body to determine whether the person is authorized to enter. (See Figure 6-6.)

Figure 6-4: A combination of a proximity card and PIN pad entry control.

Photo by International Electronics, Inc.

Figure 6-5:
A PIN-pad
entry
control.

Photo by International Electronics, Inc.

Figure 6-6:
A biometric
fingerprint
reader.

Photo by HID Corporation

The most common types of biometric controls include

- ✔ **Fingerprint:** An optical reader reads a fingerprint and compares it to the registered fingerprints on file. Figure 6-6 shows a typical fingerprint reader.

- ✔ **Hand scan:** An optical reader reads the geometry of a person's entire hand. A typical hand scan device that also includes a PIN pad is shown in Figure 6-7.

- ✔ **Retina scan:** A subject's retina is scanned by a special reader.

- ✔ **Face scan:** A camera scans a person's face and compares it to the registered image.

Other types of biometric identity verification systems include keystroke, signature, and voice.

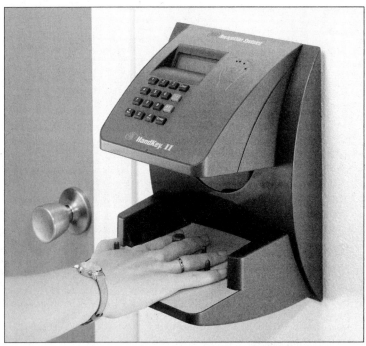

Figure 6-7:
A biometric hand reader and PIN-pad device.

Photo by Ingersoll-Rand Corporation

Man traps

Man traps are human entry mechanisms that utilize two doors, and only one door may be open at a time. Man traps can be manually operated (by a guard) or automatically operated, usually in conjunction with other access controls, such as key-card readers or PIN pads.

Here's a typical sequence for passing through a man trap:

1. Person identifies him- or herself to a guard or electronic control.

2. First door opens. Person walks into the trap.

3. First door closes with the person inside the trap.

4. Second door opens. Person exits the trap.

5. Second door closes.

6. The man trap is now available for another person to enter or exit.

A typical man trap diagram is shown in Figure 6-8.

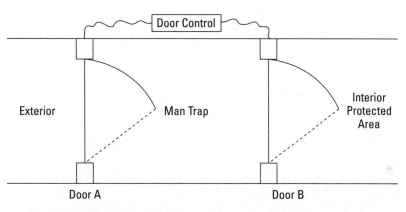

Figure 6-8:
A man trap provides one-at-a-time control for entry and exit of personnel.

The primary rules that enforce passage through a man trap are

✔ An electronic or manual control governs when each door can be opened.

✔ Only one door can be open at a time.

✔ People can travel in only one direction at a time.

Because man traps can be expensive to purchase and operate, they're usually used to protect only highest-value areas, such as data centers and cash vaults.

Security guards

Security guards are personnel who are trained and designated to perform several functions, including

✔ Checking identification of visitors

✔ Examining the personal effects of persons entering or leaving a facility

✔ Monitoring building entrances and exits

✔ Inspecting visiting vehicles prior to their entry

✔ Apprehending persons of suspicious nature

✔ Registering building visitors

✔ Operating video surveillance systems

✔ Escorting visitors

✔ Registering information about equipment that personnel are taking out of the building

✔ Receiving incoming shipments

Security guards fill a needed gap that varies from organization to organization, depending on security requirements and perceptions. The primary strength of security guards is that they possess the powers of judgment and intuition, unmatched in electronic-based control systems.

Hardened facilities

This catch-all category includes facilities that house information-processing equipment, particularly for highest-value organizations (large financial institutions, for instance) that have a lot to lose if their systems are damaged.

Some examples of features in a hardened facility include

✔ **No exterior windows:** Nothing to throw heavy objects through and no way to see from the street what's going on inside.

✔ **Bulletproof glass:** If the facility does have a *few* windows, bullets won't pierce them.

✔ **Fences:** Eight-foot–high chain link — or even solid walls — with three or more strands of barbed wire or razor wire on top. Walls make effective *pre-detonation screens* (armored shields that can stop a projectile explosive from detonating on the building itself) if you're concerned that someone may use heavy weapons against your facility.

✔ **Equipment bracing:** Equipment cabinets and racks, and the systems in them, need to be securely fastened and braced, not only for personnel safety, but also to mitigate seismic (earthquake) risks. You don't want to put a bunch of servers and other equipment up on racks only to have those racks fall down or the equipment fall off the racks, damaging the equipment and seriously injuring personnel.

✔ **Electromagnetic shields:** If you're really concerned about the continuous onslaught of electromagnetic radiation in the kilohertz, megahertz, and gigahertz bands, consider putting in shielding that blocks all of that incoming noise. These shields are sometimes called TEMPEST (Transient Electromagnetic Pulse Emanation Standard) or Faraday cages. Cellphones and pagers can't receive signals in such environments.

✔ **Window coating:** In particular, the sort that prevents laser listening devices from working.

✔ **Bollards and crash gates:** You don't want angry or determined people to drive their vehicles into your building. Figure 6-9 shows an effective retractable vehicle crash barrier in action. *Bollards* are those heavy, short vertical posts that are used along roadways and in front of buildings to prevent vehicles from driving into certain areas.

Figure 6-9:
Vehicle barriers can effectively stop unwanted vehicles from entering a secure facility.

Photo from B&B ARMR Corporation

Locking storage cabinets

Information processing facilities have a lot of valuable items that you should lock away out of sight. Some items that need to be locked away include

✔ System documentation

✔ Release media (CD-ROM and other media that contain purchased software)

✔ Backup media

✔ Spare parts

The quality of the locking storage cabinets should depend on the value of the contents they're protecting.

Equipment cabinets and cages

Usually found in multi-tenant commercial colocation data centers and companies with factions that don't trust each other, equipment cabinets and cages allow equipment to be cordoned off to prevent physical access by persons who otherwise *do* have a legitimate reason to be in the data center. Figure 6-10 shows locking equipment cabinets in a modern processing center.

Cages and cabinets can range in size from a single 30-inch cabinet to caged areas that cover hundreds of square feet. You typically lock them with metal keys or an electronic access control system, such as a PIN pad or key-card reader.

Getting charged up about electric power

Electricity is the critical ingredient for information systems and supporting equipment. Servers and network equipment get cranky when any of the common and not-so-common electrical anomalies occur, including sags, surges, spikes, transients, brownouts, noise, and outright failures.

Dirty electricity, and also frequent brownouts and blackouts, not only cause unscheduled downtime, but can also have a significant effect on the life expectancy of equipment. IT equipment requires clean — *really* clean — power.

You need some of this equipment in your facility to protect your IT equipment from power problems:

 ✔ **Remote power controllers:** These smart, network-attached plug strips let you switch power off and on to each plug. They're invaluable for remotely controlled equipment in *lights-out data centers* (centers that are unstaffed most of the time). Beats having to get dressed just to power cycle a server.

✔ **Uninterruptible Power Supply (UPS):** Absolutely non-negotiable, in my opinion. You might not need a large one, but you need one. They not only store several minutes of electricity in batteries, they also (usually) filter out all the dirty power that makes your systems sick.

✔ **Line conditioners:** A possible adjunct to UPS, line conditioners smooth out the bumps and dips in incoming power.

✔ **Power Distribution Unit (PDU):** A PDU is a device that distributes electric power to individual circuits and plugs. Some PDUs also step down voltage from 240 to 120 volts, and some have remote control capability.

✔ **Electric generator:** If your organization can't tolerate occasional utility outages, put an electric generator on your shopping list. Generators work in conjunction with a UPS: In the event of a utility power failure, the UPS immediately begins providing power from its batteries for the seconds or minutes the generator requires to start and get up to speed. Larger installations may require more than one generator, for both capacity and redundancy reasons.

✔ **Diverse power feeds:** For really critical facilities, consider having the public utility bring in two separate power feeds that enter the building from opposite ends and that feed from different substations.

✔ **Switching equipment:** Large installations with multiple power feeds, generators, and UPSs need switching equipment that can ensure the continuous flow of electricity to your systems in any situation.

In addition to the equipment in the preceding list, another highly critical aspect to power management is planning. Planning is especially important for larger installations that are utilizing newer blade technology, which consumes more power per square foot than older technologies.

Detecting and suppressing fire

Early fire detection is critical in information processing centers. If you can identify a fire in its earliest stages, you can deal with it before serious damage occurs.

When fire does erupt, you need to extinguish it as quickly as possible, with minimum damage inflicted on otherwise-uninvolved equipment. Using water to extinguish a fire in a data center isn't such a great idea, unless you want to replace all of your water-soaked equipment because some technician let his soldering iron get too hot and smoky.

Smoke and fire detection

Where there's smoke, there's fire. The old saying isn't far from the truth. Effective fire detection starts with smoke detection. When fire is in its early stages, it may emit smoke in very small amounts.

The options for smoke and fire detection are

- **Photoelectric:** Smoke scatters light in the air. Photoelectric smoke detectors work by detecting this scattering.

- **Ionization:** In a small ionization chamber, smoke alters the process of ionization and triggers the alarm.

- **Air sampling:** A network of air sampling pipes throughout the facility draws air into a centralized, highly sensitive sampling chamber. By design, this setup can detect fire earlier than other types of detectors because it can get a higher quality air sampling by using only one really good sampling device rather than many less expensive units.

- **Temperature:** When the fire becomes more active, it heats the air around it. Temperature or rate-of-rise sensors detect the change in temperature.

- **Manual stations:** People in the facility can run to the nearest fire alarm panel and manually turn on the alarm if they know that a fire has started. Similarly, an observant surveillance operator can detect smoke or fire through the video surveillance.

Many locations have laws that require a computing facility to include two or more of these detection systems.

Fire alarms and evacuation

Because human life and safety are the primary concerns in any disaster situation, fire alarms need to be properly designed and maintained so that personnel know when a fire breaks out and how to quickly evacuate the premises. You also need well-placed exit signs, of course, to help people find their way out of a building when the alarms go off.

Fire alarms in commercial buildings are commonly connected to local fire departments. This connection automatically notifies firefighters, speeding their arrival and hopefully reducing damage.

Fire suppression

When a fire has started in an information processing facility, you need to extinguish the fire as soon as possible, before it damages costly equipment. You can use several means of controlling and extinguishing fire, including

✔ **Fire extinguishers:** These portable devices are usually located through-out office buildings and data centers. Fire extinguishers come in several types for fighting different kinds of fires. Here are the kinds available in the United States:

- **Class A:** Ordinary combustibles, such as wood and paper
- **Class B:** Flammable liquids
- **Class C:** *Energized* (powered on and active) electrical equipment
- **Class D:** Combustible metals
- **Class K:** Cooking oils

Some fire extinguishers fall into a combination of the different types — for instance, an extinguisher can be classified both Class A and Class B.

✔ **Sprinkler systems:** These systems send a steady spray of water onto large areas, cooling the fire until it can no longer sustain itself. Water causes severe damage to information processing equipment, so you don't want sprinklers fighting fires in data centers. However, building codes often require sprinkler systems as a backup to other types of suppression.

You can find several types of sprinkler systems:

- **Wet pipe:** When sufficient heat reaches near a sprinkler head, a fusible link melts, releasing water through the sprinkler head.
- **Dry pipe:** The pipes are dry until smoke or heat activates the system, at which time water flows through the pipes and out of the sprinkler heads. Water flows only from heads whose fusible links have melted.
- **Deluge:** Used in locations where rapidly spreading fire is a concern. All sprinklers are *open* (they have no fusible links that must melt), and upon activation, all sprinkler heads discharge water simultaneously.
- **Pre-action:** A hybrid of dry pipe and deluge. Typically, the system requires a preceding event, such as smoke detection, which charges the pipes with water, converting the system to a wet-pipe system. When further smoke alarms, heat alarms, or heat at the sprinkler heads occur, water flows.
- **Foam and water:** As you might guess, sprinklers discharge a mixture of low-expansion foam and water.

Figure 6-11 shows a close-up of a sprinkler head. This illustration clearly shows the transparent fusible link capsule. This capsule melts in heat caused by a fire, which activates the flow of water.

Figure 6-11:
The link
capsule in a
sprinkler
head.

✔ **Gaseous fire suppression:** Most often found in data centers, these systems flood the area with an inert gas, thereby depriving the fire of oxygen. The system works by discharging the gas when someone pulls a fire alarm in the facility or when one or more smoke or heat detectors are activated. The gas is stored in large tanks inside or immediately outside the protected area. Gases often used include FM-200, Argonite, and Inergen. Organizations once commonly used Halon 1301, but it's been discontinued since the signing of the Montreal Protocol in 1989, which outlawed the use of ozone-depleting substances.

The choices you have for fire detection and suppression really depend on your locality's fire codes.

Chemical hazards

Many organizations work with hazardous chemicals and materials as a part of their business. In the United States, the Occupational Health and Safety Administration (OSHA) and the Environmental Protection Agency (EPA) have strict guidelines concerning the acquisition, storage, and use of a vast number of hazardous substances, as well as specific contingency plans for treating spills and accidental releases of these substances.

In many cases, these spills and releases may trigger disasters. Mandatory evacuations alone are enough to trigger a business disaster: If everyone has to leave a facility, how can the business continue operations?

Often, businesses are subject to not only U.S. federal laws, but also state and local laws governing the same substances. I'm not going to attempt to untangle this sticky web of regulation and substance-related contingency plans. If your business deals in hazardous substances (as defined by OSHA and the EPA, or other agencies that have jurisdiction where your business is located), you need to gain expertise in handling those substances, in addition to the more generalized disaster recovery planning that this book covers.

Keeping your cool

Information processing equipment operates very happily within a fairly narrow band of temperature and humidity. These environment restrictions becomes a challenge when the equipment consumes a lot of electricity and throws off so much heat! Getting rid of the heat at the same rate that it's produced is no small task. And with the amount of heat that newer equipment discharges per square foot of space, cooling equipment must deliver much more punch than in the past.

The life expectancy of information processing equipment drops sharply (sometimes by more than 90 percent) with just a single high temperature spike. When systems catch a high fever, they're not long for this world.

Because temperature control is so vital, an information processing center must have redundancy in its HVAC (Heating, Ventilation, and Air Conditioning) systems, so the failure (or planned maintenance) of one HVAC system doesn't put the data center at risk. Also, the control systems that manage the HVAC systems must be robust themselves, so they don't ever fail to direct the HVAC systems to do the right thing.

Because HVAC is so vital, you need to protect it by having backup power (UPS and generators) along with computing equipment. If HVAC stops operating for more than a few minutes, you need to shut down computing equipment right away to prevent overheating and damage.

Staying dry: Water/flooding detection and prevention

Information systems and water don't mix very well at all. For this reason, water-based fire suppression systems (as a first line of defense) have fallen out of favor because water discharge can severely damage computing equipment.

You can do a few things to make sure that water doesn't become a problem. You may not have to worry about some of these measures, depending on your local conditions:

- ✔ **Local flooding risk:** Find a hydrologist who can provide a realistic assessment of flooding potential for your facility. Take the results to an architect who may recommend mitigating features for your site that can ensure any flood waters are directed away from your facility.

- ✔ **Building survey:** Look for risks within your facility that may pose a water hazard. Check that roof drains and other features are operating properly.

  Here's my personal flood-in-the-building story: Years ago, a hot water heater on the fifth floor of a building exploded, sending water cascading downstairs into the second floor data center, taking a national public data network off the air for a few hours. Water was dripping out of servers. Needless to say, it pays to carefully understand the risks posed by even innocuous features in a building.

- ✔ **Emergency procedures:** If your building is prone to any sort of water accumulation, you may need to have emergency procedures and supplies on hand, such as sand bags, pumps, or other means for keeping water out or removing water if it gets in.

  Regularly test pumps or other complex apparatuses for readiness.

- ✔ **Water detectors:** Install electronic water detectors in the lowest places in your information processing center and connect them to whatever alarm management or network management system seems appropriate for proper alert-and-action capabilities. With this water-detector setup in place, if water somehow gets into your information processing center, you can find out about it while you may still have time to deal with it and avert a disaster.

- ✔ **Equipment location within a building:** For facilities in or near areas prone to flooding, you should locate equipment in the building above potential flood levels.

- ✔ **Water-resistant storage:** Get water-resistant safes and media vaults so flooding, fire suppression, and other discharges of water don't damage valuable documents and storage media.

- ✔ **Humidity control:** Have equipment for removing excess humidity on hand or readily available in the event a discharge of water occurs.

Often, preventing a disaster is far easier than dealing with one when it occurs.

Selecting Alternate Processing Sites

Despite every reasonable means available to prevent a disaster or minimize a disaster's impact, some events are so intense that you have no choice but to temporarily or permanently abandon a data processing facility and resume operations elsewhere. Extreme natural and man-made disasters do occur, and in your locale, you know which types are more likely to trigger a real disaster for your organization.

So the main question is: If you have a disaster, where you gonna go? The following sections are devoted to helping you answer that question for your organization.

You have several alternatives for relocating your systems if your data center ends up a smoking crater:

- **Cold sites:** Processing facilities with no computers installed
- **Warm sites:** Processing facilities with computers that require installation and configuration
- **Hot sites:** Processing facilities with computers that are ready to perform business processing
- **Other business locations:** Other facilities that the organization owns
- **Mobile sites:** Processing facilities in trailers
- **Contracted facilities:** Processing facilities owned by other organizations
- **Reciprocal facilities:** Mutual-aid arrangements

The following sections give you detailed explanations of the alternatives in the preceding list.

Hot, cold, and warm sites

You have a few ways to consider alternate processing sites. You can consider who owns an alternate site and the business relationship between your organization and the alternate site's owner. You can also consider the alternate site's readiness to take on the burden of production information processing — I discuss this readiness consideration in this section.

In terms of readiness, alternate processing centers are categorized in three levels: hot, cold, and warm. I describe these levels in the following sections.

 The terms hot site, warm site, and cold site aren't absolute. You use them in the same way you identify a small car, medium-sized car, and large car. You don't have an absolute boundary between the terms: They're simply general, relative categories.

Hot sites

A *hot site* is a location that's ready to assume production application processing with little or no preparation. Systems, networks, and applications are all in place and up-to-date, and perhaps live data is already on the site or can be loaded up fairly quickly. Generally speaking, a hot site can assume processing with only a few minutes' or hours' notice.

Hot sites are the most expensive because keeping a hot site ready to assume production duties requires continuous effort. But, for businesses with highly time-sensitive applications, the expense of a hot site may be well worth the cost.

Cold sites

Cold sites are generally just empty processing centers with little or no networking equipment, and few (if any) systems. Communications facilities may or may not be in place. Think of a cold site as an empty room, with physical and environmental controls in place, but no information processing equipment.

The time required to get a cold site up to full battle readiness is at least several days and possibly a week or longer.

Warm sites

Warm sites are, well, in the middle between ready-to-go hot sites and the empty shells of cold sites. Warm sites may have servers and network equipment in place, but no software or data loaded. A warm site might need from one to five days to get up and running.

Table 6-1 compares hot, warm, and cold sites.

Table 6-1	Hot, Warm, and Cold Sites		
Category	*Hot*	*Warm*	*Cold*
Readiness	Minutes to hours	Hours to days	Days to weeks
Application systems	Loaded and ready	Present but not ready	Absent; must be purchased and installed
Communications	Ready to go	Capable	Little or none
Application data	Up to date	Not up to date; must be refreshed	Not present; must be loaded
Cost	Very high	Moderate	Low

You perform the Business Impact Analysis (BIA) and determine the Maximum Tolerable Downtime (MTD), Recovery Time Objectives (RTO), and Recovery Point Objectives (RPO) early in the disaster recovery project. The results and content of these formal documents and processes determine the investment required regarding the resumption of processing capability with hot, warm, or cold sites. The cost of downtime and the long-term costs incurred by a long outage determine the level of recovery capability. You're probably not going to invest more in your recovery capability than you derive from the process you're trying to protect. In other words, this is ultimately a cost-benefit matter, taking the probability of a disaster into consideration.

Other business locations

Some businesses already have more than one processing site or have the ability to implement a second processing site in one of its premises. The capability to build your own alternative processing site may cost less than going with outside service bureaus or colocation facilities.

Some points to consider when thinking about other business locations as alternate processing sites include

- **Siting risks:** Is the site free from risks associated with airports, railroads, hazardous materials, flooding, storms, landslides, and other factors?

- **Environment support:** Does the site have sufficient HVAC and power capacity, or can you add it?

- **Physical security:** Does the other business location have sufficient physical security controls, such as fencing, video surveillance, key card systems, and so on?

- **Proximity to primary processing site:** Is the site far enough away from the existing information processing facility to not be considered in the same risk zone? Such a minimum distance might range from 100 to 500 miles, depending on the nature of the risks, such as earthquakes, volcanoes, hurricanes, tsunamis, and so on. Consult with local experts regarding the threats associated with nearby natural threats.

- **Transportation:** Is the alternate site sufficiently close to major transportation systems, such as airports, railroads, seaports, or freeways, to make those systems accessible in an emergency?

- **Supporting services:** Are supporting services near enough to the alternate site? Examples of supporting services that you may need to take into consideration include shipping, police and fire, lodging and restaurants, public utilities, building construction and repair, and network connectivity.

- **Laws and codes:** Are the building codes and laws concerning security and other matters for the alternate processing center suitable for your needs?

You may identify other factors that you think are important for your particular business activity and other needs.

Data center in a box: Mobile sites

Organizations such as APC, Sun Microsystems, and SunGard have developed emergency mobile data centers that they can deliver to a business location. These companies offer the following features:

- ✔ **APC InfraStruXure Express:** 2,500-square-foot mobile data center on a semi-truck trailer platform that includes power, cooling, 12 equipment racks, and satellite communications.

  `http://www.apc.com/products/infrastruxure/index.cfm`

- ✔ **Sun Microsystems Project Blackbox:** Self-contained data center in a shipping container that can be sent anywhere in the world by truck, ship, rail, or air. Equipped with integrated power and cooling, and a configurable selection of servers and network equipment.

  `www.sun.com/emrkt/blackbox`

- ✔ **SunGard:** Mobile data center on a semi-truck trailer platform that includes a generator, voice and data communications access, terminals and printers, equipment racks, work areas, kitchen, restrooms, lighting, and physical security. SunGard has several of these units available for dispatch within 48 hours.

  Go to `www.availability.sungard.com` and search for Mobile Data Center.

An emergency mobile data center may be appropriate for your business if you need a temporary data center up and running quickly in a location that has no other facilities available.

Colocation facilities

Commercial data centers, also known as *colocation facilities* or just *colos,* are big business in nearly every metropolitan area in the world. The big players, such as AT&T, have dozens of facilities throughout the world; many regional and local companies have carrier-grade data centers, as well.

Colocation facilities are multi-tenant data centers in which an organization such as yours leases as much space as it needs — from as little as a portion of a single rack to hundreds of square feet. The colo provides several features:

- ✔ **Physical security:** Security guards, key card entrances, video surveillance, fences, and perhaps other measures, such as hardened buildings, guard dogs, crash barriers, and so on.

- ✔ **Network/Internet connectivity:** Provides connectivity to the Internet — just hook up your router, firewall, switches, and so on.

✔ **Power, including emergency power:** Some facilities have redundant power feeds, generators, UPSs, and so on.

✔ **HVAC:** Redundant air-conditioning and humidity controls to get rid of all the heat that your servers throw off.

✔ **System monitoring and management:** Systems monitoring, management, backups, and so on, manned 24/7 by colo staff members so you don't have to.

The cost advantage of a colocation facility is potentially significant. In particular, they're expensive to build and maintain, and your organization needs to pay only its share in the form of monthly fees. Colocation facilities do have a downside: They're expensive, although less so than building one of your own.

Reciprocal facilities

Before colocation facilities came into being, one of the few options available for alternate processing sites was the reciprocal facility. A *reciprocal facility* is a legal arrangement between two parties, in which each pledges to make a portion of its facility available to the other party in the event that the other party experiences a disaster that forces it to abandon its own data center.

In plain and simple English, the agreement is, "I let you use a portion of my data center if you experience a disaster, and you let me use a portion of your data center if I experience a disaster."

In the era of mainframe computers, the reciprocal agreement applied not only to the physical space, but to the use of the organization's mainframe computer(s). So a reciprocal agreement was also a timesharing or service-bureau type agreement because an organization would permit another organization to run its programs on its mainframe.

The two organizations needed to have the same kind of mainframe computers so that application programs on one would also run on the other. The organizations needed to conduct an initial test to check the viability of a long-term reciprocal agreement and perhaps regular testing to make sure that the systems were still compatible.

In today's environment, a reciprocal agreement may or may not include the use of the other organization's systems — it may cover just the floor space and power for your systems in the other organization's data center. Still, a reciprocal agreement can cost much less than the alternative, colocation facilities.

Chapter 7

Planning System and Network Recovery

*A*lthough disaster recovery planning is all about recovering critical business functions, data, and the associated applications, application recovery can't exist or operate without support from the systems they reside on and the networks that enable communication to everything else in your application ecosystem.

DR planning, in large part, is about prevention — not preventing disastrous events, but preventing the crippling aftermath of a disaster. In the context of systems and networks, this prevention involves building consistent, resilient servers and networks that are flexible and can accommodate the processing needs for the applications they support.

In this chapter, you can figure out what you need to build and maintain the server and network infrastructure that your DR needs require. Every business is different in so many ways; so, rather than just give you the answers (which would make this book far too long), I give you everything you need to think about so that you can establish the best possible recovery plan for your critical applications and processes.

Managing and Recovering Server Computing

If data and applications are the soul of an IT-supported business process, systems are the body in which the soul resides. The system, like the body, needs to be a suitable vessel that allows the application to run correctly and provides access to that application's data.

Systems' resilience is the key to recoverability in the face of disaster. When I say systems' resilience, I indeed mean to use the plural because the entire community of systems that support an application before, during, and after a disaster need this resilience. You may need to make sure the organization has a collection of systems, in different locations, that are ready to assume operational duties when a disaster occurs.

I'm not saying that you must have a second set of servers ready to go in another location. Many organizations can't afford that kind of redundancy. Rather, your organization should have systems ready only when you need them, in the event that a disaster damages your primary servers or makes them unavailable for use. This need-specific setup could mean

- Hot servers already sharing the current workload
- Hot standby servers ready to take over at short notice
- Warm standby servers ready to take over with some preparation
- Cold standby servers ready for installation of applications and data
- Order servers when the disaster strikes, and then install your application and data on them when they arrive

Which option an organization chooses depends on the time sensitivity and business value of the applications that servers support, as well as whether the organization can invest in a given recovery capability. Whichever option you choose, you have to identify and manage numerous technical issues. And, generally speaking, the faster you want to recover your processing ability, the more complicated and costly your solution needs to be. I discuss these issues in the following sections.

Determining system readiness

A top-down DR plan defines the most critical business processes, and it therefore identifies the applications and databases associated with those processes as critical. These critical applications and databases, in turn, pinpoint critical servers and supporting infrastructure. When you determine Recovery Time Objectives (RTOs — that is, how quickly replacement servers must be up and running), you can figure out how much time you have to get new servers ready to run those critical applications. The RTOs drive the arguments for hot sites versus warm or cold sites. (I discuss determining RTO and other key values fully in Chapter 5, and I talk about the distinction between and issues about hot, cold, and warm sites in Chapter 6.)

RTOs and hot/warm/cold sites are all about timing: An RTO determines how quickly you need to recover your systems in a disaster. If you measure your RTOs in minutes, you have hot servers in a remote location that are probably already doing production work in the form of load balancing. If you measure your RTOs in hours or days, you still have a hot site, but one with a failover capability, instead. If you measure your RTOs in days or weeks, your plan probably calls for a warm or cold site. It's just about the speed of recovery.

Speed doesn't drive the argument, but consider speed to readiness as I dive into the issues that really matter for system recovery and readiness.

Server architecture and configuration

In Chapter 4, I discuss the need for inventory information at every level. When you inventory your systems, software, network devices, and other supporting assets, you can begin to identify the components that support critical business functions. After you identify these assets, you need to get the magnifying glass out and look more closely at critical application servers. At this level of detail, you have to identify every tiny detail and determine the following information for every server:

- ✔ **Hardware configuration:** Find out everything about the hardware on a server, including

  - Make, model, serial number

  - Firmware (BIOS/CMOS) versions

  - Number and type of CPUs

  - Amount and type of memory

  - Number, type, and hardware configuration of network adaptors

  - Number, type, and hardware configuration of storage interfaces (for example, SCSI adaptors)

  - Exactly how the hardware is assembled (order of adaptor cards, memory sticks, and so on)

  - Attached peripheral devices (type, model, version, and so on)

- ✔ **Operating system:** Figure out everything about the operating system (OS) that's running on the server, including but not limited to

  - Version, release date, and patch level for the OS you're using

- Patches installed (and the versions of those patches and even the order of installation, if you can find out)

- Components installed and their versions

- Boot configuration

- Recovery settings

You're probably thinking, "This is a lot of detail!" But you need to know these details to ensure that application software functions properly and predictably.

✔ **Resource configuration:** Virtual memory, disk utilization settings, memory utilization, and how the OS makes resources available to applications and system processes. In the UNIX world, these are kernel parameters; in Windows, these are mostly configured in the Registry and in some administrative user interface functions. Regardless of the OS, system administrators usually manage these settings.

✔ **Network and network services configuration:** All the usual settings, including subnet mask, gateway, DNS server, directory server, and time server, as well as tuning settings, such as number of open connections and buffer allocation.

✔ **Security configuration:** A lot of these settings deal with event logging, system auditing, system-level access control configuration, patch download and installation, and user account settings.

✔ **System-level components:** Additional components installed at the system level, including

- Firewall

- Intrusion detection and prevention

- Anti-virus and other anti-malware

- System management agents

Be sure to get the versions and configurations for all of these components!

✔ **Access management:** The whole gamut of system-level access that includes

- User IDs, user ID and password configuration

- Configurations related to any centralized user management resources, such as LDAP or Active Directory

- Shared resources, meaning directories and other resources that users can access via the network

Inventorying all the information in the preceding list for a server could take you a good long time. Multiply the effort by the number of servers you have. I envision a very wide and deep spreadsheet in your immediate future.

Those centralized system configuration management platforms are highly valued, and also very expensive because of their complexity and the high value they provide. The top tools in the configuration management space make identifying and managing the entire configuration for each server a far easier task. If you don't have any such tools, you have to manage systems the hard way (in other words, manually).

Why this level of detail is important

Critical applications and data reside and run on your servers. Your servers' intricate configuration permits your applications to run in the more-or-less predictable state that administrators and users are familiar with.

To ensure that a recovery server can support the correct and proper functioning of a critical application, configure the recovery server to match the original server as closely as possible. If you do otherwise, you introduce potential instabilities or changes in functionality that you don't want to introduce ever, especially during a real-life disaster recovery operation. In such a situation, you already have enough chaos and disruption to deal with; adding application instability because of differences in server configuration could be the difference between your business's survival and demise.

Understanding the case for consistency

If you haven't delved into the depths of server configuration detail before, you're probably gaining an appreciation for the complexity of modern operating systems and the people who manage them. If you want consistency across multiple servers in an environment, I applaud you for your wisdom. Simplicity and consistency are far easier to manage than complexity and inconsistency. Well, you can't get rid of complexity in operating systems (because of the vast number of configuration settings), but you can make the configuration of systems more consistent, server to server. Configuration management tools can help you achieve this consistency.

Configuration management can also give you other significant advantages:

- ✔ **Reduction in administrative errors:** System administrators can more easily manage identically configured systems, so they make fewer mistakes.

- ✔ **Reduction in unscheduled downtime:** When system administrators are making fewer mistakes on servers, those servers run more reliably.

Developing the ability to build new servers

You have to be able to make identical copies (well, as near to identical as is practical) of critical application servers and use those copies to run your applications when disaster strikes.

So you need to figure out how to build new servers that are like existing ones. This book isn't about Windows (or UNIX, or whatever) system administration, so I won't go too deep into that subject. It should suffice to say that you need to make new servers as similar as possible to existing ones so that applications can run on those new servers with as little fuss as possible. And this smooth transition makes building recovery systems after a disaster easier.

Building nearly identical servers for recovery purposes is one thing, but keeping those servers consistent is quite another. Server consistency requires two separate but related disciplines:

- **Change management:** The business process concerned with the proper development, analysis, and approval of changes made in a production environment, at all layers. The goal of change management is to expose potential risks and other issues that could jeopardize proposed changes before they occur. Proper change management gives you higher system availability and fewer unscheduled outages.

- **Configuration management:** The process of recording all changes made to all components (at all layers) in an environment. The central repository is known as the *configuration management database* (CMDB), which stores every detail about the systems under its management.

Typically, change management and configuration management relate to each other in this way: You use configuration management to document the changes that the change management process has analyzed and approved.

How you keep your recovery server configurations consistent depends a lot on your speed to recovery: If your DR plan calls for rapid failover to hot servers, you need to make the means for updating those hot standby servers as close to automated as possible. If you install patches or make other changes to the primary server, make those same changes to the recovery servers as soon as possible. Letting servers get too far out of sync could invite trouble during a recovery operation.

If, on the other hand, your recovery servers are stored in a closet someplace, you need to somehow queue up all of your changes and apply them only now and then so those servers aren't too far out of sync in case a disaster strikes.

Your DR plan may specify that you purchase servers when a disaster strikes and then build them after they arrive. In a situation such as this, you might invest in a set of tools that you can use to duplicate a server configuration onto another server.

The bottom line is that you must keep your recovery servers' configuration consistent with your primary servers. *How* you maintain this consistency depends on how quickly you need to begin using your recovery servers in a disaster.

Distributed server computing considerations

Many environments use a complex application architecture that includes components that reside on many servers, and not all of those servers are necessarily located in the same location. *Distributed architectures* (as these types of architectures are called) increase the complexity of an environment in steady-state and introduce additional issues that you must address in your DR planning.

This complexity is further exacerbated in cases in which other organizations own or operate one or more of the components in the application environment. With Internet-connected enterprises and application integration that's fueled by business interoperability and made possible by newer technologies, such as Service-Oriented Architecture (SOA), disaster recovery planning assumes a much higher level of complexity. Organizations need to make additional plans for recovering these increasingly complex environments if one of those organizations is hit with a disastrous event.

Architecture issues

You may encounter these issues related to application architecture during your DR analysis and planning effort:

- ✔ **Interfaces:** If you have custom interfaces between the components of your distributed environment, it'll take more effort (on the part of system developers or integrators) to improve resilience in the overall environment. Engage your application architecture personnel and urge them to develop strategic plans that include moving to standard interfaces, such as Service-Oriented Architecture (SOA).

- ✔ **Latency:** In a highly distributed environment, systems that communicate over great distances and/or over slow wide-area network (WAN) connections can experience *latency* (delays in the transmission of data from system to system). The behavior of the application may change in unexpected ways in a disaster scenario if the latency between components increases (or decreases) by a significant amount. Parts of a distributed environment may not be able to tolerate latency, and other parts that include significant latency may behave differently if the latency decreases.

- ✔ **Network considerations:** A distributed application environment that encompasses WAN connectivity needs to take network design into account. Distributed applications that were designed for, and implemented in, fast local-area networks may suffer performance degradation in a wide-area network. The cumulative effect of several lengthy hops across a WAN can slow response time and even cause network timeouts.

Operational issues

Keep these common operational issues for distributed applications in mind when doing your system-level DR planning:

- ✔ **Failure points:** Distributed systems have more *failure points* (literally, the number of hardware and software components required to support the environment) than centralized systems, and a disaster is more likely to occur when those failure points are geographically diverse, rather than in a single/central location.

- ✔ **Distributed recovery:** A disaster that occurs in one location of a distributed environment may prompt a recovery operation that involves personnel in many locations.

- ✔ **Third-party components:** If a third-party service provider that hosts a vital element to your application experiences a disaster, that service provider's priority list may differ from yours.

- ✔ **Priority:** In a distributed environment, a disaster that disables one component may have additional recovery complications. The failure of a component at a remote location may be *your* high priority, but a lower priority than other components for the remote location's organization. For instance, a database server in a remote location is only a medium priority for the organization in that location, but it's critical to your organization. If that database server fails, the organization that runs it may not be in a particular hurry to fix it, which can lead to longer downtime or a more difficult or time-consuming recovery for you.

Application architecture considerations

Because the bulk of DR planning is in preparation, an organization should consider a number of application architecture issues while developing its DR plan. You can more easily recover a resilient application that relies on standard components than you can an environment that relies more heavily on custom components and non-standard features. Figure 7-1 shows a typical application architecture.

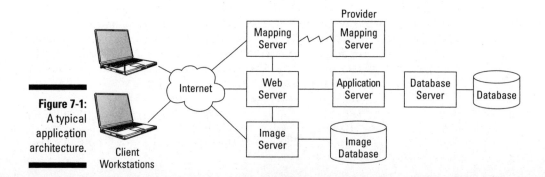

Figure 7-1: A typical application architecture.

Introduce these issues into the long-term application architecture effort:

✔ **Centralized authentication:** Application architects and integrators should seriously consider a shift towards network-based authentication services instead of relying on authentication within the application. Sure, an application may still need to perform an authentication, but authentication data should be centralized, which improves the integrity of access controls across the organization in several ways:

   • **Standard logon credentials:** Users have fewer (as few as one) user IDs and passwords that they need to remember.

   • **Streamlined authentication management:** You need fewer personnel to manage the issuance and termination of access rights.

   • **Fewer forgotten passwords:** Because workers have fewer passwords that they need to remember (as few as one), they won't forget their passwords as often, so you can spend less time performing password resets.

   Examples of centralized authentication and identity services include LDAP, Microsoft Active Directory, Oblix, and IBM Tivoli Identity Manager.

✔ **Standardized interfaces:** Application architects should put SOA (Service-Oriented Architecture), Web Services, ETL (Extract, Transform, Load), and XML (Extensible Markup Language) on their roadmaps as the means for highly agile integration between applications, both within the enterprise and with external applications.

The approaches in the preceding list permit application designers and DR planners to think about the service components that support applications, separate from the applications themselves. Developing standard and centralized services permits an organization to streamline its application environment by plugging application components into a service-oriented framework that already provides basic services, such as authentication and data management.

Server consolidation: The double-edged sword

Server consolidation has been the talk of IT departments for several years and represents a still-popular cost-cutting move. The concept is simple: Instead of dedicating applications to individual servers, which can result in underutilized servers, you install multiple applications onto servers to more efficiently utilize server hardware, thereby reducing costs.

I'm all for saving money, electricity, natural resources, and so on. Consolidating servers is a smart move to undertake, as long as you remember that server consolidation is something to undertake during *peacetime* (normal operations), not in a disaster scenario.

Security laws and regulations apply during disasters

Organizations need to protect every type of sensitive data, including

✔ Financial records and transactions

✔ Medical records

✔ Identity information, such as names, dates of birth, social insurance numbers, and passport numbers

✔ Intellectual property, including an organization's secrets

In the onset or aftermath of a disaster, you can't suspend security laws and regulations. On the contrary, disaster recovery plans must take into account all the security requirements that apply during peacetime.

Many regulations exist to protect information about citizens and corporate entities from compromise and theft. Organizations that are in the midst of a disaster recovery operation aren't exempt from these regulations, so you need to consider all applicable security regulations and requirements when developing an organization's disaster recovery plan. Also consider that a disaster declaration may result from a malicious act, possibly a deliberate attempt to get an organization to let its guard down and make information easier to steal or sabotage.

Consider an environment that's made up of dozens of underutilized servers dedicated to applications. The DR planning team wants to consider a DR strategy that consolidates these applications onto fewer servers to provide a lower-cost recovery capability.

Well, this consolidation might work, but the DR planning team should test it very thoroughly and carefully. Combining applications that previously had servers all to themselves may lead to unexpected interactions that could be difficult to troubleshoot and untangle.

If you want to undertake server consolidation, do it first in your production environment, and then take that consolidated architecture and apply it to a DR architecture. To make server consolidation successful in your DR plan, first implement server consolidation in your production environment, where your architects, designers, developers, and operations staff can become familiar with it. You can far more easily implement something in a DR environment if you're already familiar with it.

Managing and Recovering Network Infrastructure

Networks and network services are the plumbing that permits applications to communicate with each other and with the people who use them. Although networks are generally a lot less complicated than the applications they support, they're a lot more complicated than the router-firewall-hub architectures that businesses used in times past. Figure 7-2 shows a typical enterprise network architecture.

Networks are a lot more than just devices that move network traffic about. Networks perform often-invisible functions that enable communications within and among enterprises.

Ninety percent of good DR planning is knowing what makes your environment run today, especially when you're dealing with networks and those invisible services.

To a great extent, the features in a network and the issues with network recovery are one in the same. After you identify your assets and features, you can incorporate that information into your DR planning effort.

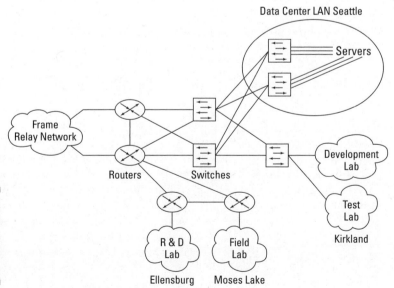

Figure 7-2:
A typical
enterprise
network
architecture.

Consider your voice network capabilities (meaning your office telephones) as part of your network, whether you use analog, digital, or IP-based phones in your environment. Voice communications are as vital as data communications in most organizations, and perhaps even more so.

Consider these voice network features and issues:

- ✔ **External network dependencies:** An organization's connection to the Internet depends on some configuration settings that external service providers maintain, including

  - **Data circuits and trunks:** Getting any sort of an Internet *data circuit* (a network circuit that connects your internal data network to the Internet) or *PBX trunk* (a network connection between your internal phone system and the public telephone network) installed takes several weeks, even with expedited orders from local telephone companies. Data circuits are also expensive, so organizations need to use some creative thinking to figure out how to set up data circuits for DR purposes. Not only are circuits and trunks expensive, but they take several weeks to install and set up.

  - **Domain name service (DNS):** DNS is the glue that associates domain names (such as `www.company.com` or `http://mailserver.company.com`) with the IP addresses that systems use. Changing an IP address for a well-known service, such as a Web site, can take hours or days before Internet users can visit the site on the new IP address.

  - **Publicly routable network numbers:** The network connection established between an ISP (Internet Service Provider) and a business includes some fixed (non-changeable) IP addresses that are associated with that particular network connection. You generally can't associate those IP addresses with another physical location.

  - **Office telephone service:** Aside from trunks, you have a lot of other considerations if you want to build or recover your voice network in a DR setting. Partner with your voice service provider to get a better idea of what issues you need to consider in order to recover your voice network.

    DNS, network addresses, and especially data and voice circuits are *long lead time items* — functions that you must build well in advance of a disaster, especially if an alternate processing site depends on them. Even for a cold site, you need to pre-order these items and put them in place, unless you don't mind waiting six weeks for connectivity at your DR site.

  - **Network Time Protocol (NTP):** You use NTP to provide accurate clock synchronization for servers and workstations. Usually, business applications just work when starting up new servers in a new environment. Still, include NTP on your system build checklist so you can make sure that this important function continues working.

✔ **Firewalls:** They stop the bad stuff, such as worms and scanning attacks, from getting in — that's the easy part. Firewalls also contain a list of rules, which permit specific communications between servers inside the enterprise with servers or networks outside the environment. Often, network administrators introduce these rules to permit specific applications to communicate with systems in other organizations. If you need to move an application to an alternate processing site, you need to know and correctly apply all the original firewalls' rules to the firewall(s) at the alternate site.

✔ **Network security devices:** In addition to firewalls, organizations frequently use a variety of other means for protecting systems and networks:

  • Intrusion detection and prevention

  • Spam filters

  • Web proxies and filters

  • Load balancers

  • Hardware encryption

  • VLANs (virtual networks)

  • DMZ (demilitarized zone) network segments

✔ **Network equipment:** Like servers, some network equipment — especially bigger routers and other non-commodity items — can take a while to obtain. You either need to have this equipment on hand in your alternate processing facility or have "first off the line" privileges with your suppliers.

✔ **Management processes:** Specifically, change management and configuration management. I describe these two disciplines in the section "Developing the ability to build new servers," earlier in this chapter. Change and configuration management are vital for network equipment and configuration, not just for servers.

✔ **Network architecture, routing, and addressing:** The internal details of a network facilitate communication within the network and with external networks. Setting up *network addressing* (the IP addresses that are assigned to systems and devices) and *routing* (the means through which systems on different networks can communicate with each other) involves a lot of detail that applications depend on.

✔ **Network management:** Medium-sized and larger organizations often use a network management application to monitor and manage all the network devices (and, often, servers) in the environment. Some organizations' networks are so tightly coupled to their network management platforms that the networks can't run without the management systems.

The completion of the Business Impact Analysis (discussed in Chapter 3), together with the establishment of Recovery Time Objectives (RTOs), largely determines the speed at which you need to recover critical business applications. A rapid speed to recovery can cost quite a lot. The process of establishing

RTOs and then determining their costs can get repetitive: A first pass could well determine that the cost of recovering an application within an arbitrary period of time would cost more than the business derives from the business process that the application supports. DR planning is, for sure, a time of soul searching and difficult decisions.

Implementing Standard Interfaces

You can often more easily extend and change an applications architecture that's based on open standards than one that's built with custom interfaces. *Open standards* are the programming and communications standards that applications and systems are built on. Here are some examples of open standards:

- ✔ **TCP/IP:** The network protocol of the Internet. Dozens of open standards fall within TCP/IP, including SMTP (Simple Mail Transfer Protocol) that makes e-mail work, DNS (domain name service) that's used to translate names into IP addresses, NTP (Network Time Protocol) that synchronizes system clocks, HTTP (HyperText Transfer Protocol) that Web browsers use to request data from Web servers, and SNMP (Simple Network Management Protocol) that's used to manage network devices and systems.

- ✔ **World Wide Web:** Encompasses protocols and standards that support the Web.

- ✔ **GSM:** The cellular telephone communication standard used in most of the world.

To make applications and systems more resilient and recoverable, organizations may have to add or change components that can facilitate recovery operations. Here are some examples:

- ✔ **Upgrading interfaces to SOA:** Service-Oriented Architecture (SOA), sometimes known as Web Services, is a newer method that you use to integrate applications without having to build custom interfaces over low-level protocols, such as CORBA (Common Object Request Broker Architecture), DCOM (Distributed Component Object Model), or .Net.

- ✔ **Implementing centralized identity management:** Centralizing authentication within the environment permits applications to do what they do best — provide access to business information. Technologies and products that provide centralized identity management include LDAP (the open standard Lightweight Directory Access Protocol), IBM Tivoli Identity Manager, Microsoft Identity Integration Server, Novell Identity Manager, Oracle Identity Management, and Sun Java System Identity Manager.

Implementing Server Clustering

Applications that are critical to important business processes often require higher availability, and you need to be able to quickly recover them in another location. Organizations that need the ability to recover these applications within minutes of a failure frequently use server clustering. Clustering is an expensive proposition, but it's the method of choice for applications that require rapid recovery.

A *server cluster* is a tightly-coupled collection of two or more servers that are configured to host one or more applications. In his book *In Search of Clusters* (Prentice Hall), Gregory Pfister describes a cluster as "a parallel or distributed system that consists of a collection of interconnected whole computers that are utilized as a single, unified computing resource." In other words, a cluster is a collection of computers that appear as a single computer to end users.

The servers in a cluster coordinate with each other to ensure that at least one of the servers is running the applications. They coordinate by communicating with each other through a fast network, using clustering software that manages a complex set of tasks. Figure 7-3 shows a server cluster architecture.

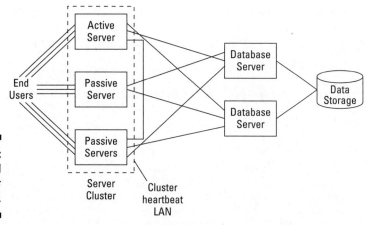

Figure 7-3:
A typical
server
cluster.

Server clusters improve the availability of the applications they serve by reducing the effects of

- ✔ **Hardware failure:** Failures in components such as CPU, RAM, bus, or boot drive result in an immediate, unplanned outage for critical applications running on the system.

- ✔ **Software failure:** A malfunction in software can result in a server lockup or crash. You may be thinking, "If a software failure occurs on one server in the cluster, wouldn't it also occur in other servers in the cluster?" Yes, possibly. This scenario is certainly worth thinking about while application and system engineers try to figure out an ideal architecture for a clustered application.

- ✔ **Network failure:** You couple a properly designed system cluster with a network architecture that has similar redundancies. If you experience a failure in the network, other network components and paths should still be available, making at least some of the servers in the cluster still reachable from client systems.

- ✔ **Maintenance:** With two or more systems in a cluster, you can much more easily perform regular maintenance activities on individual servers. You can take individual servers in a cluster offline, shut them down, and perform maintenance on them — all without affecting application availability.

- ✔ **Performance issues:** You can configure a cluster to permit more than one server in the cluster to serve applications. I discuss cluster configuration more in the following section, which talks about cluster modes.

Understanding cluster modes

Server clusters generally operate in one of two basic modes, which are based on how the servers in the cluster are configured to operate day by day:

- ✔ **Active/active:** In this configuration, all the servers in the cluster run applications. You use this mode for a load-sharing scenario in which an application runs on several servers at the same time.

- ✔ **Active/passive:** This configuration consists of servers that are hosting applications (the active ones) and other servers that are in a standby mode.

Whether an organization chooses to run its clusters in active/active or active/passive mode depends on performance, availability, and disaster recovery needs. You need specially designed applications if you want several servers hosting those applications at the same time.

Geographically distributed clusters

In the preceding sections of this chapter, I discuss server clusters that you set up in a data center, in which all of the servers in the cluster are located within a few feet of each other. When put into operation, the cluster provides not only much higher availability for the application, but also greater capacity if you configure the cluster as active/active.

This type of clustering does little for disaster recovery purposes, however. The entire cluster can be incapacitated if any of several events occur:

✔ **Fire, flood, earthquake, tornado, or hurricane:** Any of these events can directly destroy servers or render them incapable of operation.

✔ **Widespread communications or other utility failure:** A prolonged or severe event can result in communications or power utilities being unavailable for so long that short-term contingencies can't compensate.

✔ **Sabotage, vandalism, or terrorism:** Somebody with determination can render all of the systems in a processing center inoperative for hours, days, or longer. Wire cutters, a sledge hammer, a bomb, or a degausser can quickly destroy several servers' ability to host critical applications.

Any of these events can easily render all of the servers in a cluster inoperative or unreachable. Right? Not necessarily. You can make your server clusters geographically diverse. In other words, instead of placing servers side by side in a processing center, you can place them hundreds or thousands of miles apart in separate processing centers. These clusters are called *geo-clusters* or *GD (geographically diverse) clusters.*

The chief advantage of a geo-cluster is that you always have an application available, even when a widespread regional disaster completely destroys a processing center. Servers in the cluster that are located in surviving processing centers keep running, with little or no interruption. Figure 7-4 shows a typical geo-cluster configuration.

Figure 7-4:
A typical geographically diverse server cluster.

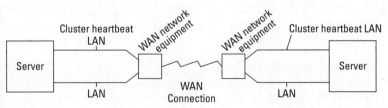

Cluster and storage architecture

The architecture of clustered servers, storage systems, and the applications themselves are tightly coupled. Applications hosted on a server cluster must be designed to properly interface with the physical architecture of storage systems and how cluster failovers work. The integrity of applications is vital to the health of the application, especially when the servers and cluster architecture can be changed in real time.

You can use several technologies to protect application data, including resilient storage, mirroring, and replication. A server cluster needs one or more of these technologies. In fact, you can develop many such possible cluster-storage architectures. The following list breaks down cluster and storage architecture into the simplest terms. Choose a technology from each of the following groups to put together a complete clustered architecture:

- **Cluster architecture:** Pick one:

    - Active/active

    - Active/passive

    You also need to figure out how many servers you want in your cluster and whether you want them located in the same processing center or hundreds of miles apart.

- **Storage architecture:** Pick one or more:

    - **SAN (Storage Area Network):** Select whether you want storage attached via SCSI, Fibre Arbitrated Loop, or a Fibre network.

    - **NAS (Network Attached Storage):** You connect storage systems to the network and access them with NFS (Network File System) or SMB (Server Message Block) network protocols.

- **Data replication:** Pick one or more:

    - **Mirroring:** The database, server OS, or storage system layers can perform the *mirroring,* in which changes to data on a storage system are copied to a remote storage system in real time.

    - **Replication:** The copying of transactions from one system to another.

- **Network architecture:** You have many choices available, including

    - **Load balancers:** For arbitrating access among several active servers

    - **Round robin DNS:** For load balancing across an active/active geo-cluster

    - **Dynamic routing changes:** For failover at the network level so that application clients are directed to active servers, wherever those servers are

The technologies in the preceding list are just the high-level details. Within every option, you have to make many more choices. And many intimate details of the application, in terms of how transactions work, matter when making choices, large and small. You can find entire books filled with information on application, storage, and cluster architecture. I have only enough room in this book to take you on a quick tour.

Chapter 8

Planning Data Recovery

*I*t's all about the data.

That pretty much sums it up. But don't close the book yet. I have a lot of details to cover about how to protect that data.

I don't blame you if you're confused because I say that it's all about the data. Security products have, in the past, been largely network-centric: Firewalls and intrusion detection systems are network-based tools, leading many IT professionals (myself included) to believe that their networks needed the protection. But your network is only your private highway that leads to what really matters — your data.

This chapter focuses on protecting your organization's data so you don't find yourself in a jam when a disaster strikes — instead, you're prepared to resume processing at a later time in your same location or soon in a different location.

Protecting and Recovering Application Data

If you know that your most valuable IT assets are your databases, protecting them is just a matter of incorporating some backup or replication scheme to make them more readily available if a disaster strikes. Right?

Not so fast.

In most organizations, although they store much of the data centrally in databases, they also store some of the data elsewhere. And probably only a few people are familiar with the details of the data that exists in the backwater places in your network.

Locating all your data requires some sleuthing. You need a process-centric view that uncovers all of the ins and outs of your data (where the data comes from and where it goes) so you don't miss any details.

Recovering critical business functions means more than just recovering the databases. It also requires recovering the capabilities for moving the data into and out of applications that support business functions.

Before we explore the various options for protecting data against loss (and making it available soon after a disaster), you need to understand some basic principles about DR-style data protection:

- ✔ **Speed increases costs.** In other words, the faster you want your data available after a disaster, the more it'll cost you.

- ✔ **Distance increases costs.** The further away you store the data that you'll need to recover quickly, the more it'll cost you. Primarily, this cost relates to private, high-speed WAN connections between two or more of your facilities.

- ✔ **Size increases costs.** The more data that you want to make available soon after a disaster, the more it'll cost you. This cost relates to the amount of storage you must purchase to achieve the storage redundancy you require.

- ✔ **Complexity increases costs.** A data protection and recovery plan that contains several different solutions for parts of the organization costs more than a simple plan. For instance, a plan that has mirroring for part of the data, replication for another part of the data, electronic vaulting for yet another part of the data, and tape backup recovery (all discussed later in this chapter) for the rest of the data costs quite a lot in terms of all of these platforms that you must build and operate over time. A simpler one- or two-tier plan is more cost effective than a complex plan with many more components.

Here's an example: During its Business Impact Analysis (BIA), an organization identifies several critical databases that it must protect and recover in the event of a disaster. While developing the Recovery Time Objectives (RTOs) for various business applications, the DR project team identifies two classes of recovery needs: a more rapid need to recover a subset of data and a less rapid need to recover the remaining data.

The project team debates these possible strategies:

- ✔ **Two-tier recovery:** They can protect and recover the most time-critical data by using a more expensive data replication mechanism and recover the rest of the data, which is less time-sensitive, from backup tapes. Members of the project team who are in favor of this strategy argue that this approach is less expensive than using costly data replication for all the organization's data.

> ✔ **One-tier recovery:** They can use the pricey data replication to protect and recover all the organization's data. Although this approach has more in upfront costs to protect all the data, the strategy is simpler and easier to implement than two separate schemes. The team members in favor of this approach argue that its simplicity outweighs the additional costs. They'll probably find this approach easier and more reliable during a recovery.

The project team needs to do more analysis to determine whether the two-tier or one-tier recovery strategy is appropriate for the organization. The team needs to weigh not only the capital costs, but also the costs of operating the environment day to day and during disaster and recovery scenarios.

Keep the data protection principles in mind when you're developing your data protection and recovery plans. You need to weigh the costs and benefits of developing either a single data recovery solution for your entire enterprise or a multi-tier data recovery solution.

Choosing How and Where to Store Data for Recovery

The process of DR planning begins with the Business Impact Analysis (BIA), which includes a risk assessment and the determination of Recovery Time Objectives (RTOs) and Recovery Point Objectives (RPOs). These steps help you identify which business processes are the most important in an organization and how quickly you need to recover them. Chapter 3 discusses BIA development in detail.

Before you can develop a viable data recovery plan, you need to identify all the data associated with each critical business process listed in the BIA. Analysis often shows that you find some of the data where you expect to find it — in application databases and other centrally managed locations. However, you probably also find much data in other places, including end-user laptops, workstations, and inside the heads of several individuals. This data-location effort is discussed in Chapter 4.

The Business Impact Analysis and data sleuthing efforts, when completed, provide two important facts:

✔ Which data is important

✔ Where the important data is located now

Knowing these facts, you can now construct a strategy for protecting the data and making the data recoverable in the event of a disaster.

Because, in a disaster, the facility or the equipment that houses the data is often destroyed, the business needs to recover the data (either in the same or a different location) on alternative equipment so business operations can resume.

The next important step in developing your DR plan (after completing the BIA) is to determine where and how to store the data so that you can recover it in the time required to support your RTOs and RPOs.

This chapter deals with the where and how of this data storage. The following sections discuss several solutions for protecting data:

- ✔ Backups
- ✔ Resilient storage
- ✔ Replication and mirroring
- ✔ Electronic vaulting

Protecting data through backups

Tape backup has, for over five decades, been a runaway favorite for protecting data against loss in the event of a disaster. People who need to back up data have favored tape for its long-term storage stability and low unit cost. The storage capacity of magnetic tape, or *magtape,* has steadily increased over time, enabling tape backup to keep up with similar advances in hard-disk capacity. Figure 8-1 shows the flow of data to and from backup media when you back up and later restore that data.

Recently, backing up data onto removable hard drives, such as those that easily plug in to RAID arrays (highly resilient disk storage systems), has become popular. From a business function standpoint, backup media, such as tapes and disks, are more or less the same: They're media that you use to store and retain copies of electronic data. Backup is defined more by the function — making backup copies of information — than by the type of media used.

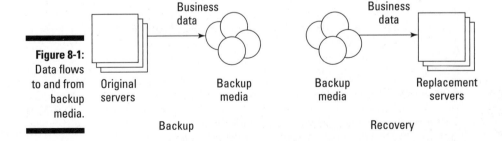

Figure 8-1: Data flows to and from backup media.

Business data → Original servers → Backup media

Backup

Backup media → Business data → Replacement servers

Recovery

Backup fulfills several purposes:

- **Long-term archiving:** Regulations often require the long-term storage of certain business records. Organizations back up such data to tape and store those tapes for long periods of time so they can meet those retention needs.

- **Data recovery:** Human error often occurs — a program bug can inadvertently corrupt data or someone can accidentally deletes files. Equipment malfunctions, such as hard drive failures, are also common. In these and similar scenarios, you can recover data from recently-created backup tapes.

- **Disaster recovery:** If a disastrous event strikes a data center in which your organization stores important business information, you can easily recover that data from backup tapes onto replacement or alternate systems.

Organizations that have no disaster recovery plan still often use tape backup for data recovery purposes, either because they know that it makes good business sense or they want to avoid repeating an incident in which an equipment failure or human error resulted in a costly data loss. With some changes in the way that the organization performs these backups, it can adapt its tape backup operation to support disaster recovery needs.

You need to consider several important issues if you want to make tape backup a part of your disaster recovery plan:

- **Data retention policy:** Before you can put a tape backup plan into place, the organization must first decide how long it wants to retain electronic data, including data in databases and in other locations. Factors that drive a retention policy include statutory requirements, contractual requirements, service level agreements, and existing operations procedures.

- **Backup media retention:** The organization needs to decide how long it plans to retain backup tapes. This timeframe should fulfill data RPOs in both directions, meaning

    - **Most recent data recovery:** This requirement supports the RPO — recovering most recent data in order to avoid re-keying or re-processing newest data.

    - **Least recent data recovery:** This requirement supports a different objective — recovering data from a particular point in time for whatever business purpose requires that data. For example, to see what a customer record looked like exactly six weeks and three days ago, you might need to retain daily backups for seven weeks or more.

Developing a tape backup media retention and rotation plan can be complex. Such a plan needs to accommodate both archival and disaster recovery functions, and it must anticipate data growth, longevity of backup media, and other business requirements.

✔ **Backup media recordkeeping:** Because you use backup media for both archival and recovery purposes, you need to establish a robust and reliable recordkeeping system for backup media. The recordkeeping system should support several functions:

- Quickly determine which backup tape contains any given data file.

- Quickly determine which backup tapes you need to completely recover a given server.

- Quickly determine the physical location of any backup tape.

- Easily determine how many times any given backup tape has been used.

✔ **Backup media protection:** Because they contain valuable business information, you need to protect backup tapes from unauthorized access and use.

✔ **Backup media location:** To effectively guard against any disaster scenario, you must locate backup media away from the data center in case that data center is damaged or destroyed. Backup tapes wouldn't be much good if they were damaged or destroyed alongside the equipment that stored the original data. I discuss where to store your backup media in more detail in the section "Deciding where to keep your recovery data," later in this chapter.

✔ **Backup media privacy:** Government regulations, as well as requirements through pervasive standards, such as PCI (the Payment Card Industry data security standard intended to protect credit card data), often require that data in backup media be encrypted, thus preventing exposure of backup data to any unauthorized parties. You can implement the encryption of backup media in a variety of ways:

- **Main storage encryption:** If data that you want to back up is already encrypted in its native location, the data may be automatically encrypted when you copy it to backup media.

- **Backup program encryption:** The software that performs the backup operation may be able to encrypt the data as it passes from the source system to the tape backup equipment.

- **Backup equipment encryption:** The equipment that you use to write data onto backup tapes may have the ability to encrypt the data before it writes that data to tape.

Table 8-1 shows several pros and cons for tape and disk backup.

Table 8-1	Pros and Cons of Tape/Disk Backup
Pros	*Cons*
Inexpensive media	Slow/sequential access
Well established	Media is somewhat fragile (applies mostly to tape)
Media has a long shelf life	
Media is easily transportable, lends itself easily to off-site storage	

You often keep backup tapes that you create for data retention purposes separate from tapes that you create for data recovery and disaster recovery reasons. You can keep tapes that contain data you want to retain for long periods of time in a different location to reduce the chance that someone accidentally overwrites such tapes.

Tape backup has been a popular choice for long-term archiving of electronic records. However, organizations don't often use tape backup in conjunction with disaster recovery planning, primarily because of the time required to restore data from tape. Backup to removable disk, replication, and mirroring are becoming the methods of choice.

Protecting data through resilient storage

Hardware failures in storage systems account for enough unscheduled downtime that these failures warrant attention and DR planning consideration. If you make the storage systems themselves resilient, you reduce the likelihood that a storage system failure will cripple a critical business function.

Here are some of the ways in which you can make a storage system more resilient:

- **RAID:** Redundant Array of Independent Drives (or Disks), also known as Redundant Array of Inexpensive Drives (or Disks). You can choose from many RAID features and configurations. But all RAID-based storage systems have the ability for the storage system to continue functioning, even if one of the hard drives fails. RAID systems also permit you to replace a failed drive without needing to power down the RAID system (called *hot swapping*).

✔ **Redundant power supplies:** Many storage systems have multiple power supplies, which permit the continuous operation of the storage system, even if one of the power supplies fails. These storage systems also permit the hot replacement (or hot swap) of power supplies, assuring continuous availability.

✔ **Redundant server connections:** Many storage systems have multiple controllers and physical connections to servers, assuring continuous operation, even if one of the connections fails.

✔ **Virtualization:** You can use large central storage systems to create virtual disk volumes that meet whatever storage needs application servers have. Storage virtualization lets you more efficiently use storage resources by allowing the organization to carve up the storage system in whatever ways meet its business needs.

Network Attached Storage (NAS) and Storage Area Network (SAN) technologies often include all of the features in the preceding list. I discuss NAS and SAN in Chapter 7.

Resilient storage by itself doesn't provide a disaster-proof storage capability because a significant event can cause the failure (or unavailability) of the entire storage system. However, resilience still supports both high availability and disaster recovery objectives for lower severity events, such as equipment failures.

Protecting data through replication and mirroring

The terms *replication* and *mirroring* generally refer to the ability to write newly introduced data to more than one storage system at the same time. Replication and mirroring differ somewhat in the details.

The two chief advantages of replication and mirroring over tape (or disk) backup are

✔ Data is copied to another storage system that a server can immediately use, in near-real time.

✔ You can access data without the need for a magtape-style restore.

You can develop a variety of architectures to support replication and mirroring, depending on the nature of the business objectives. The two primary architectures involve replication or mirroring to

✔ A secondary storage system that a server accesses (as shown in Figure 8-2)

✔ A storage system at a remote location (refer to Figure 8-3)

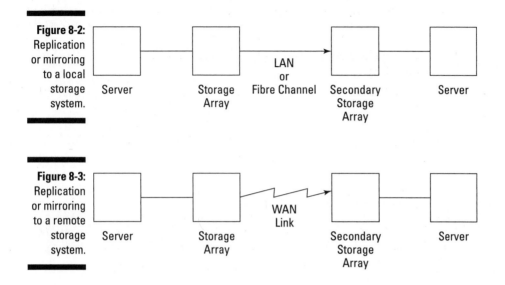

Figure 8-2:
Replication
or mirroring
to a local
storage
system.

Server   Storage   LAN   Secondary   Server
                Array   or   Storage
                                 Fibre Channel Array

Figure 8-3:
Replication
or mirroring
to a remote
storage
system.

Server   Storage   WAN   Secondary   Server
                Array   Link   Storage
                                              Array

The difference between replication and mirroring is as follows:

✔ **Mirroring:** A real-time or near real-time copying process, disk block by
disk block. Changes take place on a primary storage system and onto
one or more secondary storage systems. Here are some additional facts
about mirroring:

  • Mirroring is usually handled directly by the storage subsystem.

  • Servers often don't know that any mirroring is taking place (at least,
    when the storage hardware controls mirroring).

✔ **Replication:** A transaction-level process in which changes to databases
that occur on primary storage systems are carried out on secondary
storage systems. Additional facts about replication include

  • Replication can occur in near-real time, but it can also be delayed
    by several minutes or hours, depending on the configuration of the
    replication software, the speed of the communications link between
    storage systems, and the RTO and RPO figures.

  • Database management systems or storage systems can manage
    replication; hence, servers may or may not be aware of the details
    of replication.

You need to know these other salient facts about replication and mirroring so
you can make sure your clustered servers operate properly:

> ✔ Replication and mirroring are a part of a larger application resiliency architecture that also may include a clustering or failover capability.
>
> ✔ You can't do replication and mirroring without deep consideration for other layers in the stack, including application, server, database, and network. You must closely coordinate replication and mirroring with server cluster configuration, which in turn requires you to carefully configure the application and network devices.

Mirroring and replication are closely tied to server failover and clustering technology, so the mirroring/replication and clustering work together smoothly.

Protecting data through electronic vaulting

A popular option available for backing up data is known as electronic vaulting, sometimes known as remote backup or e-vaulting. *Electronic vaulting* is the process of sending data electronically to an off-site location through a network connection.

In the strict sense of the word, electronic vaulting can also mean sending data to another one of your business locations. I prefer to use the term *replication* to mean sending your own data to yourself at a different location.

You can use electronic vaulting for a lot of things, depending on whom you ask. Some of the possibilities include

> ✔ Using backup software on your systems to send backup data to computers run by a backup service provider.
>
> ✔ Replicating database transactions that you send off-site.
>
> ✔ Copying data to a remotely located standby system that can assume primary processing duties during a disaster.

Most people probably consider electronic vaulting a faster version of third-party off-site media storage. Off-site backup media storage provides one or more copies of data that you can use to recover systems in the event of a disaster. Electronic vaulting achieves this same objective, and it's generally much faster because you can have recovery data electronically transmitted to a recovery facility.

Deciding where to keep your recovery data

Whether your DR plan calls for backup tapes, replication, electronic vaulting, or remote mirroring, you need to think about where your data is going and how you'll get it back when you need it. In most cases, you need to decide where to store your recovery data.

Case in point: If you decide to recover your application data by using backup tapes stored off-site, at what location do you want to store those backup tapes?

Some of the factors that you need to consider when evaluating off-site locations include

- ✔ **Proximity to business locations:** Keep your recovery data close to your primary (or alternate) processing site for rapid recovery times. However, if the site is too close to your primary site, it could also be involved in a regional disaster, such as an earthquake or hurricane.

- ✔ **Physical security:** Make the measures that protect media from harm and unauthorized access at least as good as the physical security in your main processing site — perhaps even far better than your own security.

- ✔ **Proximity to transportation:** If your DR plan calls for backup media to be flown to another city, be sure that your media storage location is close enough to major transportation centers (airports, freeways, and so on) so your media can be quickly sent to a recovery center.

- ✔ **Security while in transit:** You take unnecessary risks if you have your backup media transported on a scooter or in some hitchhiker's backpack. Seriously, though, transport backup media in vehicles with security measures that ensure your media stays secure while en route to or from the storage facility. A third-party service may include secure media transit, or you may need to find a separate secure media transportation service provider.

You may have additional criteria concerning off-site storage. After you know some of the characteristics you want for the location storing your backup media, you can begin evaluating the characteristics of possible locations.

You can find a few types of data storage facilities available:

- ✔ **Commercial media storage centers:** Organizations that store backup media in highly secured facilities designed for that purpose.

- ✔ **Alternate business locations:** These locations could (and should) coincide with your alternate processing sites so those processing sites can more quickly resume support of critical business functions.

- ✔ **Third-party service providers:** Electronic vaulting and managed backup services have their own facilities for storing customer data. Due diligence is especially important — check them out for yourself.

✔ **Reciprocal processing site:** If your organization has entered into a reciprocal processing site usage agreement with another organization, you may want to have your recovery data sent to that location. Just make sure you can get to your data when you need it.

Protecting data in transit

Although the business information that you store on your systems is important, don't lose sight of the data that you transmit over network connections to or from other organizations. Not only does that data itself require protection, but you probably also need to include the means for transporting it in your DR plan, especially when transporting data into and out of your organization is a part of critical business functions.

Your hardware and software inventories, as well as the development of your infrastructure and data flow diagrams, have probably captured the facts about how you transmit data into and out of your organization. You need to include the transmission facilities that are essential to critical business processes in your DR plan. If you don't include those facilities, one or more critical business functions may be unable to operate in a disaster.

Here are some tips about how to identify and protect data transmission-capabilities:

✔ **Inventory all data transfer points.** Identify all the external systems that transfer data to or from your organization. You can look in two places:

- At any scheduling tool used to initiate data transfer connections with other organizations

- At user IDs and passwords that other organizations use to initiate connections with your system

This task is especially tedious if your organization doesn't have an existing inventory of all of the data transfer partners.

✔ **Inventory encryption keys and means.** If your data transfer system(s) uses encryption, you need to capture all the details about encryption with every external entity. Decide whether to use the same encryption keys at your alternate processing center or develop alternative encryption keys for your alternate site.

✔ **Identify associated firewall rules.** If your firewall has rules about permitting inbound or outbound data transfer sessions, you need to translate these rules for use at your alternate site. *Translating,* in this context, means mapping IP addresses between the main and recovery sites (although it may not be this simple if the DR site's architecture is different from the main site's architecture). Similarly, the entities with which you exchange data need to make adjustments in their firewall rule sets so their firewalls permit your file transfer sessions to and from your alternate sites.

For disaster recovery planning purposes, you need to protect not only business information while in transit, but also the ability to continue transmitting and receiving information from third parties.

Protecting data while in DR mode

In the preceding sections, I discuss various ways to protect data during normal operations — backups, replication, off-site storage, data transmission, and so on.

While in disaster recovery mode — during a disaster when critical business applications are operating in alternate locations — you also need all of these protections:

- ✔ Back up DR servers.
- ✔ Protect backup media, usually through off-site storage.
- ✔ Protect transmitted data.
- ✔ Store critical data on resilient storage systems.

In disaster mode, business information and processes are just as critical as they are in times of normal operations. Consequently, the systems and processes that you use during a disaster must provide the same level of protection as the primary systems and processes.

Protecting and Recovering Applications

Applications enable employees, customers, and suppliers to manage the production and delivery of whatever goods or services your organization provides. Without applications, your business data just sits there, unable to move or be seen. Applications bring data to life and give it meaning.

From a purist's point of view, applications (meaning the software itself) are just another form of business data. Although this assertion is mostly true, you need to consider many issues when recovering applications that you don't have to worry about for data. You must consider these application-specific issues and factors when building a DR plan:

- ✔ Version
- ✔ Patches and fixes
- ✔ Configuration
- ✔ Users and roles
- ✔ Interfaces

✔ Customizations

✔ Pairing with OS and database versions

✔ Client systems

✔ Network considerations

✔ Change management

✔ Configuration management

In terms of disaster recovery, applications are a good deal more complex than data. If you think that recovering applications is a simple restore-and-go process, I hate to be the bearer of bad news. You have to know and address many details — otherwise, restoring an application becomes a gamble.

Application version

Each application has a notation of its version. Many organizations lag behind the most recent version of an application, particularly in larger and more complex environments, such as ERP (Enterprise Resource Planning), CRM (Customer Relationship Management), MRP II (Manufacturing Resource Planning), and financials.

Determine the steps you need to take to recover the current version of each critical application.

Application patches and fixes

Organizations that run in-house developed applications need to keep a highly detailed history of problems, solutions, changes, patches, and fixes made to each critical application. Your organization may make these changes for a wide variety of reasons, from feature changes to stability to cosmetic adjustments.

You need to make the level of recordkeeping for application changes so good that a recovery team can use that recordkeeping to properly recover the application in a disaster scenario, rolling forward all the changes so the application can operate in the same way in the recovered environment.

For more about patches and fixes, see the section "Applications and change management," later in this chapter.

Application configuration

Applications are becoming more configuration-centric, thereby increasing flexibility and reducing the need for customizations. The overburdened IT industry has seen this development as a boon because IT departments don't have the in-house resources to maintain every application at the application code layer. Some applications can have so many configuration settings that just keeping track of all those settings can become someone's full-time job.

And many configuration changes have an effect on data and external systems. Configuration changes can alter the layout of data feeds and even database schema. They can change the way that users log in and how the application uses resources on servers and other equipment.

You need to do more than just blindly clone all configuration changes from a production system onto a recovery system. That might be a good start, but the recovery system may require different configuration settings so the application can operate as intended in recovery mode. You need to put a lot of thought into the meaning of some configuration settings to ensure that you can recover and operate the application in a recovery setting, in which business conditions and the technical environment are probably different than in day-to-day business.

I discuss application configuration more in the section "Applications and change management," later in this chapter.

Application users and roles

Users log in to applications in order to perform their specific duties, according to their roles in the organization. But logging in to an application isn't as easy as it looks. Consider some of the ways in which authentication can take place:

✔ **Local password database:** The application itself authenticates the user. One or more tables contain user IDs, and encrypted or hashed passwords. The application has its own login functions that it uses to identify and authenticate the user.

✔ **External directory service:** The application performs its own authentication, but it doesn't store user ID information. Instead, the application makes a call to an external directory service, such as Microsoft Active Directory, LDAP (Lightweight Directory Access Protocol), or Liberty. An application that relies on an external service needs to know how to find the external service and communicate with it in real time to authenticate users.

✔ **Single Sign On (SSO):** The application participates in an enterprise-wide service whereby users authenticate once, and their credentials are passed around between applications and a central session management service. SSO can use any of dozens of services, including SAML, Kerberos, HMAC, or OpenID.

Users may also use two-factor authentication in conjunction with any of the authentication methods in the preceding list. Two-factor authentication can add unnecessary (or necessary) complication to a recovery environment because of the extra hardware and software that you need.

The DR planning team needs to make some strategic decisions on how users will authenticate to applications in a recovery environment. You may use the same method currently in the normal business environment, or you may go with a different approach. If you use a different method, all users who plan to use the application in a recovery situation need to know how they can log in to that application. You need to understand security requirements and possibly contractual obligations to understand how you should implement authentication in a DR system.

If an application relies on external entities for authentication, plan so that you can accommodate the application's need to communicate with the external authentication service. You may need to make changes to firewalls, VPNs (Virtual Private Networks, for remote access), routing, and host- or network-based access control.

Roles

In all but the most simple and mundane applications, users are assigned functions and/or permitted to perform certain functions in an application. In today's vernacular, you say that a user is assigned to one or more roles. A *role* is a name (such as Revenue Clerk 1) that has specific application functions associated with it. The application also uses access control to determine what database information a given role is permitted to view, modify, or remove.

Some application environments have highly granular roles — these roles require a lot more attention and foresight on the part of DR planners if you want the organization to continue operating its applications in a recovery situation. In some environments, such as financial applications, each user's role has a paper trail for requests and approvals. You must maintain even this kind of functionality in a disaster scenario to maintain compliance with laws, regulations, and standards.

The assignment of roles may be closely tied to the way in which users are authenticated. The DR planning team needs to carefully sift through the details in order to determine how you can recover and operate such an application in a recovery situation, realizing that in many disaster situations, different people may need to use and operate the application than those who do in daily business when the sun is shining.

External users

External users can include suppliers, partners, or members of the general public.

Users of any given online application are largely unaware of the actual location of the systems they're using. In today's online world, a natural or man-made disaster can occur in some region of the world, and users don't necessarily connect such a disaster to the availability of the online application they use. They just want to start their application client program or Web browser and access the application as always, and they usually do so without a thought about the application infrastructure that's located somewhere, doing their bidding.

If external users are your bread and butter, you need to make the manner in which they authenticate to your applications consistent — so much so that they have little or no idea whether they're logging in to and using a recovery system or the original.

Application interfaces

No application is an island. Applications often rely on back-end data transfers that occur in real time or in batches. These data transfers may take place between applications in the business, and they often involve exchanging information with external entities.

I discuss this topic in Chapter 4 as it relates to identifying all data inputs and outputs for systems and the organization, as a whole. This section talks about these interfaces from the application's point of view.

The application itself may have configurations, scheduled jobs, staging tables, or other moving parts associated with data that's sent to or from the application. For each type of interface (and perhaps for each external entity, as well), you need to document and understand all the details so these interfaces (at least, the critical ones) can function in a recovery environment.

Some of the interfaces' configuration or operations details may contain specific information, such as IP addresses, user IDs, or passwords. You probably need to change some of these settings now so these interfaces can operate in a recovery environment. You must find and document these settings now if you want the recovery team to successfully get these interfaces running in a disaster.

Application customizations

Many organizations aren't quite satisfied with the off-the-shelf behaviors and functionality of applications. Often, those organizations write custom code and wedge it into the application to make that application work the way they want it to.

Customizations may have specific rewards, but they also have certain risks. These risks include, but aren't limited to, disaster recovery planning. Creating customizations and integrating them into an application require effort, and you usually need to re-implement the customizations when you upgrade the application in order to keep those customizations working, even in a disaster scenario.

Generally speaking, you should assume that an application won't work properly unless you have all of its customizations in place. So, you must apply all customizations to the recovery environment. Depending on how system developers develop and implement customizations for a given application, you may need to recover both the application itself and the development environment so that you can recompile or reinstall customizations into production systems.

Managing customizations can add considerable complexity to a recovery plan.

On an ongoing basis, an organization may be able to make some key changes so it can more easily determine whether specific customizations are critical in a recovery situation, as well as more simply install customizations.

Applications dependencies with databases, operating systems, and more

Applications are at the top of the stack, but they don't exist in a vacuum. Instead, applications depend on a great many details further down in the stack, almost to the bottom. Figure 8-4 contains a depiction of the application stack.

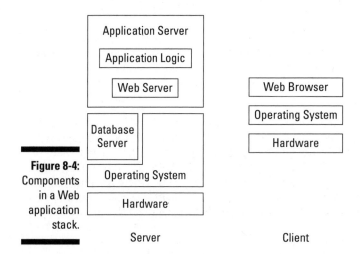

Figure 8-4: Components in a Web application stack.

A properly operating application depends on many details in the other layers in the stack:

✔ **Operating system version, patches, and configuration:** The version of the application that you want to build in the recovery environment may require a specific version of the operating system (OS). Also, you may need (or need to avoid) certain OS patches. And the application may depend on several OS configuration settings in order to work properly.

✔ **Database management system version, patches, and configuration:** An application in a recovery environment may require specific versions of the database management system (DBMS), including specific patches and configurations.

✔ **Database names and locations:** The application may look in specific locations for data or connect with specifically named databases.

✔ **Web server version, patches, and configuration:** Many Web-based applications use a separate Web server that's configured to run one or more specific applications. You often need the version, patch levels, and configuration of such a Web server for the application to work properly.

✔ **Network:** An application may have one or more external systems specifically named, either by DNS host name or by IP address. Other possible network-based dependencies include configurations of Web servers, authentication servers, and sources for external feeds.

A careful analysis of dependencies in the stack may uncover additional dependencies. Be sure to capture these details so you can make your recovery plans accurate and successful.

Applications and client systems

Applications require client systems in order to work properly. Clients allow users to communicate with the application so the users can do whatever it is they do with the application.

These clients may be

✔ **Client software:** Many applications use client software that's installed on end-user workstations. In order for this software to work properly, you may need specific versions of these clients that have particular configuration settings. In turn, the client software may impose specific dependencies on the workstation OS, patch level, and configuration settings. The topics in the preceding section may apply to client systems, as well as many aspects of server architecture and configuration.

✔ **Web browsers:** Web-based applications require only Web browsers — or do they? Often, these applications also require a Java run-time program, ActiveX controls, browser helper objects (BHOs), and other components. And Web browsers have versions, patches, and configurations of their own that often must be just right.

✔ **Terminal emulators:** PCs that run terminal emulation software, which is just another application client, often access many mainframe applications. Like with client software of other types, you have to get versioning, patches, configuration, and perhaps other factors right so that the software works properly.

Applications and networks

Applications communicate. They communicate over networks to other applications, client systems, and network-based services for a variety of reasons, including authentication. Applications depend on networks just to function, in most cases.

Some of the ways in which applications depend on networks include

✔ **Domain name service (DNS):** When applications need to establish communications with other systems (or when they want to know the name of the host that wants to communicate with them), they need to make queries to DNS servers. Most of the time, the underlying OS (on both servers and clients) contains information about server IP addresses and domain names. A common problem occurs when an application wants to communicate with a given hostname, but the application doesn't specify the fully qualified host name (FQDN), such as `fileserver.acct.company.com`, but instead just specifies `fileserver`. In a recovery environment, the network's domain name may be different (for example, `recovery.company.com`), and the desired host name may not exist in the recovery domain. You need to use a consistent approach to server naming so that applications can function correctly in a recovery environment and you can more easily maintain them in the primary environment.

✔ **Hard-coded IP addresses:** Some applications have hard-coded IP addresses for network resources. When an application needs to communicate with another system, the application usually references the system by name, but developers sometimes use IP addresses. You need to identify, document, and remedy these hard-coded IP addresses if you want the application to work properly in a recovery environment.

✔ **Hard-coded network resource names:** Instead of using a configuration file to store resource names, applications might have hard-coded network resources that include file servers, database servers, printers, and other network based resources.

✔ **Authentication service:** Applications often don't authenticate users directly, but instead rely on an authentication service, such as LDAP, Kerberos, or Active Directory.

✔ **Network configurations:** The network layers may contain configurations that facilitate proper operation of (or access to) an application. Examples include VPN connections to external entities, NAT settings, custom routes, router ACLs, and holes in firewalls.

Applications and change management

Most organizations use a change management process to control the changes that they make on production systems. The main benefit to a DR program that includes a formal change management process is that the organization has a formal record of all changes it makes to the production environment. This record can help the recovery team with the task of building the recovery environment. The team can more conveniently see the recent changes that were made, as well as why they were made.

Here are some additional considerations about change management and DR planning:

✔ Change management doesn't always record all the changes made to a production system. Routine, low-risk, and low-impact changes may be exempt from the change management process.

✔ Systems or infrastructure that support specific applications may lie outside the scope of change management.

✔ Secret changes that circumvent the change management process may not be recorded. The team that builds the recovery system has to work without knowledge of those changes, which could lead to unexpected results.

Applications and configuration management

Many organizations use configuration management to track all changes they make to their environments. You can use configuration management systems to track all changes in all layers of the stack (possibly including hardware changes), enabling an organization to know precisely what's happening on the systems that a configuration management system manages.

You can use some configuration management systems to rebuild application servers in a *bare-metal-restore recovery* (in which you recover a server in a single step — operating system, database, application, and data). Having such a capability would be potentially powerful for building recovery servers in an alternate processing center because it could simplify the server recovery procedure to just a few steps. In fact, with advance knowledge about a recovery processing center, you may be able to configure the configuration management system so that it creates application servers that would properly function at the alternate processing site. Your mileage may vary.

Off-Site Media and Records Storage

In the section "Deciding where to keep your recovery data," earlier in this chapter, I discuss off-site media storage in the context of backups. Backups are only a portion of the entire set of data that you may want to protect from loss by storing off-site. An organization should include all of the following types of data in its off-site storage strategy:

- ✔ **Backup media:** Protects the organization against loss of vital online information if a catastrophic event occurs in the primary processing center.

- ✔ **Backup records:** Information about which tapes (or disks) you used to back up which databases on which days. Vital for recovering applications from backup media.

- ✔ **Release media:** The CDs and tapes that contain the software you purchase to run on your servers. If you purchase the software by downloading it, copy that software to CD or other suitable media, and then store a copy off-site.

- ✔ **Infrastructure diagrams and schematics:** All the drawings and records that show how the current environment is assembled, including data flow, network addresses, and so on.

- ✔ **Software release and operations documentation:** All documentation that comes with software, including installation, operations, programming, release notes, and so on. If you have soft copies only (maybe you ordered the software online and downloaded it), get copies stored off-site. If you have hardcopies only, either scan or photocopy them and store those copies off-site.

- ✔ **Software licenses and activation codes:** Information that you need to activate software — for example, license codes.

- ✔ **Encryption keys:** Keys you use to encrypt and decrypt files, stored data, and communications sessions.

- ✔ **Passwords:** User IDs and passwords that gain access to key accounts at every layer in the stack so administrators can make an application fully functional.

- ✔ **Change management and configuration management records:** The information that contains changes made to applications and supporting infrastructure. Vital when a recovery team attempts to recover and restart a critical application.

✔ **Inventory information:** Lists of hardware, software, licenses, and whatever you use to track all the components in all the layers that support vital applications.

✔ **Disaster recovery plans:** All the procedures, emergency contact lists, and other information you need to recover vital applications during a disaster.

✔ **Catalog of information stored off-site:** A master list of everything that you store off-site: names, descriptions, creation dates, and so forth.

The preceding list gives you a lot of information to store at an off-site facility. Remember, store all the information you need to recover vital applications in a real disaster at this off-site facility. Assume the disaster will completely destroy the current information processing facilities and you'll need to rebuild everything from only the knowledge and information stored at the off-site data center.

By reading the preceding list of data that you should store off-site, you may realize that you need to make the security of such a facility of paramount importance. The last thing you want to have happen is a breach of security at the off-site storage facility that could result in a disclosure of a great deal of vital information about your organization!

Consider only an off-site storage provider whose primary line of business includes this activity. An employee's home or a bank safe deposit box isn't an acceptable solution for off-site storage! Here are some requirements to include in your shopping list for off-site storage providers:

✔ **Secure siting:** An unmarked building in a low-traffic area away from natural and man-made threats.

✔ **Multiple layers of physical security:** At least two or three layers of access control (main entrance, inner storage area, clients' individual storage areas) with badges or biometric authentication, video surveillance, man traps, and guards. Least-privilege access to all locations. Dual-custody access to client assets. Audit trails on all accesses. Employees with clean background checks.

✔ **Secure delivery vehicles:** Double-locked to protect client assets. Drivers who have clean background checks. Effective and secure pickup and delivery procedures.

✔ **Secure procedures:** Multiple approvals needed to retrieve assets from the secure facility. Thorough recordkeeping for transfer and storage of all assets.

✔ **24/7/365 availability:** Ability to retrieve assets any hour of the day, any day of the year.

✔ **Location, location, location!** Close enough to the primary business location so you can return assets quickly, but not so close that the off-site storage facility is involved in the same regional disaster as your primary processing site. A lot of good all your off-site storage efforts would be if an earthquake or hurricane damaged both facilities.

If your organization has several business locations — possibly including an alternate processing site — you can consider one of your own business locations as your off-site storage facility. Your alternate facility may not have all the features in the preceding list; you need to identify which features are available and perform a risk analysis to determine whether you need any additional security features.

Chapter 9

Writing the Disaster Recovery Plan

*T*he job isn't done until the paperwork's done.

Nowhere is this pithy saying truer than in disaster recovery planning. The paperwork in DR planning outlines how to jump-start the business when the big one hits. Depending on where your business is located, the big one may be an earthquake, labor strike, hurricane, flood, or a swarm of locusts.

The paperwork for DR planning simply covers the procedures and other documents that business personnel must refer to in order to get things going again after a disaster. The DR planning procedures are especially important because people who aren't the foremost experts on the systems that support critical business processes may have to read and follow those procedures. Those people have to rebuild critical systems in a short period of time so those systems can support critical processes. And the people performing those processes probably aren't subject matter experts at the business process level.

The business's survival depends on the paperwork being right. You don't get any second chances.

In this chapter, I explain how to actually write down the DR plan.

You just *love* documentation, right? Thought so.

Determining Plan Contents

Before embarking on the task of actually writing the DR plan, the team needs to agree what the DR plan is. You can describe it something like this:

> The disaster recovery plan is the set of documents that describes post-disaster emergency response, damage assessment, and system restart for designated critical business processes.

The devil, as they say, is in the details.

DR plans should contain several key elements that you can use to jumpstart critical systems and processes after a disaster strikes. Most organizations should include the following elements in their DR plan:

- A disaster-declaration procedure

- Emergency contact lists and trees

- Emergency leadership selection (the predetermined leadership team and also the procedure to quickly assemble a team)

- Damage assessment procedures

- System recovery and restart procedures

- Procedures for the transition to normal operations

- Recovery team selection (the pre-selected recovery team, as well as the process for finding others who can help when disaster actually strikes)

I cover these elements in greater detail in the following sections.

Disaster declaration procedure

Disaster recovery procedures commence when somebody says so. And when does someone say so? When a disaster has occurred.

I'm sorry if this sounds silly. Many DR planners get too hung up on how to declare a disaster. Here are a few ideas for how to declare a disaster, one of which may work for you:

- **Declaration by consensus:** You designate a core team of decision makers, probably middle or senior managers, as the DR leadership team. When a disaster occurs, the core team members contact one another and perhaps convene a conference call, if they can. When two or more of the core team members agree that the organization should start the disaster recovery plan, they make that decision. This decision triggers the execution of the DR plan. A typical declaration might go something like this:

1. The event occurs.

2. Two or more DR plan core team members discuss the event by telephone, if possible. They exchange information about what they know of the event and the potential impact on the business.

3. Two or more core team members conclude that the event has sufficient impact on the business to affect business operations.

4. The core team members decide to declare a disaster, which triggers disaster response and recovery actions, including performing emergency communications and action plans that assess damage and begin restoration of services.

You don't need to make your disaster declaration procedure much more complicated than the preceding steps.

Core team members may or may not be near the business facility when they need to make a direct assessment of the event's impact. They can make a judgment call and decide based on what they know at the time, or they can choose to gather more information before making a declaration.

✓ **Declaration by criteria:** Designate core team members as the DR leadership team. When an event occurs, one or more of them reads a short checklist, which might be a series of Yes or No questions. If certain answers, or a minimum number of answers, are Yes, the team declares a disaster, which triggers the DR plan. Here's how this process might play out in a disaster:

1. A weather-related event occurs that has widespread impact on a city.

2. DR plan core team members begin to contact one another to share information about the situation.

3. Available core team members answer basic questions on their disaster declaration checklists. The core team members decide that the results of the checklist warrant a disaster declaration. If they can't come to a consensus, either they have to gather more information or just decide one way or the other.

4. The core team declares a disaster and begins to notify other core team members, instructing them to begin working through their DR plan procedures to assess, contain, and begin recovery from the disaster.

Over the years, I've heard many people express the same concern: What if an organization declares a disaster unnecessarily? The short answer: Don't worry about it. If the core team declares a disaster, and they later decide that the situation isn't so bad, they can just call a halt to the disaster response. For example, if a severe weather event results in widespread utility outages and transportation problems, an organization might initially declare a disaster but later cancel the disaster response effort when it discovers that critical IT systems are only lightly isolated and quickly recoverable, despite feet of snow, inches of water, volcanic ash, or whatever prompted the disaster declaration.

You can make disaster declaration as scientific or unscientific as you need it to be. Don't make it too complicated, or the core team members may hesitate to declare a disaster if they can't decide whether they should.

Emergency contact lists and trees

After you declare a disaster, the logical next step in a comprehensive plan is to begin notifying the personnel who are responsible for performing DR-plan-related activities, such as communications, assessment, and recovery. The DR plan core team members who participate in the disaster declaration obviously know first when the organization declares a disaster, and the notifications move out from there to additional disaster response personnel, management, personnel who communicate with suppliers and customers, and so on.

Where will DR planning core team members be when a disaster occurs? The decidedly unscientific method in this section is based on simple probabilities.

A seven-day period contains five workdays, which total 168 hours. Presuming that a core team member has a life, Table 9-1 shows the probability breakdown for employees' possible activities, giving you an idea of where people may be when the disaster strikes.

Table 9-1	Average Percentages of Daily Activities during the Five-Day Work Week	
Hours	*Percent of Work Week*	*Activity*
48	28.6	Sleeping
48	28.6	Working at place of employment
40	23.8	Leisure activities at home
10	6.0	Commuting
4	2.4	Shopping
2	1.2	Worship
16	9.5	Other
168	100.0	Total

When a disaster strikes, employees will probably be at home, either sleeping, working, or relaxing. The next most likely place they'll be is at work itself, followed by commuting, shopping, at worship, and doing something else entirely. Table 9-1 doesn't factor in weeks of vacation or business travel. If a core team member spends a lot of recreation time away from home (boating, hiking, or whatever), that core team member will more likely be away from home when a disaster strikes.

Given the high probability that a disaster will occur when core team members are away from work, you need to make the information that core team members need both portable and easy to use. You have a lot of choices when it comes to storing emergency contact information, as well as performing other disaster declaration and emergency communications activities. Table 9-2 features these choices.

Table 9-2	Emergency Contact Storage Options	
Method	*Pros*	*Cons*
Wallet card	Compact, portable, likely available	Can't hold much information; not easily updated
Thumb drive	Compact, portable, high density	Requires a running computer to view
PDA	Compact, portable, high density	Might not be on-hand when a disaster occurs; must be partially charged
Mobile phone	Compact, portable, high density	Might not function if the network is unreachable
CD-ROM	Compact, portable, high density	Requires a running computer to view
Laptop hard drive	High capacity	User may not have it on-hand at all times; bulky; short battery life; more likely to be damaged or left behind
Private Web site or file servers	Centrally available, easily updated	Difficult to access in a disaster situation
Microfiche or microfilm	Portable, high density	Requires bulky reader and possibly electricity
Three-ring binder	Portable, easy to read	User may not have it on-hand at all times; may be damaged or left behind

Many organizations put emergency contact lists on laminated wallet cards. Wallet cards are very portable because they can fit into a wallet or billfold. And staff are more likely to have their wallets or billfolds (and therefore their cards) with them when a disaster event occurs, even if they're on vacation or away from home. People don't need electricity or any other technology to read a wallet card.

Consider putting the following items on your emergency-contact wallet cards:

- ✔ **Core team member names:** But, of course!

- ✔ **Mobile, home, and office phone numbers:** Talking live by phone is the next best thing to being there.

- ✔ **Spouse mobile and office numbers:** When you can't find a core team member, calling his or her spouse may help locate him or her.

- ✔ **E-mail and instant messaging contacts:** In a disaster, you never know what infrastructures will be down and what will still be running.

- ✔ **Conference bridge numbers:** More than one, preferably, and from different services.

- ✔ **Key business addresses:** Just in case core team members need to know.

- ✔ **Hints on disaster declaration procedures:** Jog the core team members' memories.

- ✔ **URL that contains more disaster procedures:** Disaster recovery procedures stored online. Hopefully hosted far, far away from your business, in case damage is widespread.

You might need more information than what appears in the preceding list, or you might need less, depending on your disaster recovery and business needs.

Emergency leadership and role selection

When your organization declares a disaster, who's going to lead the response team?

Actually, I think the question should be, who's *not* going to lead it? At the onset of a disaster, core team members each have a number of distinct responsibilities related to their respective departments. Each member will have enough to keep him or her busy when a disaster unfolds. But during a disaster, several decisions must be made, minute by minute and hour by hour.

Your first natural inclination might be to select, from among the core team members, the person who should be the team's leader before the recovery effort even begins. But, depending on the nature of the disaster and when it occurs, you don't know which core team members will be active at the onset of the disaster. You could rank-order possible leaders from among core team members, or you could let them figure it out amongst themselves. In disaster situations, one of the core team members will just step out and lead the rest. If your core team comes from company management, several of your core team members have leadership skills and talents. One of them will take the lead, and the others will follow. You don't need to get scientific about who will lead. In fact, you can probably just let the team members figure it out on their own.

The nature of the disaster may call for around-the-clock response for a few days, or even a long stretch of days or weeks. At least at the beginning of the disaster, the core response team should assign one of its members a duty-officer role, which involves leading the team for a period of several hours. Leaders can trade off, giving members a chance to rest if your organization need 24/7 coverage.

When a disaster response stretches into several days, the response team should set up a more formal leadership and management schedule so all team members know who's in charge at what times and on what days. But, like a few other matters in disaster response and recovery (such as leadership selection), you probably don't want to get too rigid in your DR plan. Allow the leadership and response team to make those decisions on the fly. After all, you need to consider many possible scenarios with varying damage and recovery conditions, and you'll have an unpredictable selection of personnel available to lead, manage, and recover the business.

In addition to the leadership and management roles, you also need a scribe. Somebody needs to write down the discussions, duties, findings, and decisions. Don't count on remembering these decisions later because it may all be a blur when the disaster response team can finally stand down after a lengthy recovery effort. Instead, record these decisions and other matters on the spot.

At the beginning of the disaster, scribes should operate the old-fashioned way — pen and paper. High tech solutions, such as notebook computers or voice recorders, might very well be impractical, depending on the nature of the disaster.

Damage assessment procedures

The disaster recovery plan needs to include procedures for assessing damage to equipment and facilities. The objective of damage assessment is to identify the state of the IT systems and supporting facilities that are involved in a disaster and to decide whether the systems and supporting facilities are damaged or disabled to the extent that you need IT systems in another location to continue supporting critical business functions.

Damage assessment is both an art and a science. In this section, I don't tell you how to determine whether a building is safe for occupancy — that's a role for professional civil and structural engineers. Similarly, I don't delve into whether a disaster warrants evacuation or if personnel can stay behind to help with assessment and possible recovery or restarts. These matters are important, to be sure, but they're beyond the scope of this book.

No business process is worth risking a person's life. Personnel safety must always be the top priority in any disaster recovery plan. If the hurricane, tornado, or rising floodwaters are coming — or if an earthquake or landslide has damaged a building — don't stay behind or enter buildings with unknown dangers for the sake of the business.

Damage assessment procedures focus on determining what happened to critical IT systems and the related facilities — such as HVAC (Heating, Ventilation, and Air Conditioning), network, utilities, and security perimeter — in a disaster. You also need to figure out whether you can still access or restart IT systems, or whether the business needs to implement its Plan B — the disaster recovery plan.

You don't need to use complicated damage assessment procedures, but you may find the procedures you do use a bit tedious. The tedium may lie in the number of simple checks you need to perform in order to assess the overall health and availability of systems. Here's an example to help explain what I mean:

> Acme Services (not a real company) is an organization that provides online records management to corporate customers around the world. A natural or man-made disaster has occurred (imagine a hurricane, civil unrest, tsunami, earthquake, flood, or whatever other disaster you're familiar with), and Acme's online systems have experienced a temporary interruption.

> As specified in Acme's disaster declaration procedure, the core team members who were able to contact one another determined that the magnitude of the disaster warranted the declaration of an official disaster and the initiation of the disaster recovery plan.

> After some delays related to the nature of the disaster (imagine a damaged transportation infrastructure), some emergency response personnel arrived at Acme's office building. They hesitantly entered the building (which didn't appear damaged) to find that the building had no electricity or running water. IT systems appeared undamaged. The UPS batteries had been exhausted (it took personnel over an hour to reach the facility), and the backup generator wasn't running.

> Because the Maximum Tolerable Downtime (MTD) for Acme's critical online processes was set to eight hours, the damage assessment team decides that they need to put the DR plan into full force. Even if they started the generator right away, the health of the IT systems was in question, and customers from around the world were anxious to access Acme's systems so that they could go about their business.

The preceding example is a little simplistic, but it contains an important judgment call: No people were available to start the generator. If someone had been able to start the generator, the team still would have needed time to assess the health and reach-ability of the critical IT systems. Further, a generator typically has only several hours of fuel, not enough to keep critical systems going until power is restored, which could take several days in a widespread disaster. The team's decision to invoke the disaster recovery plan was sound.

Assessment procedures are basically just checklists. You need to examine these potentially long lists of items and check either the Running or Not Running box. One or more Not Running checkmarks might mean that you need to use systems in alternate locations, unless you can quickly remedy the Not Running items. Assessment is just that: an examination of what's running and what's not. After you assess the items, you need to begin recovery and restart procedures, both of which I cover in the following section.

The personnel who carry out damage assessment procedures might not be subject matter experts. In a disaster, the preferred individuals who know the most about systems often aren't available for assessment or recovery. Hence, you need to make damage assessment procedures detailed enough so people other than the main subject matter experts can properly carry out the procedures.

You can get templates for virtually all disaster recovery procedures from a variety of sources. Chapter 14 and Chapter 15 contain sources for these and other tools and capabilities.

System recovery and restart procedures

After you develop the disaster declaration and assessment procedures, you need to create the instructions for recovering and restarting vital IT systems. You use these procedures to recover and restart IT systems that support critical business processes as soon as possible.

You likely need to make your system recovery and restart procedures pretty complex and lengthy. They need to include every tiny detail involved in getting systems up and running from various states, including *bare metal* (servers with no operating system or application software installed on them).

This list illustrates some disaster scenarios for cold sites, warm sites, and hot sites:

- **Cold site:** In a cold-site restart scenario, you may or may not have computers to start with (the typical cold site has no computers). They could be boxed up, or maybe you have to go and buy them. A typical cold-site procedure might resemble these steps:

    1. Order systems and network devices from a supplier or manufacturer to replace the systems and devices damaged by the disaster.

    2. Retrieve the most recent backup media from wherever you store it.

    3. Install network devices and build a server network. Verify connectivity to customers, suppliers, and partners.

4. Install operating systems and applications on new servers.

5. Restore data from backup media.

6. Start the applications and perform functionality tests.

7. Announce the availability of recovered applications to employees, customers, and partners, as needed.

The preceding procedure probably takes place over a period of several days to as long as two weeks.

✔ **Warm site:** With equipment and servers already on hand, a warm site recovery takes less time and is generally a little less complicated than a cold site recovery. Here's a typical warm-site procedure:

1. Retrieve the most recent backup media from wherever you store it.

2. Configure network devices. Verify connectivity to customers, suppliers, and partners.

3. Install or update operating systems and applications on new servers.

4. Restore data from backup media.

5. Start the applications and perform functionality tests.

6. Announce the availability of recovered applications to employees, customers, and partners, as needed.

The preceding warm-site procedure is similar to the cold-site procedure, but you have a head start with a warm site over a cold site because you already have computers available.

✔ **Hot site:** Ready to assume production duties with already-prepared servers within hours or even minutes. Here's a typical hot-site procedure:

1. Confirm the state of the most recent mirroring or replication activities.

2. Make any required network configuration changes.

3. Switch the state of server cluster nodes and database servers to active.

4. Perform application functionality tests.

5. Announce the availability of recovered applications to employees, customers, and partners, as needed.

Systems at a hot site are very nearly ready to take over operational duties with short notice. The exact procedures for a cutover to hot site servers depends on the technologies you use to bring about the readiness — whether transaction replication, mirroring, clustering, or a combination of these.

I deliberately omitted many details from the procedures in the preceding list. You need to take many additional factors into account when you develop your system recovery procedures:

- ✓ **Communications:** Throughout the recovery operation, recovery teams need to be in constant communication with the DR core team, as well as customers, suppliers, partners, and other entities.

- ✓ **Work areas:** Establish an area where critical IT workers can work during and after the recovery operation. IT systems in a recovered state might be somewhat more unstable than they were in their original production environments, and they might require more observation, adjusting, and tuning.

- ✓ **Expertise:** Make the recovery procedures general enough so that people who are familiar with systems administration duties, but not necessarily *your* systems, can recover your systems without having to make guesses or assumptions. Step by step means step by step!

The people who write the system recovery procedures should assume that whoever reads and follows those procedures in an actual disaster has no familiarity with your particular system's environment.

Templates that you can get from several sources have outlines for system recovery procedures. I discuss these templates in Chapter 14 and Chapter 15.

Transition to normal operations

After the disaster occurs and you recover critical IT systems at an alternate processing center, recovery activities have restored the original processing and work facilities. When you recover the original processing center, you need to reestablish IT systems there and shut down the alternate site.

The timing of the cutover back to the original processing center (or a permanent replacement facility if the original facility was completely destroyed) depends on many factors, including

- ✓ **Application stability:** If applications running in the recovery site are a little unstable, consult the personnel maintaining the applications to determine the best time to transition back to the main processing site.

- ✓ **Business workload:** Transition back to the main processing site at a time when workload is low so any users or related systems will better tolerate the actual cutover.

- ✓ **Available staff:** Have sufficient staff at both the recovery site and the main processing site to switch processing back to the main site.

> ✔ **Costs:** Additional costs associated with operating the recovery site may bring pressure to transition back to the main processing site as soon as possible.
>
> ✔ **Functional readiness:** Operating and supporting critical IT applications at the main processing site must meet some minimum criteria so the applications can function properly after you transition them back to the main site. In other words, are you ready to get back to normal operations?

Write down the procedures for transitioning systems back to primary processing sites. These procedures aren't the same as the recovery procedures. The state and configuration of systems in the alternate processing site probably won't be precisely the way you planned them. For whatever reasons, you may have had to make some changes during the recovery procedures that resulted in the recovery systems not being configured or architected precisely as you intended. In other words, the starting point for transition back to the main processing sites may not be exactly as the DR planners anticipated. So, the procedures for getting back to the main site won't exactly fit, either. Figure 9-1 illustrates the fact that transitioning back to the primary *site* doesn't necessarily mean transitioning back to the primary *state*.

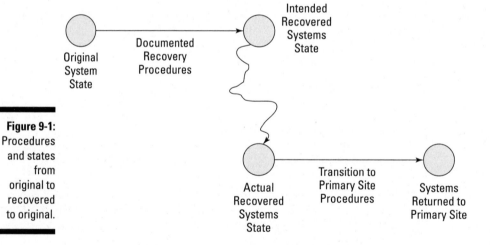

Figure 9-1: Procedures and states from original to recovered to original.

You need to write procedures that explain how to transition from the temporary DR systems back to systems in the primary processing site. How can you write a procedure to get to the desired end state when you don't know exactly what the initial state (the recovery systems) will be?

Testing can help with this conundrum. Full testing, including a failover test, forces recovery team members to actually construct application recovery systems and infrastructure, and then transition them back. During those tests, you should uncover most of the variables that may occur in an actual disaster, so the transition-to-normal procedures should very closely resemble reality. I describe the various types of tests in Chapter 10.

Finally, you can incorporate issues you uncover during testing into *release notes* (a detailed description of systems and procedures) that recovery personnel can read to better understand any issues they may encounter during recovery and transition-to-normal operations.

Recovery team

When the disaster strikes, who can the core team depend on to perform all of the tasks associated with communications, assessment, system recovery, and transition-to-normal operations? Anyone they can find. Remember, you can choose your recovery team in advance, but a disaster can render some of those team members unavailable for various reasons.

Seriously, depending on the type of disaster, many of the normal operational staff many be unavailable for a variety of reasons, including

- ✓ **Family and home come first:** When a regional disaster occurs, workers with families and homes attend to those needs before thinking of work. When workers have things under control on the home front, then they can turn their attention to the workplace and their work responsibilities.

- ✓ **Transportation issues:** Regional disasters can disrupt transportation systems, making it difficult for workers to travel to work locations.

- ✓ **Disrupted communications:** Workers can often perform many recovery tasks *over the wire,* through VPN (Virtual Private Network, for remote access) connections from their residences to business networks. But a widespread disaster can disrupt communications, making such work difficult or impossible to perform.

- ✓ **Evacuations:** Often, civil authorities order mass evacuations that prevent workers from being able to travel to work locations. Sometimes, evacuations work in reverse, preventing workers from leaving work to travel home, which introduces a whole other set of challenges.

- ✓ **Injury, illness, and death:** Regional disasters are often, by their nature, violent, which can lead to injuries, disease, and fatalities.

You can't handpick your recovery team members. The disaster selects them for you. For this reason, you need to make recovery procedures specific enough that anyone with the basic relevant skills can carry them out confidently and correctly.

Structuring the Plan

The preceding sections in this chapter discuss the contents of a disaster recovery plan in the very pragmatic sense — the sections and words that you put into the DR plan documents. In all but the smallest organizations, several people write sections of the plan, and many more people are involved in document review. In the following sections, I describe some of the approaches and methods that you can use to assemble a disaster recovery plan.

You don't have to write the plan from scratch. You can get templates from several sources listed in Chapter 14 and Chapter 15.

Enterprise-level structure

This section looks at some ways that an organization can slice and dice its DR plans. You might adopt one of these approaches or tailor one to fit your business needs.

Multi-unit organizations doing large DR plans have to figure out how to write these plans for critical processes and applications that span departments or business units. Should DR plans align with applications, or should they align with the business units? It's difficult to say; your DR development team needs to weigh the options and decide. Figure 9-2 shows an application versus business-unit point of view.

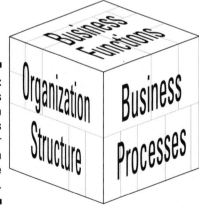

Figure 9-2:
DR plans align with business functions, or they align to the organization.

Here are some considerations that can help you understand how to approach this big-picture issue:

- ✔ **Geography:** Disasters, for the most part, strike a geographic region, regardless of the organizational or political structures of the organizations located in those regions. Writing DR plans that take care of business in the regions hit by disasters may make the most sense for your organization. In a large company, DR plans need to reference business units and functions that are located in other locations, particularly when those units and functions are on the critical path for business processes affected by a disaster.

- ✔ **Organization structure:** Different segments of a large organization may push forward on DR planning at different rates. One segment's lack of progress shouldn't impede another segment. Think of this type of situation as a DR plan for each cog in the organizational wheel. If you do things in your organization business unit by business unit, you may want to build the DR plan in pieces, asynchronously.

- ✔ **Business function:** The point of disaster recovery planning is to recover and restore critical business functions as quickly as possible, regardless of the geographical or political makeup of the organization. With this purpose in mind, DR plans should address whole business processes, regardless of where specific functions are located.

The preceding list of considerations is somewhat idealistic. Although idealism doesn't factor much into real-world business, consider these points of view when you try to figure out how your organization needs to structure its DR planning.

Document-level structure

Like any formal project in which important business information appears in documents, consider setting up some structure within individual disaster-recovery documents. Yes, I'm talking document templates. Your templates may include the following:

- ✔ **Standard document and file naming:** Make the names of different documents (what appears on the title page), as well as those documents' file names (the name of the document in a computer), consistent.

- ✔ **Standard headers and footers:** Include the document name at the top of each page (header) and information such as Company Confidential, page number, date, and version number at the bottom of each page (footer).

- ✔ **Title page:** Create a formal title page that includes all the document metadata, including title (but, of course!), version, date, and so on.

✔ **Table of contents:** A table of contents helps the reader quickly find sections in the document. Larger documents may also need an index, list of figures, and list of tables.

✔ **Copyright and other legalese:** Helps protect the organization's intellectual property.

✔ **Modification history:** Helps you keep track of the changes made from one version to the next, as well as who made those changes and when.

✔ **Document version:** Call me picky, but it helps.

✔ **Standard headings and paragraphs:** A consistent appearance makes the DR documents easier to read and work with. You might even consider doing nested section numbering (such as Section 1, 1.1, 1.1.1, and so on) if you have a really big DR plan.

Depending on the maturity of document management in your organization, the template structure in the preceding list might be too heavy, too lightweight, or just right — just like in the timeless story, "The Three Bears."

Managing Plan Development

Unless you have just one person writing your organization's DR plan, you need to establish some process and procedure for this effort so the pieces of the plan come together smoothly without getting tangled. You need formal document management, including these kinds of activities and capabilities:

✔ **Formal document templates:** I discuss templates in detail in the preceding section.

✔ **Version control:** Keep track of document versions manually, perhaps by putting the version number of each document in that document's name. You can also use a formal document management product that performs functions such as document check-out, check-in, and version management. You can find several good document management products available today, and maybe your organization has one already.

✔ **Document review:** Establish a formal document review procedure in which a document's author circulates each document to specific reviewers who can make edits and comments. Some document management products manage document review.

This book covers just the high-level basics of document management so you can better organize the development of DR plan documents if you have several people writing those documents and more people reviewing them.

Preserving the Plan

When you have completely written, reviewed, corrected, revised, and examined the plan, you need to protect that plan from harm and loss. In other words, you need to make the DR plan itself disaster-proof! What good is a good DR plan if it's trapped inside inoperable systems that were damaged or destroyed in a disaster?

You need to preserve your DR plan, along with a lot of supporting information, against loss, just in case a significant disaster occurs. Think worst-case scenario, whatever that might be in your part of the world. Here are some methods you can use to preserve your DR plan, just in case the unthinkable happens:

- ✔ **Three-ring binders:** Often, the low-tech way is best. Binders don't need power cords or power supplies. Make binders for each core team member, as well as other key personnel. Make a set for work and another set for home. One downside is the difficulty in keeping them all current. I didn't say DR planning was easy!

- ✔ **CD-ROM or USB keys:** These devices are compact and lightweight, and they have a lot of capacity. On the downside, you need a working computer to access them.

- ✔ **Internet-accessible servers:** These servers are a good idea, as long as you locate at least some of them far away from the main business centers so a regional disaster won't affect them. A possible downside is that you need Internet connectivity to access these servers.

- ✔ **Off-site storage:** Chances are, most organizations use off-site media storage for backup media safe-keeping. Often, these off-site storage firms also store paper records in addition to electronic records, so why not have them store your DR plans?

Taking the Next Steps

After you write your DR plan, are you done? Hardly. You have many tasks still ahead.

You need to test your DR plans to be sure that they'll actually work in a real disaster. DR-plan testing is covered in Chapter 10.

After you finalize and bless your DR plan, are the underlying software and data architecture, business processes, and supporting IT systems going to stop changing? No way! Disaster recovery plans need to be kept up-to-date, which I cover in Chapter 11.

Part III
Managing
Recovery Plans

"Well, whoever stole my passwords was sure clever. Especially since none of my reminders are missing."

In this part . . .

This part focuses on work that continues after you develop the disaster recovery plan. The discussions in these chapters represent more advanced disaster recovery planning practices.

Chapter 10 discusses the need to test DR plans. It gives you some methods that you can use to prove your disaster recovery procedures will actually work in a real disaster.

Chapter 11 introduces the tasks you need to perform to keep your DR plans current and train your personnel in disaster recovery procedures.

Disaster prevention is the topic of Chapter 12. Although you can't prevent natural or man-made disasters, preparation can reduce the impact of those events significantly.

Chapter 13 takes a more detailed look at many disaster scenarios, including many types of natural and man-made disasters, and examines how you can reduce your risks and the impact of these disasters.

Chapter 10

Testing the Recovery Plan

. . . .

In This Chapter

▶ Diving into DR plan testing

▶ Conducting paper tests, walkthroughs, simulations, parallel tests, and cutover tests

▶ Deciding how often to perform tests

. . . .

And you thought you were done when you finished writing your plan! You've only just begun.

Testing a DR plan is the only way to know if it's any good. In this chapter, I describe the different types of testing that you can use, from simple paper tests to full-on cutover testing.

And, even after you finish testing, you aren't done with the plan. But, as with a good murder mystery, I shouldn't spoil the ending by giving it away (no, the butler didn't do it).

Testing the DR Plan

Disaster recovery plans aren't much good if they don't work. And if they don't work, you pretty much waste the time devoted to their development.

Decision makers in businesses, especially executives, like certainty. They want to have confidence that things will go as planned. And although no one plans a disaster, execs want to know that the recovery effort after a disaster will work.

The survival of the business may depend on it.

To see if your DR plan will work, you can always take it to a fortune teller, but I wouldn't put much stock in that. Why not just try it?

Why test a DR plan?

Disaster recovery plans contain lists of procedures and other information that an emergency response team follows when a natural or man-made disaster occurs. The purpose of the plan is to recover the IT systems and infrastructure that support business processes critical to the organization's survival. Because disasters don't occur very often, you seldom can clearly tell whether those DR plans will actually work. And given the nature of disasters, if your DR plan fails, the organization may not survive the disaster.

Testing is a natural part of the lifecycle for many technology development efforts today: software, processes, and — yes — disaster recovery planning. Figure 10-1 depicts the DR plan lifecycle.

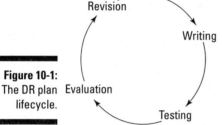

Figure 10-1:
The DR plan lifecycle.

When you test the DR plan, note any discrepancies, and then pass the plan back to the people who wrote each section so they can update it. This process improves the quality and accuracy of the DR plan, which increases the likelihood that the organization will actually survive a disaster if one occurs.

Another great benefit of DR plans and their tests is the likelihood that, by undertaking them, you can improve the organization's everyday processes and systems. When teams closely scrutinize processes and figure out how they can protect and recover those processes, often the team members discover opportunities for improvement. Sometimes the question, "How can we recover this system?" gives people the opportunity to answer the question, "How can we improve the existing system?" Be open to those opportunities because they'll come, sometimes in droves.

The types of testing that I discuss in this chapter are

- ✔ Paper tests
- ✔ Walkthrough tests
- ✔ Simulations
- ✔ Parallel tests
- ✔ Cutover tests

These tests range from the simple review of DR procedure documents to simulations to running through procedures as if you're experiencing the real thing.

Developing a test strategy

DR testing in all its forms takes considerable effort and time. To make the best possible use of staff and other resources, map out a test strategy well in advance of any scheduled tests.

Structure DR testing in the same way you structure other complicated undertakings, such as software development and associated testing. Just follow these steps:

1. Determine how frequently you should perform each type of test.
2. Test individual components.
3. Perform wider tests of combined components.
4. Test the entire plan.

When you perform DR testing as outlined in the preceding list, you can identify many errors during individual tests and correct those errors before you do more comprehensive tests. This process saves time by preventing little errors from interrupting comprehensive tests that involve a lot of people.

Virtually every enterprise that builds actual products performs testing as outlined in the preceding list. Businesses have found this test methodology to be the most effective way to ensure success in a reasonable timeframe. Figure 10-2 shows the flow of DR testing.

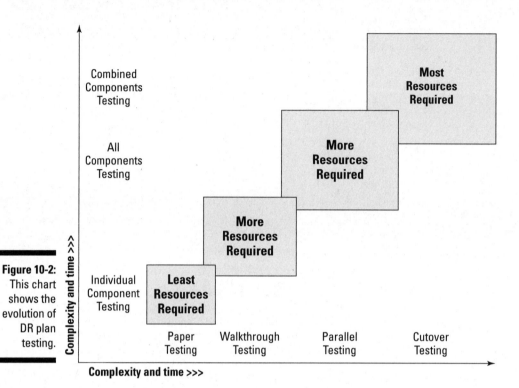

Figure 10-2:
This chart
shows the
evolution of
DR plan
testing.

Developing and following test procedures

You're probably anxious to get to testing, but you should know some procedures that are vital for every type of test. Follow these basic steps for every DR test:

1. **Determine what you want to test and the type of testing you need to do.**

   Create a detailed list that includes every step of the disaster response procedure so you can be sure to test each step and record the results.

2. **Define and document explicit goals and objectives for each test.**

   Also determine success criteria.

3. **Determine who will perform the test.**

4. **Schedule the test.**

   Confirm that the assigned person(s) are available at that time.

5. **Make sure the assigned person(s) perform the test and record the test results.**

6. **If any part of the test was unsuccessful, you must correct the DR procedures and reschedule the test.**

The preceding steps give you the minimum that you must do. If your organization does less for its DR plan testing, you risk a recovery effort failing when it matters most, which can jeopardize the future of the organization.

Conducting Paper Tests

A paper test is usually the first type of test that you perform for a recovery procedure. A *paper test* is a review of disaster recovery procedures and other response documentation, such as contact lists. In a paper test, individual staff members review these documents on their own. Ask them to make annotations or comments so you can verify the accuracy of a DR procedure, prior to performing tests that are more labor-intensive and complex.

The procedure for performing a paper test is fairly simple. Just follow these steps:

1. **Assign staff members to perform the test.**

   The staff members you choose should range from subject matter experts to near-novices. You never know who might be carrying out the procedure in a real disaster!

2. **Have these assigned people carefully review the recovery procedure.**

   They should read the procedure with a critical eye to verifying the facts, as well as making sure the documents are clearly written.

3. **Have the assigned people note, step-by-step, which items are correct and which ones need changing.**

   They need to note errors that are factual in nature (for instance, the misspelling of a command) and procedural in nature (for example, a missing step). Also, ask for suggestions on how you can improve the procedure. The assignees may use any internal or external reference materials they need to confirm the accuracy and appropriateness of the test procedure.

4. **Get the test results in writing, including the details that the tester notes in Step 3.**

5. **Collect these results from all test subjects.**

6. **Give the results to the project manager or the person who owns the procedure (probably the same person who wrote that procedure) so he or she can revise and retest the procedure.**

The people who perform these tests should do so alone and at their own pace. You have opportunities in walkthrough tests (which I talk about in the following section) to have groups of people review procedures together.

Good recordkeeping is essential in DR plan procedure testing. Creating a plan for coordinating testing, issuing test assignments, gathering results, and passing results back to document/procedure owners helps assure the success of the DR plan.

After all the reviewers complete paper testing, and you make all revisions and carry out retests, you can advance the procedure to further testing, such as

 ✓ **Paper tests in which you combine the procedure with others:** For example, you can combine a procedure for restarting a server with other procedures related to starting all the servers associated with an application.

 ✓ **Walkthrough testing:** See the following section for details.

Conduct paper tests periodically to make sure that they remain accurate over time. I discuss the long-term schedule for DR plan testing in the section "Establishing Test Frequency," later in this chapter.

Conducting Walkthrough Tests

A walkthrough test is similar to a paper test — it's a review of a written recovery procedure document. But you perform the walkthrough test with a group of experts, rather than a single expert working alone.

A walkthrough test takes place after you complete paper testing. Paper testing eliminates many of the errors in the procedure, so the group reviews a much higher quality procedure in walkthrough testing. You make the walkthrough a more valuable activity if you remove most of the errors before it takes place. A recovery procedure that's rife with errors makes a walkthrough test a waste of everyone's time, slowing down the group and making the test less effective.

In a walkthrough test, the test participants discuss each step in the procedure. In this group setting, participants talk their way through each step and decide whether that step is properly worded, and they consider what happens in each step. The ensuing discussion provides opportunities to find errors, as well as opportunities to make improvements.

Walkthrough test participants

Who should participate in the walkthrough test? You need several parties:

- ✔ **Facilitator:** Someone with established facilitation and people skills who has no vested interest in the outcome of the walkthrough. The facilitator needs, um, facilitation skills — keeping the participants on track, making sure the pace of the discussion is appropriate, and so on.

- ✔ **Scribe:** This person needs to take good notes throughout the walk-through. These notes include things that went well and things that didn't go so well throughout the walkthrough.

- ✔ **Business process owners:** The people in the company who perform the business process that the walkthrough focuses on. They're usually familiar with the workings of supporting applications, but they have a point of view that's quite different from IT developers and operations.

- ✔ **Recovery team members:** Staff members whom you select to perform actual recovery operations if and when a disaster occurs.

- ✔ **Subject matter experts:** Staff members or outsiders who have expertise in the processes or technologies related to the test.

- ✔ **Auditors:** In a regulated or audited organization, auditors can provide valuable insight. The security and audit requirements for a business process and its supporting application(s) aren't relaxed during a disaster!

- ✔ **Senior management:** They provide invaluable big-picture insight when they observe and participate in the walkthrough. Often, they know about business matters that others might miss during a walkthrough.

Walkthrough test procedure

Follow these steps to perform a walkthrough test:

1. **Identify the people you want to participate in the walkthrough.**

2. **Identify potential locations for the walkthrough.**

   You need a large and comfortable meeting room that can easily accommodate all the participants, as well as space for setting up and eating any meals the group requires.

3. **Estimate the length of time required for the walkthrough.**

   You usually need an entire day.

4. **Assign a facilitator and a scribe for the walkthrough.**

   I can't overstate the importance of a scribe; when comments, issues, and proposed changes to the DR plan arise, the scribe writes these down so the plan can be updated later. Other people in the room may be too caught up in the discussion to write down all of the issues.

5. **Schedule the walkthrough.**

   Be sure that you allocate enough time for the test — half a day or more. Arrange to provide one or more meals so people don't have to interrupt the walkthrough by leaving to eat.

6. **Distribute the procedure to the walkthrough participants in advance.**

7. **Conduct the walkthrough (or let the facilitator lead the walkthrough).**

   During the walkthrough, the most important task — which the scribe performs — is to record the results of the test: What went well, what didn't go well, and what changes you need to make in the procedure to ensure its success. You most importantly need to discover dependencies — meaning when a step in a procedure depends on an external item — and record the details and issues regarding those dependencies.

8. **Prepare the written results and feedback, and pass them to the owner/creator of the procedure.**

   The owner/creator of the procedure should make any needed revisions to the procedure.

Scenarios

The test facilitator — and possibly other walkthrough test participants — needs to select one or more scenarios as the subject of the walkthrough. Choose the scenarios from among the types of disasters that can actually occur in the organization's region. Possible scenarios include

- **Severe storm:** A severe storm could be a tornado, hurricane, cyclone, ice storm, windstorm, or other storm that causes widespread transportation and utility outages.

- **Earthquake, volcano, landslide, or avalanche:** Consider any of these scenarios if they're likely to occur in your region.

- **Flood or tsunami:** If your business is located in an area where these events may occur, you can use them as a walkthrough test scenario.

- **Utility outage:** Human error or a natural event can cause a power or communication outage lasting several days.

- **Pandemic:** A widespread illness can result in high rates of absenteeism and government-mandated quarantines.

- ✔ **Man-caused event:** Can include civil unrest, strikes, acts of terrorism, or war.

- ✔ **Other disruptions:** Consider including scenarios such as building evacuations, corruption of a critical database, failure of a critical server, a large-scale network outage, and so on. One or more participants may have experienced one of these events, which can help make the walkthrough more realistic and expose more issues.

Describe the scenario you choose in detail at the beginning of the walkthrough. Whoever reveals the scenario should describe its location, as well as what impact the event has on the region. Include a description of damage to the facility and which staff members are or aren't available to help.

Using a real-life scenario puts a face on the walkthrough and makes it more real. It may be easier to imagine a more realistic and likely scenario that can get the adrenalin flowing. The participants have a greater sense of urgency and concern because their own imaginations help them see the impact of a real disaster and how an organization has to make a best effort to recover critical business processes with few available resources.

Walkthrough results

At the end of the walkthrough, the facilitator should lead a discussion. He or she should solicit from the participants examples of what went well and what didn't. Of course, the scribe should have written down these items as they occurred, but in recounting the event, the participants can think about how well the walkthrough went and how they could improve it.

Even if the walkthrough exposes serious deficiencies in the DR plan, you can consider it at least a partial success if the participants identify areas you can improve in the DR plan.

You may or may not need to re-perform the walkthrough. If the first walkthrough didn't go well (which could happen for a variety of reasons), perhaps you need to repeat the walkthrough after you update the procedures and any supporting materials. If the first walkthrough resulted in only minor revisions, you may not need to repeat it.

Properly record the results and details of all walkthroughs so you know the status of each walkthrough and can note and record any required changes.

Debriefing

The team may want to conduct a debriefing session that takes place one or more days after the walkthrough. The purpose of a debriefing is to discuss the results of the walkthrough, after the participants have had some time to analyze the results and perform any needed post-walkthrough research or number crunching. The debriefing should include the facilitator, scribe, management, and any senior managers or executive sponsors.

Depending on the size and complexity of the walkthrough itself, a debriefing may range from very informal to highly structured. The debriefing needs a clear purpose and may range from extended discussions about procedures, results, and problems you ran into during the test to strategizing/brainstorming.

Next steps

After you perform walkthroughs for all procedures in the DR plan and correct all errors and discrepancies, the DR plan team can consider doing parallel testing, in which response teams actually perform the recovery procedures to see how well they work. I cover parallel testing in the section "Conducting Parallel Testing," later in this chapter. Also, consider simulation testing, which I talk about in the following section.

You need to conduct walkthrough tests now and again. I cover test frequency in the section "Establishing Test Frequency," later in this chapter.

Conducting Simulation Testing

A simulation is more than a walkthrough (which I discuss in the section "Conducting Walkthrough Tests," earlier in this chapter), but it shares many characteristics with a walkthrough. A simulation is basically an on-location walkthrough test with props. Here are some relevant facts about simulations:

- A simulation's setting is a credible and likely disaster scenario.
- Simulation participants are recovery team members.
- The simulation takes place in a designated emergency operations center or a location resembling one.
- A simulation usually takes an entire day — maybe even two or three days.
- A well-orchestrated simulation usually takes weeks or months to plan.

Probably the most important characteristic of a simulation is that it's highly choreographed. Script the disaster scenario to take place over a period of several hours. For instance, in a simulation that begins at 8:30 a.m., the moderator issues a number of verbal and written statements at predetermined times, such as the following:

✔ **8:30 a.m.:** Announcement of a nearby earthquake (tsunami, tornado, ice storm, and so on) with a description of the immediately known damage.

✔ **8:35 a.m.:** Announcement of early reports of damage to roads, the regional airport, and broadcast facilities.

✔ **8:45 a.m.:** Announcement that a ruptured natural gas pipeline is burning, forcing mass evacuations and disrupting businesses and transportation systems.

✔ **9:00 a.m.:** Announcements of specific public utility outages, transportation disruptions, and telecommunications outages.

As the disaster response team hears these announcements, they spring into action, declaring a disaster and mobilizing resources. Design further announcements to constrain their abilities and give them the feeling that these events are actually occurring.

A simulation test is primarily a test of personnel — how they'll respond and take charge during a real disaster. A simulation reveals the characteristics of leadership, communication, cooperation, and creative thinking among the disaster response team. The information you get from a disaster scenario simulation can provide tremendous insight into the ways in which members of the response team will conduct themselves during a real disaster.

Similar to a walkthrough test, a simulation test should have a scribe and a facilitator, and it should include a post-simulation debriefing in which participants and senior management can discuss the simulation and its results.

Conducting Parallel Testing

The disaster recovery plan paper and walkthrough testing that I discuss earlier in this chapter takes place in the minds of the participants. Team members discuss many details, but they don't actually do anything. Paper and walkthrough testing exercise the imaginations of the subject matter experts who play various roles in the organization and in the DR planning teams.

With parallel testing, disaster response personnel actually perform the steps in their response procedures. When the procedures say build a server, the personnel build a server. When the procedures say start the applications, the personnel start the applications.

In short, parallel testing finds out if the disaster recovery plans actually work. Well, almost.

In a parallel test, the personnel who are actually delivering services to customers continue doing so. IT systems that support those services continue to run. Customers who do business with the organization don't see any difference because you make no real changes to the systems that support the services they use, but the disaster response personnel perform DR procedures as though a disaster had actually occurred.

A parallel test involves the use of recovery systems in parallel with primary systems (hence the name!). The primary systems continue to support the business.

Parallel testing considerations

Parallel testing is quite different than paper testing and walkthroughs. In a parallel test, bits actually flow through recovery systems, so you can get a more reliable idea whether the DR plan will work in an actual disaster. You need to take a number of considerations into account before performing a parallel test:

- ✔ **Do no harm to infrastructure.** Don't interrupt or interfere with existing networks, systems, databases, and applications in a parallel test. Existing systems still perform actual business and support existing business processes that must continue.

- ✔ **Do no harm to staff.** Similarly, a parallel test may involve additional employees working in the presence of staff members who are carrying out their regular duties. Recovery test personnel must not interfere with the real staff members.

- ✔ **Acquiring replacement equipment.** In some DR plans, you use systems that the organization already owns as recovery systems. In others, the organization must purchase recovery systems. For purposes of parallel testing, you may need to alter the plans somewhat so those purchases don't actually happen. A viable alternative would be to lease the systems that you need for the duration of the parallel test.

- ✔ **Side-by-side transactions.** Depending on the nature of the business process and IT systems you're parallel testing, you may be able to run some, or all, of the actual business transactions through both the actual systems and the parallel test systems. The DR project team needs to decide what criteria to use when determining which transactions to run on the DR systems.

- ✔ **Actual load or simulated load.** The nature of the business might require that you perform only a small portion of transactions to validate the test. But for the test to be valid, the recovery system may need to take a full workload, even if you run only dummy data through it. Testing may also require both types of tests (small numbers of real transactions, plus a full workload test) to validate the correct operation of the systems.

✓ **External interfaces.** Make the parallel test as much like the real production system it's mimicking as you can. But you need to simulate some parts of the test so you can avoid certain undesirable events. For example, if an application sends transactions to a bank or payment processor for payment, you might want to avoid having the test system also transmit those transactions, or else your organization incurs twice the number and amount of payments. You may also need to apply this principle to other internal applications.

✓ **Make the test as real as possible.** Despite all of the limitations I mention in this list, the point of the parallel test is to determine if your DR plan will work during a disaster. Consequently, leave the DR test personnel alone to figure out the hard stuff. The procedures won't be perfect, and you should constrain the test personnel somewhat — and somehow — so they can't cheat by overcoming obstacles more easily than they would be able to during an actual disaster.

Even with seemingly adequate precautions, things can go wrong with parallel testing, which can interfere with ongoing business processes. But you can get considerable benefits from parallel testing: Real-world experience in building and starting recovery systems and running them through their paces to see if they can support critical processes in a real disaster.

Although parallel testing is considerably more valuable than walkthrough testing for validating plans, parallel testing falls short of actually supporting critical business processes. Another activity, however, can erase all doubt as to whether recovery systems can do the job — cutover testing. I discuss cutover testing in the section "Conducting Cutover Testing," later in this chapter.

Next steps

After you successfully complete a parallel test, you should have a very clear idea of how your response team and IT systems will respond in a real disaster. The parallel test should provide you with information that you can use to further improve recovery procedures.

You may want to carry out one or more simulations (see the section "Conducting Simulation Testing," earlier in this chapter) so you can better understand how personnel will respond in a real scenario. And if you're ready to climb higher into the rarified air of cutover testing, proceed boldly to but plan thoroughly for this most comprehensive and challenging form of disaster recovery testing, which I cover in the following section.

Conducting Cutover Testing

Parallel testing, which I talk about in the preceding sections, gives you an opportunity to actually build recovery systems to find out if they can perform the type of activities you need to support critical business functions. But parallel testing stops short of actually supporting those processes. If you absolutely must know whether your recovery systems can support actual business workload, consider performing a cutover test.

In a *cutover test,* the recovery team builds and readies recovery systems that can support critical business functions. A cutover test is the real thing. If the recovery systems don't work, the business processes they support will really be interrupted. That could be a real disaster!

Cutover testing is deadly serious business. It is, without a doubt, the DR test with the highest amount of risk. A cutover test is kind of like a heart-lung bypass during open-heart surgery — the consequences of failure are tremendous! However, the rewards are equally great: The positive outcome of a cutover test gives the organization a high degree of confidence that the DR plan can assure the continued operation of critical business processes if a real disaster strikes. Walkthrough and parallel tests can't provide the same level of assurance.

You can usually perform a cutover test more easily than a parallel test for a number of reasons:

- ✔ **No more simulations:** In a cutover test, you don't need to take special care to stop certain things from happening, such as double transactions to external systems. Managing these possible missteps is a tricky issue in parallel testing, but it's practically a no-brainer in cutover tests.

- ✔ **No more double work:** In a parallel test, you need to perform some operations on both primary and recovery systems to validate and reconcile the proper operation of the recovery system. In a cutover test, you have only one system performing transactions.

- ✔ **Less human interference:** Some operations in a parallel test may require certain staff to perform their procedures differently for the sake of the parallel test. In a cutover test, staff procedures are probably more like their day-to-day routine than what they do during a parallel test.

Performing a cutover test is like jumping out of an airplane and betting that the parachute (or the reserve 'chute) will work perfectly. Jumping out of a perfectly good airplane can be pretty unnerving, and it can make you question whether you did the right thing. One thing is certain, however — after you begin, you're committed!

Don't let testing create a disaster

Typical cutover testing involves disconnecting or shutting down primary systems and transferring operations to recovery systems. This task isn't risk-free, and a number of things can go wrong:

✔ **Inability to start recovery systems:** Despite practice, the DR team might run into an unexpected problem and be unable to get recovery systems running. If you've already shut down or disconnected primary systems, you could experience an outage of greater-than-expected duration.

✔ **Inability to start applications on recovery systems:** If the DR team can't get applications running on recovery systems, more downtime could result.

✔ **Inability to retain transaction data on recovery systems:** Cleanly transferring transactions from system to system can be very complicated in large, complex, or distributed applications. You may find maintaining transaction integrity, particularly during cutovers, really tricky.

Any of these scenarios can result in unplanned downtime. Depending on the nature of the organization, this unplanned downtime may be crippling. Perform thorough paper, walkthrough, and parallel testing — and examine the test results deeply and carefully — before you begin any cutover test.

Cutover test procedure

In a cutover test, you turn off (or disconnect) production systems and start up the recovery systems, right? Well, maybe. Although you do need to perform full end-to-end testing, you may want to give yourself some accommodations so your testing doesn't actually interrupt running business processes.

Suppose that a DR plan establishes a two-hour RTO (Recovery Time Objective), which means you need to have recovery systems up and running in less than two hours. Parallel tests may show that you can get those systems up and running in 90 minutes. But do you really want to interrupt running business processes for that long? Remember, this is a parallel test, not a real disaster. Even for the sake of end-to-end DR testing, you may not want to incur that much actual downtime. What you do in your cutover test depends on the type of business you're in and how much downtime executive management is willing to endure for the sake of a test.

You may actually want to tell your customers and suppliers that you're running a cutover test because this announcement can give them confidence in your organization — that you're taking steps to remain operational in a disaster. Why keep it a secret?

Assuming you don't want to take a full hit on downtime during a test, follow these steps to perform a cutover test:

1. **Develop the entire cutover test plan and circulate it for review to a wide audience of stakeholders and experts.**

   Include validation criteria that you can use later to determine whether each step of the test was successful.

2. **Brief the entire test team prior to the test so you can address any remaining concerns.**

3. **Begin the test. Notify the team members that the test has begun and that you need them to begin building and/or preparing recovery systems.**

   You may or may not take main production applications offline, depending on whether executive management is willing to tolerate an actual outage.

4. **After the team has prepared and readied the recovery systems, configure those systems to assume full production workload.**

5. **Carefully observe the recovery systems, now actually supporting critical business processes, to ensure that they're performing all functions properly.**

   Also observe interfaces to other systems (whether internal or external) to make sure those interfaces are also operating properly.

6. **Carry out any specific test scripts or plans that you developed for the test.**

7. **After you carry out all desired functions and tests on the recovery systems, revert production workload back to the primary systems.**

   Note: You must work out a plan for transferring transactions back to primary systems so you can do the switch back smoothly. Primary systems need to have full knowledge of transactions that the recovery systems perform, as though the primary systems had actually performed those transactions.

8. **After the primary systems resume all duties, carefully examine the recovery systems to ensure that they were in fact performing their functions correctly.**

   Personnel participating in the parallel test, as well as all staff members affected by the test, must report any unexpected results to the testing team immediately.

9. **The test team and test organizers need to fully document the procedure, issues, and results of the test.**

   Compare test results with the validation criteria you develop in Step 1 to determine whether each step of the test was successful.

10. **Circulate the test report to a wide audience of stakeholders and other personnel.**

11. **Debrief the test team to provide them an opportunity to discuss the test and its results.**

   Valuable insights, when you document and act on them, can further improve the quality of the DR plan and increase its effectiveness.

Cutover testing considerations

You need to address several issues long before you conduct a cutover test. Some of these issues include

- ✔ **Practice first:** Test virtually all the tasks associated with building and recovering an application prior to the cutover test. Before the test begins, personnel should become familiar with the procedures that they'll carry out.

- ✔ **Workload:** Recovery systems must be able to handle the entire workload. Don't necessarily expect recovery systems to perform at the same level as primary systems, however. Depending on the nature of the systems you're testing, you may need to perform volume testing and/or stress testing to be sure that the recovery systems (and all of the supporting infrastructure) can support workloads as expected.

- ✔ **Reach-ability:** Customers, users, suppliers, and other parties must know how to reach your systems during a cutover test. Ideally, they'd access your recovery systems in the same way they normally do, but the nature of the applications you're testing may influence this access.

- ✔ **Notification and communications:** Certainly, some staff know that you're performing the cutover test. But do you tell everyone in the organization that the test will occur or is occurring? I don't have easy answers for this question — the DR planning team needs to talk it out with senior managers or executives present.

- ✔ **Transaction integrity:** The recovery system needs to cleanly record the transactions — or whatever the applications perform. At the end of the test, transfer those records back to the primary system. The method and timeframe for transferring work done on recovery systems back to primary systems depends on the nature of the applications and the processes they support.

- ✔ **Transaction source:** Your application should know on which systems it performed transactions. That way, if something goes awry later, after a cutover test, you can figure out which system (primary or recovery) performed a certain transaction.

✔ **Controls, regulations, audits, and security:** If your organization is bound by any regulations or audits that impose requirements on your systems and applications, the systems must conform to those requirements at all times. You can't relax or set aside controls during any DR test. Auditors and regulators aren't likely to be compassionate on account of some omission during a DR test. Make all regulatory, audit, and security requirements and controls a part of the DR plan from the very start.

If cutover testing is starting to sound scary, that's good! This type of DR testing is very serious and should invoke fear because the risks of failure are great. The rewards for success are even greater, however, so you should figure out how to turn your fear into positive energy and proceed with intention.

Cutover tests have risks associated with them, and you must perform those tests carefully. Properly planned, a cutover test can provide valuable insight into the viability of an organization's disaster recovery procedures.

Planning Parallel and Cutover Tests

Performing a parallel or cutover test requires a great deal of planning and also a planner or project manager. If you don't believe me, have a knowledgeable person begin to write down all the tasks that you must perform before the actual test takes place, all the tasks associated with the test itself, and finally all the tasks that you must perform after you complete the test.

You need a project plan for several reasons:

✔ **You need to do many tasks.** Unlike walkthroughs, you have to do a lot of things to get ready for a parallel or cutover test.

✔ **Many tasks depend on other tasks.** You can't load the data until you install the database, and you can't install the database until you install the operating system, and you can't install the operating system until you have a computer to install it on. So, on and on it goes — many tasks depend on many others.

✔ **All tasks require people.** You can very easily build a project plan until you have to assign people to the tasks in that plan. Most project managers find that they have too few people for the job, which makes the job take a lot longer than originally expected.

✔ **People are busy with other things.** Staff members also have other responsibilities; the project planner can find out how much time each task takes and when people will be available to carry those tasks out.

✔ **The project plan is the schedule.** A thoroughly developed project plan serves as the de facto project schedule. The project plan contains a list of tasks, when those tasks are supposed to occur, and who's supposed to perform them. After you identify all the tasks, dependencies, and resources, the project plan begins to become real. When you plug in start dates, the dates for important milestones begin to have credibility with the planning team and executives.

✔ **You need to identify and resolve conflicts.** Some of the milestones are going to conflict with other events that occur in the organization. You need to identify and consider significant events, such as heavy business periods (retailers before holidays, for example) and fiscal month-, quarter-, and year-ends, so the cutover or parallel test can avoid the significant events in the business's overall calendar.

✔ **You need a way to measure progress.** After you complete the project plan and start the project, marking the completion of important milestones gives you a good measure of progress.

✔ **The plan can help identify costs.** Although plans are task-oriented, analysis of each task can give you information about hard costs (actual dollars spent) and soft costs (such as extra time needed to perform tasks) associated with each task. Costs that you can easily figure out include hardware and software purchases; more difficult ones include consultants and contractors, facilities rental, and so on.

✔ **A solid plan helps to shape expectations.** Senior management will certainly ask basic questions about the test — how long, how much, and who will do it. A well-developed plan can help you answer those questions with confidence.

Clustering and replication technologies and cutover tests

Environments that use clustering and replication technologies to establish recovery systems usually can more easily perform cutover tests than organizations that have systems that use manual cutover procedures. In local and geo-clusters, the recovery systems are already running and, if you manage them properly, already have the current application software and system configuration.

In such environments, you can perform a cutover test nearly as simply as executing a command on the recovery system's cluster program that says, "Make me the active server in the cluster." Execute that command and *voilà*, the passive recovery system now becomes the active system in the cluster, processing real transactions, or whatever the application does to pass the time.

But if only it were that easy. Clustering and replication work closely together, and they must, so applications can properly perform and record all transactions, particularly those transactions that start on one system and end on another. If this book focused on clustering, transaction processing, and replication, I'd have entire chapters on each of the topics that I mention in this paragraph. Someone in your organization must fully understand clustering and replication, together with the intimate workings of the applications that run on these technologies, so all your applications can work properly when the active server in a cluster ceases to function in a cutover test or in a real disaster.

Next steps

In disaster recovery planning, it's not over, even after it's over! After a successful cutover test, an organization knows that it has the right stuff to weather a real disaster. Make sure that you document all the notes, results, and reports of the cutover test, debrief participants and management, and put the next cutover test on the calendar.

If you focus your DR testing on technology, you might want to try a simulation (discussed in the section "Conducting Simulation Testing," earlier in this chapter) to help you understand the human dynamic that plays out during a disaster and has such a powerful influence on the success (or failure) of a response team.

Establishing Test Frequency

After you complete your testing, you can just send everyone back to their regular jobs, right? Well, yes — but not forever. Remember this constant of business processes and IT systems: They're always changing! The test plans that worked last month might not work next month. Changes in processes and IT systems have a direct impact on recovery procedures. Does that mean you need to perform DR testing monthly? Well, not necessarily, but in some cases, maybe.

The following factors may increase or decrease how often you need to test:

- ✔ **Cost:** The more a test costs, the less often you probably want to perform that test.

- ✔ **Risk:** The risk of recovery failure in an actual disaster increases test frequency so you can be sure that recovery operations will actually succeed.

- ✔ **Frequency of change:** In a business environment in which processes and/or systems change frequently, you need to perform testing more frequently to keep up with these changes.

- ✔ **Training:** More testing makes recovery personnel more familiar with recovery procedures, making a smooth and successful recovery more likely.

✔ **Customer or partner demands:** Customers or partners may want (within the context of a contract or not) more frequent testing so they can be sure that the organization will survive a disaster and not disrupt other organizations, preventing "your disaster becoming my disaster."

✔ **Regulation:** Regulation may define test frequency in some industries or locations in which laws or regulations require certain types of tests at a minimum frequency, regardless of cost.

For most organizations, the following testing schedule will suffice:

✔ **Paper tests:** As often as procedures change

✔ **Walkthroughs:** Quarterly

✔ **Parallel tests:** Annually

✔ **Cutover tests:** Annually or biennially

Paper test frequency

Keeping DR procedures current is a chore, there's no doubt about it. But the further that recovery procedures diverge from the systems and processes they support, the higher the risk that recovery procedures won't work.

Wait — this isn't just a sales pitch about maintaining recovery plans: It's also a pitch about testing frequently.

You need to perform paper tests as frequently as the recovery procedures change. But that statement's not really true, nor is it sufficient. You need to review paper tests regularly — at least quarterly and maybe more often. The periodic review of a recovery procedure serves two purposes: First, it helps operations staff remain familiar with recovery plans by keeping them aware of recovery procedures on the systems or processes they work every day. Second, review of a recovery procedure may uncover the need for a recovery procedure update.

Here's an example of a procedure review triggering an update of that procedure: An IT operations staff member reads through a recovery procedure that discusses restoring data from tape backup. The staff member recalls that the backup program was upgraded last month and that some of the user interface (UI) elements have changed. If someone who's a little less familiar with the backup system became responsible for recovering backup data in a real disaster, he or she might find the change in the backup program's UI confusing, leading to errors and delaying system recovery and restart. Not good. So, the staff member's review of the recovery procedure, and his realization that it needs a change, triggers upgrades to that recovery procedure.

You should *not,* however, routinely identify changes by using procedure reviews. At the same time, make sure all personnel associated with DR planning, training, and operations are alert to these types of little discrepancies that can require minor adjustments.

The correct way to update procedures, by the way, is to make reviewing and changing recovery procedures a part of the normal procedure for making changes to business processes and IT systems. I cover the task of keeping DR plans current in Chapter 11.

To keep people fresh and thinking about DR, review procedures monthly. If, however, you have so very many procedures that reading a department's entire recovery procedure would be too time consuming, review a different portion of the entire procedure each month. You can then test different parts of the procedure library every month — so it might take two, three, or even six months to get through the entire library.

Walkthrough test frequency

When you perform paper tests, you're tying up one person at a time. With walkthrough tests, you're corralling a lot of people at the same time, or so you hope.

As I describe in the section "Conducting Walkthrough Tests," earlier in this chapter, walkthrough tests are community events. Group discussions with experts helps to uncover issues that paper tests may have missed.

Given the rate of change in business processes and IT systems, you should perform walkthroughs quarterly. You don't have to organize a full caucus with all the stakeholders from up and down the protocol stack every three months. If systems haven't undergone significant changes since the last walkthrough, you may need only a smaller group to participate in the walkthrough. On the other hand, if you have many new hands on deck, you may need to hold a larger event to at least get the new people familiarized with your DR plan, in general, and the recovery procedures associated with the processes and systems they work with every day, in particular.

If you need some specific ideas for organizing walkthroughs, start with the following and adapt them to your specific needs:

 ✔ **First walkthrough — the big event:** After you first develop the DR plan for a given process or application, you need a large audience of participants to talk through every step and nuance of the recovery procedure so you can make sure that the procedure is complete and accurate.

 ✔ **Next two or three quarters — smaller events:** As long as you don't make any major changes in systems or processes, you may need only a small core team of participants to determine whether the recovery procedure is still sufficient and identify little changes that you may need to make.

✔ **New staff members:** All new staff members, regardless of their place in the process or system ecosystem (whether they're likely to be on a disaster recovery team), need to participate in the next walkthrough. Senior staff need to indoctrinate newer staff members on details and insights that may fall between the lines in a disaster recovery procedure.

✔ **Changes to processes or systems:** If the organization has made significant changes to systems or processes, more people need to participate in the next quarterly walkthrough — all those who designed changes, implemented changes, and perform processes or operate systems under the new changes.

✔ **Major upgrade or system replacement:** If you've overhauled a process, or upgraded or replaced an IT system, a full-on walkthrough is called for. Depending on the impact and scope of the change, you may want to wait for the next quarterly walkthrough, or perhaps you need to conduct a walkthrough before you finish the upgrade or replacement (or shortly after you do). The precise schedule for a walkthrough test in an environment with major changes depends on many factors, especially risk. In other words, can the organization afford to put in a new system and then wait to do its first DR walkthrough, or is DR important enough to do the walkthrough before the new system or process goes live?

✔ **Tuning the frequency:** If your environment is nearly static and you have few major changes and low staff turnover, you could stretch out your walkthrough schedule, perhaps to twice per year. On the other hand, if you work in a high-risk environment (for example, ICU patient telemetry or a building fire control system), you should conduct walkthroughs more frequently than my suggested quarterly schedule. Frequent system or process changes, as well as higher staff turnover, also favor testing more often.

Parallel test frequency

Although parallel tests aren't quite the real thing, they do give you an opportunity to walk the walk and see if the recovery system has what it takes to do real work. Parallel tests are tricky and require a lot of coordination, but if you never do them, it's difficult to know whether your recovery systems will even work in a real disaster.

Difficult as it sounds, an organization has to step up and perform parallel tests, even if it doesn't perform them often. How often you conduct these parallel tests depends on many factors:

✔ **Level of effort:** You may want to bring in a lot of employees for a parallel test. After all, it's probably a rare event, and you want as many people as possible to partake in the activity so they can learn from it. But such testing begins to add up when you figure what other activities your test participants don't get done because of their involvement in the test.

- ✔ **Cost:** Performing a parallel test might require some hard dollars for recovery systems (if your plans call for purchasing recovery systems), consultants (for their expertise or their two hands), and other incidentals.

- ✔ **Risk:** You have to look at risk from two perspectives — the risk of doing the test (and what could possibly go wrong) and the risk of not doing the test. You need an experienced risk analyst to figure out the risks. The answer won't be a clean "Yes" or "No." Instead, your analyst should give you an answer more like, "Here are the things that could go wrong, and here's what you can do to reduce the risk somewhat."

- ✔ **Regulation:** Ever the trump card, regulations in some industries and locales require real DR tests, regardless of cost, risk, and effort.

If you still aren't sure how often to perform parallel tests (or whether you should perform them at all), try doing your parallel test one or two times per year. Adjust this frequency up or down, depending on factors that only people in your organization can know.

Your first parallel test probably takes far more effort and causes far more pain than subsequent tests. Things you figure out in the first test can help you improve the outcome for future tests.

Cutover test frequency

Cutover tests aren't wholly unlike parallel tests: They require the involvement of many staff members and managers, can disrupt business, and have risks associated with them. Cutover tests are decidedly riskier than parallel tests because of their disruptive nature — recovery systems get in the middle of critical business processes and support those processes (or try, anyway).

Depending on your processes, your architecture, and the type of business you're in, you may need to do only parallel tests and never do cutover tests. But, probably, you do need to do cutover tests to make yourself more confident in your DR plans.

The arguments for doing cutover tests more, or less, frequently are the same as for parallel tests (which I talk about in the preceding section). It all depends on effort, cost, risk, and regulation. Say you can do a cutover test every one to two years. Working with the results from that test, you can then assess the risks associated with your applications and what you use them for. If your application keeps heart-lung machines and patient telemetry running, you might run parallel tests every month (or even more frequently than that!). However, if the applications do something nowhere near life-critical or even business-critical, a lower frequency of testing may suffice.

Chapter 11

Keeping DR Plans and Staff Current

Change is a constant force in organizations of all shapes and sizes. Updates in technology, modifications to business processes, and other changes prompt you to revisit and revise your DR documents, including you Business Impact Analysis (BIA) and disaster recovery procedures. This chapter can help you understand the types of changes you need to make to your disaster response procedures and plans when changes in the business occur.

Speaking of changes, personnel changes often happen. People come, people go, and people move around on the *org chart* (who reports to whom). These new people in new roles require training and retraining to keep teams and departments ready if a disaster occurs.

Understanding the Impact of Changes on DR Plans

By their nature, businesses are undergoing continuous metamorphoses. Businesses change their business models, org charts, product and feature sets, and SLAs (Service Level Agreements) as frequently as you change your underwear.

In the following sections, I discuss the types of changes that occur in businesses and the impact those changes have on disaster recovery plans. I group these changes into five categories:

✔ **Technology changes:** Upgrades or changes in software, hardware, and other technologies.

✔ **Business changes:** Changes in processes, mergers and acquisitions, and relocation.

✔ **Personnel changes:** Changes to the org chart, attrition, changes in department and individual responsibilities, and so on.

✔ **Market changes:** Over time, you change the way you make and price products or services, and your consumers change how they consume and think of those products or services.

✔ **External changes:** Other events that occur outside of the business itself that change your business's risks in some way.

If you don't think the preceding list was detailed enough, the following sections put each of these areas under a powerful electron microscope. Remember not to squint too long, or your eyes will hurt.

Technology changes

Paper tape gives way to punch cards, which reel-to-reel magtape displaces, which yields to tape cartridges, and then optical media . . . technology just marches on and on. Every step of the way, technology upgrades require revisions to disaster recovery procedures. The following sections give you some examples of technology changes.

Upgrades to IT systems

Changes at every layer in the stack (application, database, operating system, and network) can mean you need to change DR procedure documents. Some examples of such changes include

✔ **Network devices and software:** New routers, firewalls, load balancers, and even just software upgrades.

✔ **Server, storage, and tape library hardware:** With new hardware, the buttons are always in new places and the labels look a little different. Are your DR procedures still accurate?

✔ **Operating system (OS) change-outs or upgrades:** If you change from one OS to another, you need to rewrite your DR procedures. But even upgrades may require edits to procedures if command options or other OS procedures have changed.

✔ **Changes or upgrades in higher layers:** Such as in the database management system (DBMS) or application server. It seems like change is the only constant, which means you need to make changes to your disaster recovery procedures. Will it ever end?

✔ **Media changes:** Whenever backup media, archival media, or software release media change, you may also need to change the procedures for recovering systems.

Introduction of new IT technologies

New technologies are rolling in all the time — from USB tokens to optical media to biometrics. Whenever you incorporate any of these new technologies into an application or infrastructure, you probably need to change your recovery documents.

Business changes

Senior managers and executives in organizations sometimes make decisions that have a moderate-to-profound impact on the entire business. These range from changes in existing business processes to more significant changes such as mergers and acquisitions, outsourcing and insourcing, and changing business locations. All of these changes require you to review DR documents on some level to make sure they're still relevant and accurate.

Business process changes

Organizations change their processes with frightening regularity. The trouble is, some businesses make these changes subconsciously — meaning the businesses don't plan the changes, they happen spontaneously and aren't well documented or communicated. On the other hand, many organizations have a process for changing processes, so hopefully the *process-change process* (the process for changing processes) includes a step to review and edit disaster recovery procedures.

Mergers and acquisitions

A *merger* (when two businesses become one) or an *acquisition* (when one business purchases another) can upset the boat like few other changes can. When a merger or acquisition occurs in an organization, priorities can suddenly change or go sideways. The ramifications include

✔ Highly critical business processes may become less critical.

✔ Business processes previously considered not critical may suddenly become critical.

✔ Processes may alter.

✔ Processes often combine.

✔ Sometimes, your business scraps a process in favor of a similar process in the acquiring (or acquired) business.

✔ A merger or acquisition wreaks havoc on org charts. (I discuss these types of changes in detail in the section "Personnel changes," later in this chapter.)

✔ Business or personnel often relocate.

✔ IT applications face big changes — winning applications survive and losers get scrapped.

✔ The new organization may place more value on disaster recovery, changing all the results in the Business Impact Analysis (BIA).

An organization that undergoes a merger or acquisition should consider revisiting its BIA to reevaluate the MTD (Maximum Tolerable Downtime), RTO (Recovery Time Objective), and RPO (Recovery Point Objective) figures relating to post-merger/acquisition processes. You may have different priorities and thresholds in the new organization. Newly placed executive management may also have new opinions on the importance of disaster recovery.

Changes in business locations

Businesses that change their business locations may have a few — or many — changes that require a review of disaster recovery procedures. If a business is moving a short distance, make changes to the procedures just to reflect changes in the physical environment. But if your business moves a significant distance, you may need to change some of its suppliers (such as off-site media storage), as well as some of its technical architecture. (Moving gives you a good excuse to make changes to processes, which translates into changes in recovery procedures.)

Outsourcing and insourcing

When a part of an organization transitions from insourced functions to outsourced functions (or vice versa), you must change any DR plans related to the part of the organization that was insourced or outsourced. Here are some examples of outsourcing changes that require consideration:

✔ **Newly outsourced function:** If you have a DR plan for this function, the business needs to coordinate the development of recovery procedures with the new service provider.

✔ **Newly insourced function:** If you need a DR plan for an insourced function, develop new recovery procedures and train staff in the organization on those procedures.

✔ **Changes in dependencies:** Sometimes, a process's big picture changes in a way that alters dependencies on internal or external resources. For instance, if the DR plan for a process depends on the services provided by a department that's now outsourced (or insourced), you need to change the recovery plans to accommodate the changes introduced by the outsourcing or insourcing.

I don't have any magic formulas for how you need to change DR plans when insourcing or outsourcing occurs. You need to carefully analyze all affected business process and recovery plans, and make adjustments that permit the DR plans to work, even after the business makes the insourcing or outsourcing changes.

If your business switches an outsourcing partner, revisit any DR plans associated with the process(es) performed by that partner to make sure the services provided by the new partner are still compatible with existing DR plans.

Personnel changes

Organizations fire, hire, and rearrange their workforces on an almost daily basis. It's no wonder that companies don't publish their org charts as often as they used to: By the time the chart's printed, it requires another update. These types of changes have a bearing on DR planning, as I discuss in the following sections.

Organization chart changes

Even if no one leaves your organization and you don't bring anyone in, just changing the command and control structure may have some — perhaps a significant — impact on disaster recovery plans. Here are some examples (as told by a department manager):

✔ **That's not my department's job any more.** The experts who wrote disaster recovery plans and manned the recovery teams may suddenly be unavailable. You need to train new staff members, and you may have to edit the DR procedures.

✔ **They took my staff away.** See the preceding bullet.

✔ **That's my function now.** The opposite of the preceding bullets. A manager is newly responsible for a function covered by the DR plan. Your staff may need training, at least, and you may need to change your DR procedures to accommodate the staffing changes and possible process changes that result from the change in responsibility.

> ✔ **That dependent function is now out of my control.** Processes always have dependencies. A team that previously handled the DR plan for a business process is now split up. Can the former team still function as a team? Management needs to discuss these changes and what you need to change (if anything) in DR plans and procedures.

At the risk of sounding preachy, I want to say to managers at every level when facing the challenges of the reorganization of the month: Be responsible and figure it out. No one said it would be easy.

Relocation of key employees

Relocation involves an employee moving to a different town or city. To be more specific, one or more key personnel whom you depend on in a disaster situation now lives 20, 50, or 100 miles away. In a disaster, such personnel may not be able to travel this distance to be on-hand as part of a recovery team.

In the best-case scenario, you simply need to train personnel who live closer to business locations. In the worst case, you don't have any suitable trainees who live close enough to be there when a disaster strikes — a problem without an easy solution. Maybe you need to offer that employee who moved away more money to live closer, or perhaps you can hire another expert who lives close by (and hope he or she doesn't move away). Those pesky employees, always making life decisions that don't put work ahead of other considerations! (I'm kidding, of course — your employees are your most valuable resources.)

Telework

Technology and changing business attitudes have led to people living further and further away from their places of work, and many work permanently from home. This shift especially applies to information workers who are technically savvy and can use technology effectively from any location, whether in the office or hundreds of miles away.

Having access to the wider community of gifted workers can make finding new talent easier, and you can hire that talent without requiring that they live within a short drive of your business location. But the telework equation can go awry during a disaster. For many reasons, you may need those workers all on-site when disaster strikes — but if half of them live out of town, fat chance of that!

This situation does have an up side: If a regional disaster strikes your business location, many of your local employees may be wrapped up in the disaster, caring for family members or just trying to keep their belongings safe. But your out-of-town teleworkers may be unaffected by the disaster (because they live far enough away, out of the disaster zone), so they don't have any of the disaster-related distractions keeping them from working. As long as your business has enough infrastructure still working (such as VPN/remote access and telecommunications), your teleworkers can keep on working over the wire. They can carry out their usual duties, and perhaps they can even perform most or all of the procedures in a disaster recovery plan.

Staff attrition

It's a fact of life — people come and people go. You need to periodically train new personnel on disaster recovery procedures. Attrition can cause real problems if you no longer have any subject matter experts who can perform critical recovery functions. Smaller organizations that have only one expert in several subject areas can really suffer from such an extended absence. For this reason (and many other reasons), make your disaster recovery procedures highly detailed so non-experts can carry them out without fear of making deadly assumptions or mistakes.

Market changes

Whatever your business does, the market is always changing. Products and services grow and change, and the dynamics of the production of your company's goods and services never stand still. Sometimes, these changes are profound enough that your BIA results change, which impacts MTDs, RTOs, and RPOs, all of which can change your recovery procedures. The following sections look at some of these factors.

New production or delivery methodologies

The ways in which businesses such as yours develop and deliver goods and services change slowly over time, and sometimes bigger, more disruptive changes radically influence how you do what you do. Here are some examples:

- **Increased outsourcing:** As a flanking move, one competitor outsources a part of its operation to save costs, and other competitors follow suit to retain competitive parity. Outsourcing critical functions has a profound effect on DR plans and who carries them out.

- **More efficient production or delivery:** Innovation sometimes introduces new methods that make the production or delivery of products and services more efficient. Innovation changes the entire cost (and, often, pricing) structure for an organization, which in turn affects all of the MTD, RTO, and RPO formulas, affecting your overall BIA results.

These kinds of changes sometimes occur slowly, and at other times, quickly. Sometimes, you don't recognize them until well after the fact. Revisit the BIA every year or two, or more often in rapidly changing industries, just to make sure that the numbers still support the level of DR planning and testing activities currently taking place.

New competitors and changes in market share

Every time a competitor enters or leaves a market, or when any given organization has a significant change in market share, the economics of production and delivery change. These changes can greatly influence MTD, RTO, RPO, and BIA formulas and results.

Supply-chain changes

In complex business ecosystems, changes such as innovations, big price swings, or sea changes among partners or suppliers can profoundly influence your own business operations. For example, consider a big rise in energy costs due to hurricanes disrupting oil production and the ripple effect that those price increases have on many industries.

Sometimes, this influence is big enough to force you to revisit your BIA, MTD, RTO, and RPO figures. Sometimes, the changes increase the need for DR response capabilities, but at other times, those changes decrease the pressure to respond quickly to a disaster.

External changes

An entire class of changes can take place outside of the business. These kinds of changes can influence risk (up or down) or impact recovery procedures. The following sections by no means give you a complete list; other events and situations can also affect your DR plans and procedures.

Nearby construction

Major construction projects that take place near your business premises may change your business's risks in some way. For instance, if a factory is built nearby that handles hazardous materials, the chances that you may need to evacuate your own premises increases somewhat. If a new freeway is constructed near your business, you may have better transportation options, which may improve regional transportation capabilities during a disaster. If a facility that provides or promotes controversial services is built next door, you have an increased chance of nearby protests or civil unrest. Or, if that gasoline pipeline that passes your business is aging, a gas pipeline rupture and fire may soon happen too close to your business. Changes in nearby businesses may also affect crime rates.

Utilities changes

Changes in power grids, telecommunications, and natural gas delivery affect your organization. Over time, electric power and telecommunications may become less effective because of aging facilities, resulting in more frequent or lengthier outages.

Regulation

It may take just one significant event to motivate the government to pass a new law. Sometimes, these regulations indirectly influence your DR plan by changing the fundamental economics of businesses in a particular location or sector. These changes can, in turn, influence your DR plans.

Political events

Changes in local, regional, and national government leadership sometimes result in big changes in certain industries — some favorable and some not so favorable. The fortunes of businesses large and small sometimes hinge on elections and other political events. If I haven't struck a chord with you, perhaps your organization is immune to the political winds that blow. But will it always be?

Disasters

Besides the obvious and immediate effects on a business, disasters sometimes have longer-term effects in a region. Often, local or regional government invests in infrastructure that can better withstand future disasters. Sometimes, the changes that take place affect building codes and may even require your business to retrofit your safety systems.

Some of these changes can help a business by reducing the impact of future disasters, but they can also raise costs directly or indirectly.

Changes — some final words

Some changes, such as technology changes, require only changes in disaster recovery procedures. Other changes, such as mergers and acquisitions, are so profound that you must redo the entire Business Impact Analysis (BIA) to recalibrate business priorities.

I don't have a magic way to classify changes as big or small. But if your organization has instituted a DR plan steering committee, that group should make those judgments if and when needed. When the events discussed in this section occur, whoever in the organization has overall management responsibility for DR planning needs to enact reviews of BIAs, RTOs, RPOs, MTDs, and recovery procedures. These documents and figures probably won't get up on their own and begin updating themselves. Someone high up in the organization's management structure must have his or her finger on the pulse of the entire organization so the events discussed here can precipitate proper reviews in disaster planning and response.

Incorporating DR into Business Lifecycle Processes

Organizations use processes as a part of introducing changes into their processes. Yes, that was a recursive statement — using processes to change processes. More mature organizations use a specific set of procedures when making changes to its business processes.

But only some businesses consciously realize that they actually use a process to modify their processes. Many organizations change their processes spontaneously and without a lot of planning or analysis.

Regardless of whether your organization effectively manages its processes, consider the impact of every process change on your DR plan, and vice versa.

The following sections discuss three areas of lifecycle processes:

- Systems and services acquisition
- Systems development
- Business process engineering

When you make disaster recovery planning a part of these key processes, you make the organization naturally more proactive by including disaster recovery planning as a part of doing business, rather than as an add-on.

Systems and services acquisition

When an organization considers the acquisition of a new IT application or service provider, you need to devote a lot of thought and planning to ensure that the organization chooses the right application or service. Make sure the application or service has the right features and configurations that can meet your organization's needs.

Keep this key point in mind, particularly during the decision-making process for a new application or service: The application or service needs to support the needs of the business process(es) that it supports, not the other way around. Often, an organization makes a poor choice by selecting an application or service that doesn't meet the needs of the business; as a result, the business has to change its processes — sometimes in significant ways — so it can use the application or service.

DR planning is, first and foremost, a business activity in which business decision makers identify the most important business processes and how quickly the business must recover those processes if a disaster interrupts them. After you identify these key items (primarily your Recovery Time Objectives, or RTOs), the business needs to make all necessary changes to processes and IT systems to support those objectives.

Similarly, when the organization considers purchasing an application or service that supports a critical process, make sure the application or service meets established recovery needs. If you apply this principle to the systems and services acquisition process, whenever you acquire a new application or external service, you're on the right path to ensure that you can achieve your established DR objectives, particularly Recovery Time Objectives (RTOs) and Recovery Point Objectives (RPOs).

Meet these objectives in the systems and services acquisition process by incorporating your DR requirements into the complete set of requirements that you submit to each potential vendor. Then, when the vendors respond to each requirement, you know which vendors are more likely to deliver what you need. I discuss the development of requirements and standards in the section "Establishing DR Requirements and Standards," later in this chapter.

Systems development

Although the trend for software and systems development has leaned heavily towards acquiring applications, many organizations still opt to build some business applications themselves. Also, many organizations still use applications that they developed in the past (as long as a decade or more ago).

Organizations that purchase COTS (common off-the-shelf) applications still need to develop custom software so these applications can communicate with each other. Many organizations develop customizations for COTS applications so they can get needed custom reports or analytical databases that the applications themselves don't provide.

Whenever your organization embarks on new software development — whether for a complete application, or for customization or integration purposes — you need to make many decisions so the resulting software meets the organization's needs. Those needs include hardware and software standards, security and privacy, and disaster recovery.

Often, DR standards are manifested through standards for hardware, software, database, and application. This helps to ensure that any new applications run on systems for which the organization has already developed resilient architectures and recovery processes. For instance, if an organization has developed product standards such as Sun, Solaris, and Oracle for applications that require DR capabilities, the organization can more easily recover any additional applications, customizations, or integrations that also run on Sun, Solaris, and Oracle by using existing DR plans and procedures.

I discuss the development of specific requirements and standards in the section "Establishing DR Requirements and Standards," later in this chapter.

Business process engineering

Whether they use a formal lifecycle and methodology, or make spontaneous changes, organizations exercise *some* level of discipline in their practices of business process engineering (BPE). I've been in organizations at both ends (and in the middle) of the discipline-and-formality spectrum. Generally speaking, organizations that are newer or smaller tend to make process changes more spontaneously, without fully considering the consequences of the changes that they make. Probably the only advantage of living on the low end of the process maturity spectrum is that you can make changes quickly — even instantly! But, oftentimes, those changes have unintended and unwanted consequences that you discover later on.

Towards the formal and disciplined end of the spectrum, organizations spend more time analyzing, planning, and designing their business processes. Organizations that spend more time planning tend to have processes that better meet their needs. The downside to this level of discipline is that it takes more time to make changes in business processes. Some organizations can spend so much time analyzing changes that they never seem to actually make any changes. I like to call this phenomenon *analysis paralysis*.

Business process engineering is similar to software development: Done right, both have lifecycle processes that include concept, requirements, design, testing, implementation, and maintenance.

I emphasize the requirements part of business process engineering in this section. Simply put, when you develop requirements, you first need to write down all the necessary characteristics of a business process before you design and implement the process. Or, if you have an existing business process that needs changes, you still apply the requirements, making sure that changes still support those requirements.

Any time you develop or modify business processes, you must carefully analyze the consequences of the new or changed process. Business processes need to support business policies about security, privacy, and disaster recovery. Establish new and existing processes in such a way that you can recover and restart them during a disaster, possibly working with only inexperienced personnel. Thoroughly document the processes themselves, as well as all the procedures and tasks in them, and include recordkeeping tasks.

Establishing DR Requirements and Standards

Creating a library of formal requirements for IT development and procurement projects can really drive consistency into an organization's technical environments. Companies often develop such requirements in several categories, including the following:

- ✔ **Hardware:** Using computing hardware from as few vendors as possible reduces support costs.

- ✔ **Operating system (OS):** Basing everything on a common OS standard permits an organization to support more systems with fewer IT support staff.

- ✔ **Database:** Common database standards permit an organization to manage all of its corporate data as a more cohesive whole, not as separate, disconnected islands.

- ✔ **Application services:** Centrally managing functions such as authentication, messaging, and audit logging helps to streamline application management.

- ✔ **Network protocols:** Common routing, messaging, and management protocols simplify network architecture and management.

- ✔ **Service layer:** A distributed computing service layer, such as Service-Oriented Architecture (SOA), facilitates integration between applications.

- ✔ **Application components:** Common environments based on Rich Internet Application (RIA) technologies, such as AJAX, Adobe Flex, and Silverlight, can improve the user experience by making the application more visually appealing or easier to use.

And, starting in recent years, organizations are developing requirements and standards in two new areas:

- ✔ **Security:** Common security protocols, programs, and devices make protection and security management simpler than if different parts of an enterprise use disparate features and products.

- ✔ **Privacy:** Common means and methodologies within applications, databases, and operating systems for protecting employee and customer private information.

Organizations that realize the need for consistency in their environments for disaster recovery purposes can add a new category of requirements and standards:

✔ **Disaster recovery:** DR requirements and standards should include the selection of certain brands and technologies for new IT systems. The organization can then easily incorporate these new environments into existing DR plans without having to develop new procedure sets for each related technology.

Requirements and standards should lower support costs by driving the organization toward a more consistent environment, in which IT systems and applications use common standards, protocols, and technologies. This sameness provides a lower TCO (total cost of operations), making it easier for the organization to bring DR capabilities to more applications.

Without common standards and requirements, an organization's IT environment would resemble a computer museum that has one of everything. You'd need complete and separate sets of skills, procedures, DR plans, and support contracts for each system. I don't know many organizations that have that much money to spend on their systems.

A Multi-Tiered DR Standard Case Study

In this section, I describe a moderately complex DR standard that a hypothetical organization, a relatively large enterprise that has a multitude of IT systems and a mature DR plan, develops. In honor of one of my favorite cartoon characters, I call this organization Acme Enterprises — or Acme, for short.

Acme has many dozens of IT applications that support its various critical business operations. Acme has performed many Business Impact Analyses and has developed several DR architectures over the years.

Acme settled on three sets of technology standards that it aligns with its RTO and RPO (Recovery Time Objective and Recovery Point Objective) groupings. Acme establishes its standards as follows:

✔ **Tier 1 DR standard:** The highest resilience that provides the fastest recovery time, almost immediate

✔ **Tier 2 DR standard:** Provides recovery time measured in hours

✔ **Tier 3 DR standard:** Provides recovery time measured in days

The three standards in the preceding list align with the three levels of recovery requirements that support virtually all business functions that require DR support.

Table 11-1 describes the three DR standards established by Acme in more detail.

Table 11-1	Acme Enterprises Tiered DR Standards		
Specification	*Tier 1 DR Standard*	*Tier 2 DR Standard*	*Tier 3 DR Standard*
The RTO (Recovery Time Objective)	3 minutes	8 hours	5 business days
The RPO (Recovery Point Objective)	1 minute	15 minutes	8 hours
Hardware manufactured by	Sun (servers) and Hitachi (Storage Area Network, or SAN)	Sun (servers) and Hitachi (SAN)	Sun or HP
Operating system	Solaris	Solaris	Linux
Database management system	Oracle	Oracle	MySQL
Web server	BEA	BEA or Apache	Apache
Clustering system	Solaris World-Wide Cluster	Solaris Metro or World-Wide Cluster	None
Data recovery	From mirror	From replicated data or backup tapes	From backup tapes
Testing requirements	Paper testing (whenever documentation is updated) and cutover testing (monthly)	Paper testing (whenever documentation is updated) and cutover testing (monthly)	Paper testing (quarterly), walkthrough testing (quarterly or after any major upgrade), cutover testing (annually)

Business requirements drive Acme's DR standards, specifically its RTO and RPO, not the other way around (some organizations fall into the trap of letting their technology and DR capabilities define business requirements).

Systems that meet Tier 1 SR standards support Acme's most critical business processes. Acme has written a common set of DR procedures for Tier 1 systems; those procedures for recovering servers and data are virtually identical for all Tier 1 applications.

Similarly, systems that meet either Tier 2 or Tier 3 standards support Acme's important (but not critical) business processes. And like Tier 1, the recovery procedures for Tier 2 are practically identical to each other, as are the Tier 3 recovery procedures. In fact, the only variants in the recovery procedures within any of the three tiers are those steps specific to individual applications. The recovery procedures within each tier at the hardware, operating system, and database management layers are identical.

Acme developed a three-tier DR standard, instead of using just one standard (the Tier 1 standard) and making all systems that need disaster recovery conform to it, mainly because of cost. Building Tier 1 systems costs more than Tier 2 or Tier 3 systems because Tier 1 systems include clustering and mirroring components (which add costs). Systems that you can recover in days rather than minutes don't need to have the same expensive components that Tier 1 systems need to produce their near-real-time recovery. Acme has a lot of applications that require varying levels of recoverability, and it made sense to stratify DR needs into the three standards that they developed. This standards structure made documentation and training far easier than if each system had its own unique recovery procedures, RTOs, and RPOs.

Developing business-driven standards not only provides consistency that lowers TCO (total cost of operations), the organization also gets disaster recovery capabilities that actually meet business needs.

Maintaining DR Documentation

The consummation of disaster recovery planning is the completed disaster recovery plan and recovery procedures. Those written documents are the culmination of a great deal of effort that has a single purpose — the survival of the organization in the face of a disaster.

In the following sections, I discuss many facets of DR documents, including

- How to manage documents
- How to update documents
- How to publish and distribute documents

Many people look at documentation as a necessary but altogether evil pastime. Although it may be mundane at times, it's the central fixture of disaster recovery planning. You have to get it right because the survival of your organization depends on it!

Managing DR documents

Document management is a lifecycle proposition. Given the document-centric nature of disaster recovery planning, you need to keep those DR documents locked up safe and allow only authorized and qualified individuals to touch them. Seriously — treat high-value documents such as Business Impact Analyses (BIAs) and DR procedures as reverently as software source code.

Protecting DR documents

Protect the official DR source documents so only authorized people can access them. Ideally, you should keep them in a *vault* — a database that's a part of a document management system. Authorized people must identify themselves by logging in before they can perform any operations on any DR documents.

Managing official DR documents

You need to manage official DR documents, including Business Impact Analyses, DR procedures, and many more, through manual or automated means. The document management process should include these basic functions:

- ✔ **Check out:** When someone needs to make changes to a document, they first have to check out the document from the doc management system. After someone checks out a document, the doc management system optionally blocks others from checking out the same document until the person who first checked it out returns it. Whether you program the doc management system to block others from checking out the document is a policy decision that you make when you set up that system.

- ✔ **Review:** When a person makes changes to a document, he or she can circulate it for review by others in the organization. A full-featured doc management system may handle this review automatically, capturing comments and perhaps even proposing changes.

- ✔ **Check in:** After the document author receives and incorporates comments from others, he or she can finalize the document and check it back in to the system. When a person tries to check in a document, most doc management systems query that person for several pieces of information:

    - **Change reason:** A few words describing the change, such as ERP Upgrade or Migration to Hitachi SAN.

    - **Change description:** A longer description of the change — a couple of sentences.

    - **Author:** Name of the person who made the change, usually the person checking in the document.

- **Version number:** Some document management systems create and increment version numbers automatically, others don't.

- **Approved by:** The name of the person or group who approved the changes.

- **Reviewed by:** The name of the person(s) who reviewed the document.

✔ **Update:** Sometimes tied to check in, an update causes a newly checked-in document to become the new official document. You can think of updating as a make current function that identifies a version of a document as the official version.

✔ **Version history:** A function that permits the user (not just anyone, but someone authorized to access the document management system) to view information about each prior version of a document.

✔ **Retrieve older version:** Doc management systems permit an authorized user to retrieve an older version of a document.

Doc management systems have many other functions associated with the management of documents under their control. The preceding list describes only the common functions that these systems use.

If your organization doesn't have a formal document management system, you can perform these steps manually by storing versions of documents on a file server and using spreadsheets or other means for tracking document activities such as check ins, check outs, and updates.

Document content

Any official documentation should have a consistent style and appearance, DR documentation included. Elements such as headers, footers, versions, and modification history are all vital to the integrity of DR documents. I discuss this topic fully in Chapter 9.

Updating DR documents

When you make the decision to update a DR document, you assign someone to actually perform this task.

Updating a DR procedure involves more than just editing the changes into the document. The document editor needs to perform some tasks, or read system or process documentation, to understand exactly how to change the content in the procedure. He or she might need to test the procedure on a test system to make sure the document describes the procedure accurately. He or she might need to include screen shots and other actions for clarity.

In terms of the actual document editing, the word processing program will need to be configured to show the changes made to the document. In Microsoft Word, this feature is called *Track Changes;* in FrameMaker, it's called *Track Edited Text.* This important feature permits reviewers (either other staff members or outsiders) to easily see precisely what changes have been made to a document. <u>This is an example of a sentence that's been added.</u> ~~This sentence has been removed.~~

Highlighting changes that are made to a document does have a disadvantage: Reviewers might focus too much on the changes and lose sight of the entire procedure. Document reviewers need to understand their responsibilities and know that they're checking not just for grammar, but for accuracy. And who knows — they might even be the ones who perform the procedure in an actual disaster!

When the document editor finishes making changes to the DR document, he or she can perform whatever check-in and updating tasks your organization uses.

After changes have been made to a DR procedure, you may need to test that procedure. Someone in the organization needs to track these updates and make decisions about when you need to test the recovery procedure if significant changes are made. A DR program doesn't run itself — it needs some management oversight so important activities don't fall through the cracks.

Set up a document review calendar that includes some sort of reminders for staff members to review documents in the DR library. Here's a suggested calendar for review:

- ✔ **Emergency contact lists — monthly:** Attrition and organization changes may happen frequently enough that you need to work hard to keep these lists fresh. Sometimes, people simply change their office, mobile, and home phone numbers, as well.

- ✔ **Recovery procedures — quarterly:** Little and big changes in applications and supporting environments may affect the accuracy of recovery documents.

- ✔ **Architecture documents — quarterly:** Document changes in application and infrastructure architecture so recovery personnel can become familiar with the architecture supporting each application's native environment.

- ✔ **Business Impact Analysis (BIA) — annually:** Changes in business priorities and market conditions may influence recovery objectives, such as your Recovery Time Objective (RTO) and Recovery Point Objective (RPO).

Publishing and distributing documents

After you update DR documents, particularly recovery procedure documents, key personnel need to know about these changes.

For most ordinary documents, you simply update the document and make it available via your business's customary means (a file server or portal, for instance). But DR documents, especially procedures, aren't ordinary documents. You need to do more than simply publish them and let people download them at their leisure. The following sections explain.

Registered users

Send all disaster recovery documents' updates to all registered users via e-mail or whatever means are right for your organization.

Disaster recovery procedure documents (as well as others that I mention in the following list) are so important that members of recovery teams need to have their own soft copies and maybe even hardcopies.

Someone needs to actively manage the list of recovery team members and others who need the newest versions of recovery procedures and other documents. Tracking users is tedious and mundane, but the survival of the organization may depend on it.

Here are the documents that you need to publish and send to registered users:

- ✔ **All recovery procedure documents:** 'Nuff said.

- ✔ **Updated architecture documents:** Descriptions and diagrams about how individual applications, networks, systems, and the entire environment is put together and how it works.

- ✔ **Emergency contact lists:** Essential for all recovery personnel, particularly in disasters in which communications are affected.

- ✔ **Communications procedures:** If the DR team has developed procedures for emergency communications, you need to keep this document fresh and in everyone's hands.

- ✔ **Wallet cards:** If you maintain wallet cards with essential contact info, you must send new versions with updated names and contact info to registered users whenever you update those cards.

- ✔ **Indexes to more documents:** The organization needs to maintain copies of documentation that hardware and software vendors produce so recovery teams can have easy access to product manufacturers' documentation, even during a disaster when communications may not be so good.

Recordkeeping

Keep detailed records about all document updates, including the individual names of people who send hardcopies (or CD-ROM, or whatever form) to whom and when. These and other records that an organization's DR program produce are vital, and you must care for them well. Keeping accurate records helps to ensure that DR documents are well managed and distributed to all the right people. Ensure that these records are always up to date, accurate, and available to everyone who's authorized to access them by using good document management practices, as well as security and backups.

Training Response Teams

You may have noticed that this section is short, and I have a good reason for it. But I'm not going to give the secret away just yet. You need to understand enough about DRP so you don't have to come running back to this book every time you need an answer (but I also don't want this book to gather dust on your shelf — that would be an equally tragic outcome).

Over in Chapter 10, I discuss testing DR plans. Done properly, performing those tests can take care of the training issue, all by itself.

Types of training

Company staff have several levels of training available:

- ✔ **Paper testing:** Circulate recovery procedures to a fairly wide audience. Include all the personnel who are likely perform the actual recovery effort. By carefully reading and testing the recovery documents, they mentally step through the recovery procedures.

- ✔ **Walkthroughs:** You can use these group events to indoctrinate new staff members and refresh existing staff with disaster recovery procedures. New faces can introduce new knowledge and wisdom, which benefits all parties.

- ✔ **Parallel tests:** There's nothing like hands-on testing to keep recovery personnel familiar with recovery procedures. New staff members benefit from parallel testing by observing more experienced staffers in action.

- ✔ **Cutover tests:** A cutover test is a kind of controlled crisis — or, at least, a scheduled crisis in which the stakes are high. Personnel can benefit from the intensity of the experience.

Practice makes perfect. If you carefully and properly choose the participants for each type of test, simply performing the test provides the participants with the necessary training.

Indoctrinating new trainees

Train new employees in the organization, particularly those who are likely to be on recovery teams, as soon as possible. I suggest the following scheme for getting new staff members up to speed on recovery procedures:

- **Procedure review — week one:** Make one of the earliest assignments for new staff members a review of all DR recovery procedure documents.

- **Business Impact Analysis (BIA):** Have new staff members read through the BIA to help them see the big picture about the business's critical processes.

- **Walkthroughs:** Invite new staff members to walkthroughs, even if they're only observers. Observing a walkthrough exposes them to the thought behind the BIA and the recovery plans and procedures.

- **Simulations:** See what kind of management and leadership skills your new staff members may possess.

- **Parallel and cutover tests:** Involving new staff members in these tests spreads the experience around. You never know who'll be available to help out in an actual disaster, so the more people who have hands-on experience, the better.

- **Formal goals and milestones:** If you incorporate involvement in all levels of testing as part of employee goals and milestones, you give new employees additional incentive to get involved and up to speed. You also send a message that the organization is serious about disaster recovery planning.

- **Formal and informal training:** Introduce new employees to the culture of disaster recovery planning in the organization by setting up formal training classes and brown-bag lunch events.

The activities in the preceding list can help influence new employees early, and many organizations make preparation for disaster a top priority.

You probably don't need to develop an entire curriculum for training potential recovery personnel. Just include them in all of the review, revision, and testing activities that need to take place, and they can get their training through OJT (on-the-job training).

Chapter 12

Understanding the Role of Prevention

Throughout a disaster recovery planning project, and perpetually there-after, the DR planning team needs to continually watch for opportunities that can help prevent disasters or lessen their impact on the organization.

"An ounce of prevention is worth a pound of cure," the old saying goes. Although he was a prolific inventor, Benjamin Franklin couldn't have envisioned the Internet when he first penned that phrase. In disaster recovery planning, prevention is key — but it's often overlooked.

You have many places to look for prevention opportunities:

✔ Facilities

✔ Processes

✔ Technology

✔ Personnel

✔ Security

✔ Resilient architecture

The opportunities you find may not necessarily be huge, but smaller things often reduce risk in some way.

This chapter focuses on reducing risk where you find it to minimize the effects of disasters. In some cases, you can even prevent disasters. I'm talking about the man-made kind of disasters, of course — I don't want you to start thinking that I have a formula for preventing hurricanes, earthquakes, volcanoes, or floods. Perhaps a more accurate title for this chapter would be "Understanding the Role of Risk Reduction," but I still like the term *prevention* better because this chapter talks about preventing the effects of disasters.

Here are some disaster prevention rules of thumb:

- ✔ You can't prevent natural disasters, but you can take measures to reduce their effects.
- ✔ You can prevent some man-made disasters, and you can also take measures to reduce their effects.

As long as you understand these principles, you're on the right track.

This chapter gives you a different view of the same material you can find elsewhere in this book. Most of this book talks about analysis and response because most people think in terms of actions during a disaster. However, prevention is a worthwhile destination in disaster recovery planning, so I dedicate this entire chapter to it.

Preventing Facilities-Related Disasters

Today's most modern and secure Internet Data Centers (IDCs) are practically fortresses in their own right. *Internet Data Centers* are commercial server hosting facilities that house customers' Internet-reachable servers. The data center operators have a good reason for the security they use: They're reducing many types of risks that, left unchecked, could precipitate man-made disasters. And many of the features of these hardened data centers also help to reduce risks associated with natural disasters, as well.

These facilities are expensive to build because both their construction methods and the special equipment they use aren't cheap. You can often justify these costs by the very high availability and stability that these facilities provide.

Organizations don't need to be Fortune 20 companies to be able to afford such facilities. You don't need to build one; instead, you can rent as much or as little space as you need. Indeed, hundreds of such facilities exist throughout the world. You can rent as much as hundreds of square feet, or as little as 1U of rack space (a unit, or U, of rack space is 1.75 inches in height). Either way, applications running on equipment in such a facility have the potential for extremely high availability because of the supporting facilities, such as Uninterruptible Power Supplies (UPSs), generators, and so on.

The facility-related areas in which you can reduce risk are

- ✔ Site selection
- ✔ Fire prevention
- ✔ HVAC (Heating, Ventilation, and Air Conditioning) redundancy
- ✔ Power system redundancy
- ✔ Protection from civil unrest and war
- ✔ Avoidance of industrial hazards

I discuss all the areas in the preceding list and the secondary effects of facilities-related disasters in the following sections.

Site selection

A building's destiny is heavily governed by its location. A building's location, relative to a number of natural hazards, plays a major role in whether the building and its contents and occupants may be subjected to the effects of natural events.

Here are some of the natural events that good site selection can mitigate:

- ✔ **Hurricanes:** To reduce the effects of hurricanes, locate sites away from coastlines and on high ground in hurricane-prone areas. If your organization fears the damaging and disrupting effects of hurricanes, don't locate data processing facilities near hurricane-prone areas. You may need to locate such facilities hundreds of miles away from office locations. Figure 12-1 shows Atlantic hurricanes from the 2005 hurricane season, which included Hurricane Katrina. Use maps covering several decades of hurricanes to assess hurricane risks if your organization is located in the southeastern United States.

- ✔ **Tornadoes:** Although you can't absolutely avoid tornadoes, organizations can choose to locate offices and data processing facilities away from the highest-risk areas. You can at least figure out the risks of being located in tornado-prone areas and how you can minimize damage and loss of human life. Figure 12-2 shows those high-risk areas within the continental United States.

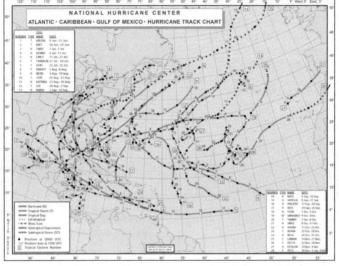

Figure 12-1:
The 2005
U.S.
hurricane
season
chart.

Source: Wikimedia

Figure 12-2:
A United
States
tornado risk
map.

Source: U.S. National Oceanic and Atmospheric Administration (NOAA)

✓ **Floods:** Usually associated with heavy rainfall and spring runoff, but also connected to catastrophes such as levee and dam failures and natural events such as hurricanes. Floods cause significant damage around the world each year. In the U.S., you can get Flood Insurance Rate Maps (FIRMs) that show the statistical likelihood of flooding in specific areas. The U.S. Federal Emergency Management Agency (FEMA) publishes these maps, and the insurance industry uses them to set rates for flood insurance. Figure 12-3 shows a FIRM for a small part of New Orleans, Louisiana.

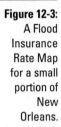

Figure 12-3:
A Flood Insurance Rate Map for a small portion of New Orleans.

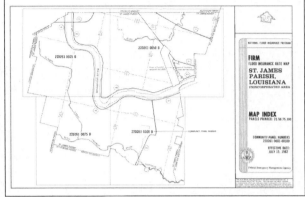

Source: U.S. Federal Emergency Management Agency (FEMA)

✔ **Earthquakes:** Many regions of the world experience frequent earthquakes, usually spaced years or decades apart, and earthquakes are difficult to predict. Larger earthquakes cause significant damage to buildings, infrastructure, and communications and can result in major loss of life. Areas prone to earthquakes have strict building codes to reduce injuries and potential damage to buildings. The Global Seismic Hazard Map, which illustrates relative risk of damage from earthquakes, is shown in Figure 12-4.

✔ **Tsunamis:** Great ocean waves that strike coastlines around the world, *tsunamis* are usually caused by undersea earthquakes that involve a significant displacement of the ocean floor. You usually get only a few hours' warning (if you get any at all), which gives you too little time for even emergency salvage. The December 26, 2004 tsunami in the Indian Ocean that resulted in over an estimated 200,000 deaths and 1.6 million displaced persons has resulted in a resurgence of interest, awareness, the development of warning systems, and an effort to identify high risk areas around the world.

✔ **Volcanic eruptions:** A volcanic eruption is often — but not always — preceded by some warning. An erupting volcano emits molten lava and clouds of ash that damage property, claim lives, and can cause widespread disruption over vast areas. The 1980 eruption of Mount St. Helens in the United States created an ash fall that plunged many cities, even those located hundreds of miles away, into total darkness and paralyzed transportation, public services, and emergency services for days. Figure 12-5 shows the Mount St. Helens volcanic eruption in 1980.

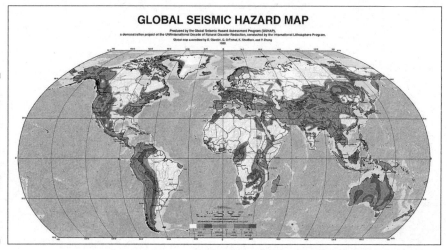

Source: Global Seismic Hazard Assessment Program, United Nations

Figure 12-4:
The Global Seismic Hazard Map shows relative risks from earthquakes around the world.

Source: U.S. Geological Survey (USGS)

Figure 12-5:
The 1980 Mount St. Helens volcano eruption.

The most significant volcanoes in the world (classified as such because of their history of large, destructive eruptions and proximity to populated regions) are

- **Avachinsky-Koryaksky:** Kamchatka, Russia
- **Colima:** Jalisco, Mexico
- **Galeras:** Nariño, Colombia
- **Mauna Loa:** Hawaii, USA
- **Mount Etna:** Sicily, Italy
- **Mount Merapi:** Central Java, Indonesia
- **Mount Nyiragongo:** Democratic Republic of the Congo
- **Mount Rainier:** Washington, USA
- **Mount Unzen:** Nagasaki Prefecture, Japan
- **Sakurajima:** Kagoshima Prefecture, Japan
- **Santa Maria and Santiaguito:** Guatemala
- **Santorini:** Cyclades, Greece
- **Taal Volcano:** Luzon, Philippines
- **Teide:** Canary Islands, Spain
- **Ulawun:** New Britain, Papua New Guinea
- **Vesuvius:** Naples, Italy

If your organization is located near any of these volcanoes, you need to do additional risk analysis to ensure that your DR plans adequately address the risks associated with the nearby volcano.

✔ **Wildfires:** In many locales, wildfires are a significant problem and result in evacuations, road closures, airport closures, and (occasionally) property damage.

✔ **Landslides and avalanches:** The sudden downhill movement of rock, earth, snow, or ice can strike without warning, damaging buildings and transportation systems, and claiming lives. Although you can't really prevent landslides and avalanches, an organization can take care to not locate its premises in a potential landslide or avalanche path. However, a landslide or avalanche that occurs even a great distance away from business facilities can disrupt transportation and communications systems.

Each kind of natural hazard presents its own set of risks, as well as measures that you can take to reduce the effects of the events if and when they occur. Each type of hazard requires creative planning if you want to adequately mitigate the risk. To mitigate the risks associated with natural hazards that can create extensive regional disruption, you need to locate alternate facilities far enough away that they don't become involved in the same natural event. For instance, placing an alternate processing center 300 miles away but on the same earthquake fault line just isn't prudent risk mitigation!

Preventing fires

When fire suppression systems and fire fighting crews fail to extinguish a fire in a business location (or simply take too long to extinguish the fire), a disaster results if critical business functions are affected. Preventing fires gives you perhaps the most notable means of actually preventing a disaster.

Fire damage

Fires destroy and damage buildings and their contents, and claim thousands of lives each year throughout the world. Fires cause damage in several ways:

- **Injuries and death:** People who are trapped in burning buildings are often injured or killed by flames, smoke, or the collapse of the building itself.

- **Direct destruction:** Fire itself damages or destroys flammable materials, including business records, furniture, and equipment.

- **Smoke damage:** The smoke from a fire can significantly damage the contents of a building, even areas the fire doesn't reach. Smoke inhalation is a major cause of death in fires.

- **Water damage:** Water is the most common agent for extinguishing a fire in business locations. Usually used in heavy volumes, the water used to fight a fire is almost as damaging to business equipment and records as a flood.

- **Extinguishment operations:** To reach a fire in a building, fire fighters often have to cut through roofs, ceilings, walls, and floors.

Also, when a building experiences a fire, the local fire marshal or other local official often closes the entire building until the fire marshal can complete a damage assessment and forensic investigation. If you can't enter a building, not being able to access business assets can lead to a disaster!

Whenever an organization analyzes the potential detective and preventive measures for fires, it must give human lives the highest priority over all business assets and other concerns.

Fire prevention

Many locales have building codes that require fire detection and suppression equipment. Fire marshals and other inspectors regularly examine work locations to make sure you have these systems in place and working, and that you're not performing unsafe practices, such as blocking emergency exits and exit corridors, or accumulating flammable materials (such as empty boxes).

Often, inspections include tests of fire detection and alarm systems to make sure they'll properly function if a fire occurs.

Many organizations purchase a fire insurance policy, which compensates the organization if a fire damages its building and equipment. Often, the fire insurance company conducts its own inspections to make sure your facility has a reasonably low risk of fire. A fire insurance company also notes the distance between the nearest fire station and the business location. Disaster recovery planners should also make note of the closest fire station in their risk assessments so they can know and mitigate fire-related risks appropriately.

In areas that commonly experience wildfires, fire marshals require residents and businesses to clear flammable materials from around the outside of their structures, to reduce the likelihood of property damage from wildfires.

Fire detection

Because fires can cause such heavy damage to a business and its assets, you can best reduce the effects of a fire by detecting it as early as possible. Detecting a fire in its earliest stages can more effectively suppress it and disrupt your business less, well before an actual fire erupts and escalates into a more serious event.

Several types of smoke and fire detectors are available:

- Infrared smoke detectors
- Ionization smoke detectors
- Aspiration smoke detectors
- Heat detectors

I discuss fire detection apparatus more fully in Chapter 6.

Fire alarms

Alarm systems consist of loud bells, sirens, alarms, and annunciators that alert personnel when a smoke or fire detector somewhere in the building detects a fire. Because fire can spread quickly under certain conditions, the primary purpose of fire alarms is to alert people that they need to evacuate the building immediately. Fire alarms do little to protect business equipment and property — but the most important things in the building are the people!

Fire alarms often connect electrically to local fire departments so rescue personnel are quickly alerted when your alarm system detects a fire. Although this connection usually saves only a few minutes, those minutes can make a huge difference in the amount of property damage your organization suffers, as well as injuries to personnel.

Fire suppression

Many buildings have automatic fire suppression in the form of water sprinklers in work areas. Rooms containing IT equipment often use more sophisticated inert gas fire-suppression systems because water can easily damage computers. Often, these suppression systems connect directly to alarm systems, so fire suppression can begin immediately and automatically.

Most businesses also have hand-held fire extinguishers that office workers can use to fight small fires before fire crews arrive. Using these extinguishers can prevent a small fire from growing and threatening an entire facility.

HVAC failures

Although heating and air conditioning primarily provide only human comfort in most parts of the world, air conditioning is a necessity for the survival and health of IT equipment. In data processing facilities that house large collections of IT equipment, the failure of a central air conditioning system can cause permanent damage to IT equipment in minutes.

When air conditioning (A/C) failure occurs in facilities that have no backup A/C system, IT personnel have barely enough time to power everything down before damage occurs. Often, personnel don't have time for an orderly shutdown of systems. If the systems support critical and time-sensitive business processes, you need one or more backup A/C systems. Larger facilities that have vast numbers of IT systems usually rely on a larger number of smaller (but still quite large) A/C systems, which provides more flexibility for scheduled maintenance.

You can prevent IT equipment failures related to too-high temperatures (which can lead to a disaster) through good capacity planning and design. You always want enough HVAC capacity to meet your cooling needs — no matter what.

Chapter 6 covers HVAC concerns in more detail.

Power-related failures

IT equipment is gluttonous when it comes to electric power. IT equipment wants its power steady and clean, and that equipment is intolerant of bumps, spikes, brownouts, and other mishaps that occur in power systems. Spikes, surges, and other unwanted noise in incoming power often can damage IT equipment. Fixing that damage can require costly and time-consuming repairs and equipment replacement. Businesses that rely on IT systems to support critical, time-sensitive business processes can't tolerate these events.

You can almost entirely eliminate disasters caused by power-related anomalies through proper prevention techniques. You can prevent these three types of unwanted events:

✔ **Noise (spikes, surges, and so on):** You can prevent these potentially damaging effects by using Uninterruptible Power Supplies (UPSs), which clean incoming electric power and feed very clean, noise-free power to IT equipment.

✔ **Short-term outages:** You can prevent power failures that last only a few minutes by using UPSs that usually contain banks of batteries. With this battery backup, UPSs can generate electricity even when utility power has failed. Usually, UPS systems can generate power for a portion of an hour; but you can find some UPS systems equipped with larger numbers of batteries, which permit the UPS to generate power for up to several hours.

✔ **Long-term outages:** You need an electric generator for facilities that need to continue processing even when utility power has been down for more than an hour. The amount of fuel you store on-site, plus any deliveries you can get, determine the amount of time that electric generators can provide electricity. Most facilities store no more than seven days worth of fuel. In most parts of the world, you very rarely experience an outage of seven days or more.

UPS systems and electric generators work together to provide continuous electric power to processing facilities. Neither can do the job alone:

✔ **UPS systems:** Generally can't deliver power for more than a portion of an hour. You need a generator to provide long-term electricity.

✔ **Generator:** Requires a few minutes for startup and stabilization before it can begin delivering electric power. You need a UPS to fill the gap.

I cover power supply protection more fully in Chapter 6.

Protection from civil unrest and war

Protests, strikes, and general mayhem sometimes get out of hand. Civil and political events can incite large numbers of people to take to the streets and damage everything in their path. Notable riots in recent history include

✔ **1992 Los Angeles riots:** Thousands of people protested the jury's verdict in a high-profile criminal case and went on a rampage that resulted in 53 deaths, widespread looting, and the burning of dozens of businesses and cars over a period of four days.

✔ **2005 civil unrest in France:** The deaths of two teenagers sparked a three-month period of civil unrest that resulted in the burning of many public buildings and almost 10,000 cars. Over 2,900 suspects were arrested.

These two events, and dozens of others, have disrupted businesses, some to the point of failure. But, in addition to large-scale civil protest, small groups and even individuals can wreak havoc in many ways, including by using vehicles as weapons. You can take some measures to help reduce the risks associated with mob violence:

- ✔ **Put up barricades and fencing.** Prevent unwanted people from approaching buildings and personnel.

- ✔ **Use shatter-proof windows or no windows at all.** Well, this measure won't make for very attractive buildings, but it's hard to throw a stone or a brick through a solid wall.

- ✔ **Locate away from large cities.** Not that civil disturbances don't happen in smaller communities, but some organizations consider this measure because it seems such violence occurs less often in smaller communities.

- ✔ **Keep a low profile.** Keeping a low profile means different things to different companies. Maybe you don't put up big signs or place advertisements that could incite strong emotional outbursts. Maybe you locate yourself away from other businesses.

All bets are off when it comes to war. In warfare, fighting factions have weapons that can inflict damage from great distances, so measures such as fencing and stronger windows don't help you much. If your business is in a war zone, try to locate it in an area that's not on someone's list of targets. And keep your passports nearby and your other options open.

Avoiding industrial hazards

You can control a lot of things about your organization — where it's located, for instance. Some of the hazards that can turn into disasters have a lot to do with where a business is located. In the section "Site selection," earlier in this chapter, I discuss floods, tornadoes, hurricanes, volcanoes, and other hazards. In this section, I discuss man-made hazards:

- ✔ **Nearby facilities with hazardous materials:** If your organization is close to a facility such as a chemical facility, oil refinery, munitions depot, nuclear power plant, mine, or heavy manufacturing facility (this is by no means a complete list!), you may need to evacuate your business if something goes amiss in a nearby facility.

- ✔ **Hazardous materials in motion:** Nearby railroads and petrochemical pipelines may also have their mishaps, resulting in damage to and evacuation of your business location. Figure 12-6 shows a train derailment that included a fire and a chlorine gas leak.

I certainly don't include a comprehensive set of examples in the preceding list. But maybe the examples I do have can help you become more aware of the risks associated with nearby industrial activities.

Figure 12-6:
This train
derailment
disrupted
nearby
businesses.

Source: Wikimedia Commons

Preventing secondary effects of facilities disasters

I feel the need to slip in some recommendations about backup tapes:

- ✔ Don't store backup tapes in even the most secure processing facility.
- ✔ Use the services of a secure off-site media storage provider.

Even the most secure processing facility is vulnerable to incidents that can destroy both servers and backup media — fires, floods, accidental discharge of fire retardant, hazardous material spills (think about that large UPS battery room), earthquakes, and don't forget malicious people who can do serious damage with a *degausser* (a device used to erase backup tapes) or a big hammer. As long as you store backup media close to the systems they back up, you reduce your ability to recover applications in another location.

Preventing Technology-Related Disasters

As long as you have IT systems — and other electrical and mechanical apparatus — that support business processes, you may have disasters caused by their breakdown. You need to design, build, and maintain the systems that support your processes to help keep those systems from failing.

These two principles can help you understand this concept:

- ✔ Failures happen, and you can't absolutely prevent them.
- ✔ Don't allow failures to cause a full-scale disaster.

Dealing with system failures

Anyone who's been in IT for any length of time has seen many kinds of IT failures that cause applications to fail. Here are some examples:

- ✔ **Hard drive failure:** For one reason or another, hard drives just stop working. Long ago, you had to worry about head crashes, but you don't hear about those kinds of failures any more. Hard drives still do fail sometimes, however.

- ✔ **Power supply failure:** Power supplies generate a lot of heat, and this heat can stress components to the breaking point.

- ✔ **Circuit board failure:** Motherboards, controllers, and network adaptors all have a finite life span.

- ✔ **Cabling failure:** Although it happens less often than in decades past, cabling still occasionally goes bad.

- ✔ **Operating system and software bugs:** These days, operating system, database, server, and application software is unbelievably complex. Sometimes, an organization has the bad luck to present a unique and deadly combination of circumstances that the software didn't anticipate, causing that software to malfunction. The worst kind of failure occurs when you don't know of the failure right away and some form of damage slowly spreads through your data.

- ✔ **Data corruption:** Sometimes, you simply can't access or create data, usually because of a failure elsewhere (in hardware or software).

Systems don't run forever. The following sections discuss ways to keep the failures from the preceding list (and others) from turning into full-scale disasters.

Minimizing hardware and software failures

Software and hardware failures aren't wholly preventable, but you should do all that's reasonable to prevent failures while still preparing for them. The following list contains many measures you can take to prepare for hardware and software failures when they do happen:

✔ **Perform regular data backups.** Copying data from main hard drives to other hard drives or backup tape is the best insurance in cases of hard drive or related failure.

✔ **Perform regular data restores.** Just because you can perform data backups doesn't mean you can get that data back! Test your organization's ability to restore data at least once per month to make sure that backups are working and that you can actually recover data from backup tapes.

✔ **Keep spare systems.** In some cases, you might more easily recover an application or database onto a different system than diagnose or repair a problem on a primary server. You might be able to use development servers, test servers, and servers for less-critical applications as spare systems.

✔ **Keep spare parts.** Having spare disk drives, memory, motherboards, and power supplies gives you more choices when you experience a hardware failure.

✔ **Have service manuals.** You never know who may need to open up one of your servers or storage systems. The usual experts may not be around when you need them.

Pros and cons of a monoculture

In computer terms, a *monoculture* is an environment whose systems are all of the same operating system and hardware type. Having a network and server monoculture has certain advantages and disadvantages. Table 12-1 outlines monoculture pros and cons.

Table 12-1	Pros and Cons of a Monoculture
Pros	*Cons*
Lower support costs	Dependent on a single supplier
Lower training costs	A software bug or malfunction affects all systems
Ability to cannibalize other systems for spare parts	Security vulnerability affects all systems

A monoculture isn't altogether bad, and you don't necessarily need to avoid it. It has many obvious advantages. But monocultures do have certain risks that you need to analyze and deal with.

Years ago, some New York-based investment banks that were concerned about monocultures built interesting application architectures. One such organization built an active/active cluster by using two different types of transaction servers that recorded the purchase and sale of investment securities — these servers handled tens or hundreds of thousands of transactions per day. The cluster consisted of two sets of servers:

- ✔ IBM running the AIX OS with a DB2 database
- ✔ Sun running the Solaris OS with an Oracle database

The organization was so concerned about the risk of a software bug taking down their entire cluster that they built their cluster with entirely different hardware and software. Thus, the organization got peace of mind, knowing if a bug or malfunction occurred in one server's hardware, software, or database, that bug or malfunction appearing in the other system would be extremely unlikely.

Although you can't prevent failures, you can prevent those failures from escalating into disasters.

Building a resilient architecture

The suggestions listed in the section "Minimizing hardware and software failures," earlier in this chapter, may work for processes that have an RTO (Recovery Time Objective) of a day or more. But many business processes can't be without their supporting IT systems for more than a few minutes. In these cases, you need a resilient architecture — one that can continue supporting applications on almost a non-stop basis, one that's impervious to failure, even a disaster that renders an entire processing center unusable for hours or days at a time.

The methods for building a resilient architecture are

- ✔ **Server clustering:** By using special clustering software, you can apply an active/active configuration to two servers in which both are performing the full application load in a sharing basis. Or you can apply an active/passive configuration in which one server processes application transactions and the other is ready to take over at a moment's notice. You can store servers in a cluster in the same room, the same city, or thousands of miles apart.

- ✔ **Data replication and mirroring:** Copying transaction data from one storage system to another. If one storage system fails, the other has an up-to-date copy of all recent transactions.

Clustering and replication can work closely together to create an application architecture that can continue running — despite the failure of a minor hardware component or the complete destruction of a processing center.

Chapter 7 explores clustering in a lot more detail. Chapter 8 takes up the subject of data replication and mirroring.

Preventing People-Related Disasters

An organization can have a brilliant application architecture, resilient business processes, and superbly engineered server clusters, and disaster can *still* occur. If the people who operate the IT systems and perform business processes aren't familiar with what they're doing, a simple mistake can trigger system failure, causing a disaster.

You can take several measures to prevent disasters caused by human error:

- ✔ **Accurate documentation:** Procedures for routine and not-so-routine actions, at every layer in the stack, from the wiring plant to application instructions. Periodically review such documentation to make sure it's up to date.

- ✔ **Configuration standards:** Also known as *server build standards* and *database configuration standards*. Documented configuration settings that all systems in an enterprise use. Consistency makes actions more routine and outcomes more predictable.

- ✔ **Training:** General training in the skills associated with each job description, plus specific training on the architecture, development, and operations of your systems and applications.

- ✔ **Pre-employment screening:** Make sure that the workers you hire have the skills required to competently perform their duties.

- ✔ **Change management:** This formal management process says that nothing gets changed in the environment until each change has been formally reviewed and approved.

- ✔ **Configuration management:** The tools and procedures that keep an accurate record of the configuration for each system in the enterprise. In larger organizations, this level of recordkeeping can be very time consuming; you can find enterprise-level tools available to handle this task automatically.

More than just innocent mistakes can cause a disaster. An employee's ill intent can also be disastrous. These measures can help to reduce those risks:

- ✔ **Pre-employment background checks:** Prior to hiring someone, an organization should verify that candidate's employment history, education, and credentials.

- ✔ **Pre-employment criminal background:** An organization should verify that the candidate doesn't have a criminal record that would disqualify him or her from employment. Each organization needs to develop its own criteria for filtering job candidates.

✔ **Periodic background checks after hire:** Check to make sure an employee's criminal record stays clean after you hire him or her. This routine check is especially important for employees who have been working in an organization for several years. Who knows — maybe that extended vacation was spent in jail!

✔ **Formal employment agreements:** An organization should have employment agreements, contracts that formally outline what the organization expects of the employee, as well as the consequences for not meeting those expectations. Such agreements can serve as useful deterrents, making an employee think twice about carrying out some malicious action that could harm the organization.

✔ **Audit logging:** When employees know that the organization monitors their activities, they're less likely to do something they wouldn't want to be caught doing. But you should trust your employees — logging exists to provide a history of events on systems that you can use as a troubleshooting aid.

None of the measures in the preceding list actually prevents an employee from carrying out a malicious action, but these measures can help the organization do a better job of selecting candidates and observing them after hire.

Preventing Security Issues and Incidents

The absence or failure of a security control can lead to some man-made disasters. Indeed, many security incidents can seriously harm an organization in the same way a prolonged outage caused by a natural disaster can. The types of security incidents that can become disasters include

✔ **Computer break-ins:** Hackers and other cyber-criminals can use some means to gain access to a system so they can

- **Steal data:** Most often, cyber thieves go after the money — credit card numbers, bank account numbers, and other personal information that they can use to steal money from citizens or perpetrate identity theft.

- **Alter, damage, or corrupt data:** Hackers also love to alter or corrupt data — a far more serious action because the organization may not immediately recognize it.

- **Embarrass the organization:** A hacker may want to embarrass an organization by defacing its public Web site. Figure 12-7 shows an example of such a defacement.

- **Malware:** This inclusive term means viruses, worms, Trojan horses, and so on. The specific purpose of malware is to disrupt, disable, or destroy systems, including those running critical applications.

- **Denial of Service:** Both Denial of Service (DoS) and Distributed Denial of Service (DDoS) attacks have a specific purpose — to render a server or group of servers unusable by the intended users. You can defend against a DoS or DDoS, but it can cost you.

- **Social engineering:** A variety of activities in which outsiders — often posing as employees, tech support, law enforcement, or Microsoft — contact various employees in order to obtain company secrets. Social engineers can use their new-found knowledge to commit further criminal acts, such as computer break-ins.

- **Damage by former employees:** Often, those who do the most harm to an organization are its former employees, now outsiders, who are familiar with people, technology, architectures, and weaknesses. Now and then, you see news stories about former employees who cause damage to their former employers' property, including computer systems and data.

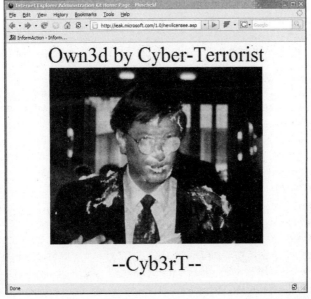

Figure 12-7:
A defaced
Web site —
yes, it can
even
happen to
Microsoft.

Source: Neohapsis

Hacking: Not just for kids anymore

The stereotypical hacker is a lonely teenage boy who's intelligent, curious, bored, and likes computers. Without the responsibilities of adulthood, teen hackers have way too much time on their hands, and they use their computers, their brains, and their spare time to figure out how to manipulate computers, including how to break into them.

The recreational teen hacker is giving way to a new breed of hackers — professionals who hack for pay. Organized crime discovered that the Internet is a safer and easier place to prey on people and businesses, and they're highly successful at it. In 2005, the U.S. Treasury Department reported that proceeds from cyber-crime had surpassed the proceeds from drug trafficking, starting in 2004.

When a corporate profit motive spurs an activity (even if the corporation is organized crime), the people involved in the activity are going to be more determined than before, now that cash is involved. Hence, organizations that have highly valued information and assets need to take added precautions to protect those assets (and their reputations).

So, although computer-savvy teenage boys still like to break into computers, they now have a career path that lets them earn a living doing what they love.

You can use several measures to reduce security risks:

- ✓ **Anti-virus software:** Used to detect and block all sorts of malware, including viruses, worms, and Trojan horses. Every server and workstation running any Windows operating system should have anti-virus software that blocks malware in real-time, updates its *signature files* (a database of known viruses and other malware) daily, and performs a whole-disk scan weekly.

- ✓ **Security patches:** One of the chief ways that hackers break into systems and networks is through well-known vulnerabilities. Most often, you can find security patches available for these vulnerabilities, but many organizations don't apply these patches quickly enough.

- ✓ **Firewalls:** These devices block access to an organization's network through the Internet and any directly connected partners. Firewalls are configured by network administrators with rules that permit specific types of connections to specific systems while blocking all other attempts at communication.

- ✓ **Application firewalls:** These firewalls examine the contents of communication to application servers (including Web servers) and block any communications identified as malicious in nature. Hackers who want to break into an organization's networks or servers often attack that organization's Web sites.

- ✓ **Vulnerability scanners:** Security people in an organization use these devices to identify vulnerabilities in its systems, applications, or network devices that a hacker could use to break in. When the devices discover vulnerabilities, security people notify operations personnel about the problems.

- ✓ **Intrusion detection system (IDS):** Network- and server-based systems that monitor network traffic and generate alerts that they send to operations personnel when an attempted break-in or intrusion appears to be in progress.

- ✓ **Intrusion prevention system (IPS):** The newer and better IDSs also function as intrusion prevention systems by actually blocking suspected malicious communications before they can cause harm.

- ✓ **Video surveillance:** You can use cameras and video recording equipment to detect intruders and prove their presence in a court of law. And visible video cameras provide a deterrent effect by discouraging illegal activity.

You can use many other means, beyond those in the preceding list, to improve the security in an organization's applications, servers, and networks so they don't fall prey to the wide variety of attacks that frequently occur.

Prevention Begins at Home

In a regional disaster, employees often aren't available to help the disaster recovery team because they're attending to a more important concern — their families. After that earthquake, hurricane, flood, or other occurrence, most employees with families attend to those needs before even considering showing up at work to be on the disaster recovery team. Until they can take care of their families, employees aren't coming to work, no matter how bad things are there.

Prevention at home can help. If you inform employees about the measures they can take to be better prepared for a disaster, you can help make sure employees' families are better taken care of in a disaster. If his or her family is secure, an employee is more likely to make him- or herself available to assist in disaster recovery operations.

Employers have a key role in prevention. While they conduct their Business Impact Analysis (BIA) and risk analyses, DR team members can probably get disaster response and prevention information, such as preparation tips, from local civil authorities. Such information can help business DR planning efforts, and those same sources frequently have family disaster prevention information. Obtain those family prevention flyers or booklets in large quantities and make them available to employees to increase the likelihood that they'll take steps to make their families more prepared for disasters.

The DR project can go one step further and actually assist key recovery personnel with information and even supplies for their families. The better prepared personnel are to take care of themselves and their families, the more likely they are to be available to assist in recovery operations.

Chapter 13

Planning for Various Disaster Scenarios

In This Chapter

▶ Getting your business ready for natural disasters

▶ Preparing for man-made disasters

*N*atural or man-made disasters throw in wild cards that can make carrying out recovery operations more difficult for your organization. In this chapter, I discuss the primary and secondary effects from a variety of disaster scenarios, and I explain how you can improve your recovery plans for the best chances of success.

Planning for Natural Disasters

Nature can throw a lot of surprises that make planning, rescue, and recovery operations difficult. Violent natural events can directly effect property and equipment, and they can also have secondary effects on communications and transportation systems, which hamper recovery efforts and may have greater impact than the event itself.

Earthquakes

Earthquakes strike with little or no warning and cause widespread damage. The violent side-to-side motion in an earthquake can cause considerable damage to buildings, equipment, and IT systems. Earthquakes often damage transportation infrastructure, particularly bridges and elevated roadways in large cities, requiring extensive repairs that can take weeks or months to complete.

Generally speaking, earthquakes occur in areas with a history of them. An earthquake rarely strikes an area that doesn't have prior earthquake history.

Transportation considerations

When a major earthquake strikes a city, people will be spending the next several hours wherever they happen to be at the time. Transportation is usually the hardest hit infrastructure, particularly bridges, tunnels, and elevated roadways.

After human life, transportation systems are often the next most important attention-getter in an earthquake. Emergency supplies in appreciable volumes arrive by truck or rail. In severe situations, authorities and aid organizations can airlift emergency supplies, but airlifts usually bring only the absolute necessities — drinking water, food rations, and emergency medical supplies. Red Cross helicopters don't bring in Sun servers or Cisco routers — not by a long shot!

Communication considerations

Communications networks tend to be highly congested after an earthquake, both because of damage to facilities and high usage. Many people make a quick phone call to say, "We just had an earthquake, and we're okay." Other people use communications facilities for longer periods of time to convey more detailed information.

The diversity in voice and data communications presents some opportunities after an earthquake. Because carriers' networks are often located in different physical locations, one or two may suffer significant outages in an earthquake, and others may fare a little better. Text messages may fare better than voice communications over congested cellular networks.

Recovery considerations

You may want to incorporate some of these items into your DR plan if any of your business locations are at risk for earthquakes:

- **Emergency supplies:** In the event that employees are at the workplace when an earthquake occurs and can't travel home for a few days. Also, keep supplies that disaster response personnel need when they do arrive at the business location. Emergency supplies should include food, water, medical supplies, and blankets.

- **Equipment protection:** Even if building codes don't require it, protect equipment with extra bracing and other means so storage racks don't fall down in an earthquake and equipment doesn't fall off racks and shelves.

✔ **Emergency power:** If public utilities are damaged, but your processing facility is otherwise workable, you may be able to use generator power to keep the work location running. In a severe earthquake, however, fuel trucks may have a difficult time working their way around damaged roadways to deliver fuel for the generator.

✔ **Supplemental communications:** Landlines and cellular networks may be congested or damaged. For really critical needs, consider satellite phones from Iridium, Inmarsat, or Globalstar, and VSAT network connectivity. A hand-crank or solar-powered radio can also help you receive news from the outside world.

✔ **Replacement IT systems:** In the event that an earthquake damages some IT systems. Include replacement user workstations because systems in employee work areas aren't usually braced, so they may fall during the quake and be damaged.

Wildfires

Many factors contribute to the amount of warning you receive before a wildfire disaster strikes — from as little as several minutes to a few days. Transportation infrastructure may be blocked if fires approach roadways. Communications and electricity may be cut off if fires burn through areas that contain wooden power poles.

Because of the threat to human life and property, local authorities may order the evacuation of personnel if a wildfire threatens a facility. You usually have only enough time to quickly gather personal belongings before leaving. Staff don't know how quickly they can return to the facility or whether public utilities will be cut off during their absence. You might have time to quickly gather backup tapes before leaving, but a DR plan can't count on those tapes being rescued because a wildfire can occur after hours. In that case, personnel may not be able to reach the facility because roads may already be closed.

Transportation considerations

Although roads may be closed for several hours to a few days, they're rarely damaged. And in most situations, personnel don't find themselves as stranded as in an earthquake. More often, roads are closed due to poor visibility caused by heavy smoke or to provide easier access for fire fighting crews. But road closures may prevent personnel from leaving or entering the facility for a day or more.

Communication considerations

When wildfires damage communication facilities, you may have to wait at least a few days before communication is restored. So, although your facility may escape direct damage, you might be forced to go without communications for as long as several days.

A fire marshal may not allow you to occupy a building if communications are down.

Recovery considerations

Consider adding these measures to a DR plan for facilities in areas threatened by wildfires:

- ✔ **Emergency supplies:** In the event that employees are at the workplace when a wildfire strikes and can't travel home for a few days. You may want facemasks and/or air filters in case a lot of smoke blows toward the facility. Have disaster response personnel bring additional emergency supplies in case you exhaust the supplies stocked in the facility before their arrival.

- ✔ **Firefighting equipment:** Employees stranded at a work facility with an approaching fire can use saws, shovels, and other gear to remove flammable materials from around the building.

- ✔ **Supplemental communications:** A wildfire may damage landlines and cellular networks. For really critical needs, consider satellite phones and VSAT network connectivity. You can also use a hand-crank or solar-powered radio to stay in touch with the outside world.

Volcanoes

In most cases, volcanoes provide warning before they erupt — but not always. Volcanic eruptions can be violent and devastating when they do occur, so personnel at a work location should take every means and opportunity to evacuate if ordered by civil emergency authorities or law enforcement. Just get the heck out!

Volcanic eruptions are characterized by huge clouds of smoke and ash, lava flows, *pyroclastic flows* (fast-moving currents of hot gas, ash, and rock), and significant landslides and debris flows that can travel dozens of miles over land and through river valleys.

If any office location or workers reside within one hundred miles of an active volcano, gather information from local civil authorities regarding precautions, preparations, and evacuation procedures. I live within twenty miles of one active volcano and eighty miles from three others, so I made myself familiar with this information for my location. But volcanoes in different parts of the world have vastly different behavior, so what's good for me may not be much help for you.

Transportation considerations

If you live or work near a volcano that may erupt with little notice, you need to be able to evacuate quickly and take next to nothing with you. If an active eruption is about to take place, staff may not be able to return to the work facility for days or weeks, and worse yet, an eruption can damage or completely destroy homes and work locations.

Recovery considerations

If a volcano is located near a primary work location, the entire business may have to start over in a different location if a serious eruption occurs. Discuss the actual risks associated with a specific volcano with civil authorities and insurance company officials.

Floods

Floods typically occur as a result of excessive rainfall in a short period of time or unusually warm weather that causes a heavy springtime snowmelt. Floods can threaten a business in several ways:

- ✔ **Direct building damage from flood waters:** If a work location is near a stream or river, flood waters may threaten the actual structure, as well as any assets and equipment located inside.

- ✔ **Damage to transportation systems:** Even if employees' homes and the work facilities are on high ground, major nearby transportation systems might not be. Flood damage to nearby highways can force some workers to stay home (or at work) and disrupt the shipment of supplies, materials, and products.

- ✔ **Damage to communications and public utilities:** Flooding may damage and cause widespread interruptions in communications and public utility infrastructures. So, although a particular business may escape the direct effects of flooding, a communications or electric power outage may still render a business location inoperative for several days.

- ✔ **Forced evacuations:** Civil authorities or law enforcement may require that you evacuate work locations and residences to prevent loss of life during a flood.

Transportation considerations

Floods can cover or wash away roads and bridges, paralyzing transportation for many days. People get stuck wherever they were when the flood waters rose, whether at home, work, or elsewhere.

Communication considerations

In areas in which flooding occurs, communications may not be severely disrupted, although outages may still occur. Even in rivers that do flood from time to time, the characteristics of each individual flood may vary enough to make damage and disruption less than predictable.

Recovery considerations

You might incorporate some of these items into your DR plan if any of your business locations are at risk for floods:

- **Emergency supplies:** In the event employees are at the workplace when flooding occurs and can't travel home for several days. Also, disaster response personnel need supplies when they arrive at the business location. Emergency supplies should include food, water, medical supplies, and blankets.

- **Supplemental communications:** Landlines and cellular networks may be congested or damaged. For really critical needs, consider satellite phones from Iridium, Inmarsat, or Globalstar, and VSAT network connectivity.

- **Emergency power:** If floods have damaged power systems, but a processing facility is otherwise workable, you may be able to use generator power to keep the work location running. In a severe flood, however, fuel trucks may not be able to deliver fuel for the generator.

- **Replacement IT systems:** In the event that flooding damages some IT systems. Be sure to include replacement user workstations.

- **Alternate work locations:** You may not be able to use buildings damaged in a flood for days or weeks. The organization may need to do business elsewhere for quite a while, and you may not be able to enter the premises to retrieve important equipment or records.

Wind and ice storms

Although they're far different from each other, wind and ice storms inflict similar damage to buildings and property. Although you usually get some warning before a wind or ice storm, you don't have enough time to do anything but pack a few things and get to wherever you want to be stuck for a while — work, home, or someplace else.

Probably the biggest effect of wind and ice storms is widespread power outages caused by one of the following:

- Wind blowing over trees, which then damage power and phone lines
- Ice that causes trees to collapse onto power and phone lines
- Ice that directly damages power transmission systems and telephone networks

Transportation considerations

In wind and ice storms, many trees fall over, often blocking roadways, making travel slow and difficult. In ice storms, roads are also icy. Civil authorities or law enforcement may close roads. Hence, people get stranded wherever they are.

In severe situations, delivery of supplies may be interrupted for days at a time. Workers can't get to work (or get home *from* work).

Communications considerations

Communications can be hard hit in wind and ice storms. Where the storm doesn't directly damage phone lines themselves, widespread power outages can cause cell sites and remote nodes to exhaust their emergency battery supplies. Locations that have emergency generators can work for a while after emergency battery supplies run out, but even these generators fail when they run out of fuel. In severe storms, communications can be out for several days — even a week or more.

Recovery considerations

DR plans for businesses located in areas subject to wind and ice storms might consider the following:

- ✔ **Emergency supplies:** You may need significant stocks of food, water, medical supplies, and blankets in areas hit by these storms. Recovery personnel who can make it through should bring additional supplies if they can obtain them.

- ✔ **Supplemental communications:** Landlines and cellular networks may be congested or damaged. For really critical needs, consider satellite phones from Iridium, Inmarsat, or Globalstar, and VSAT network connectivity.

- ✔ **Emergency power:** Generator power may keep the work location running for a few days. But in a severe wind or ice storm, the power may be out for so long that generators run out of fuel, and fuel trucks may not be able to deliver fuel for the generator. In severe situations, damaged transportation systems may hamper emergency services and delivery of all kinds of emergency supplies.

Hurricanes

Hurricanes are the perfect storm: They include rain, wind, and flooding, each in potentially cataclysmic proportions. Big Category 4 and Category 5 storms cause widespread, severe damage that can take years to recover from. Hurricanes Camille (1969), Andrew (1992), and Katrina (2005) are prime examples of the devastating power of hurricanes.

Transportation considerations

Historically, evacuations ahead of hurricanes are slow and take days because everyone takes to the roadways. All staff members should evacuate when ordered to by civil authorities so they don't have to remain behind to ride out the storm. Because of the colossal potential for damage and loss of life, businesses should emphasize the need to just leave when so ordered.

Communication considerations

Communications after a hurricane can be out for several days, even a week or more. Even if phone lines aren't damaged, power outages cause cell sites and remote nodes to exhaust their emergency battery supplies. Cell sites and remote nodes that have emergency generators can work for a while after their batteries run out, but eventually even the generators fail when they run out of fuel.

Recovery considerations

Businesses that lie in the path of a hurricane should hope for the best but prepare for a complete loss of all business assets. Businesses in hurricane-prone areas may want to consider the following in their DR plans:

- **Emergency supplies:** For those unfortunates left behind to ride out a hurricane, emergency supplies need to include food and water, medical supplies, and rain gear — enough for several days, at least.

- **Supplemental communications:** Hurricanes can completely knock out landline and mobile phone systems. For really critical needs, consider satellite phones that completely bypass landline and cellular systems, and VSAT network connectivity. A hand-crank or solar-powered radio can help you receive news from the outside world.

- **Emergency power:** You may need only generator power to keep the work location running for a few days. But in a hurricane, the power may be out for so long that generators run out of fuel. Remember that fuel trucks may have a difficult time delivering fuel for the generator.

- **Alternate processing facility:** Locate a recovery center far away from areas threatened by hurricanes and have systems at this recovery center assume duties. The best time to invest in an alternate facility is after the hurricane season is over, when demand for such facilities should be lower.

Tornadoes

Extreme winds are associated with tornado funnel clouds during severe thunderstorms in the U.S. Midwest and other parts of the world. Tornadoes strike with little or no warning, and they can completely destroy a residence or business location.

The area affected by an individual tornado is quite small — usually just a few square miles. But portions of the U.S. and other parts of the world are struck by tornadoes at a disturbing rate. Unless you moved there yesterday, if you're in tornado country, you probably already know it.

Transportation considerations

Because tornadoes strike and travel fairly quickly, wherever a person is when he or she receives the tornado warning is where he or she will be when it strikes. Many people get into their vehicles and attempt to out-run or out-maneuver a tornado, but trying to change locations during a tornado can be risky — and often fatal. Stay in the building you're in when you receive the tornado warning and head for a designated safe area where occupants should gather during a tornado.

Communication considerations

Because tornadoes are so localized, any communications outages are usually repaired quickly, within a day or two at the most. Most cell tower structures and telephone company switching centers are built to withstand the heavy winds of a tornado. However, damage can occur, causing localized outages that can last hours to days.

Recovery considerations

Businesses located in tornado-prone areas should be prepared for the total loss of business facilities. But because of the highly local nature of tornadoes, you probably don't need to locate your backup facility more than a few dozen miles away (unlike earthquake and hurricane disasters, which strike much larger regions). If your business is in an area prone to tornadoes, consider putting the following preparations in place:

- ✔ **Emergency supplies:** Emergency supplies need to include food and water, medical supplies, and rain gear — enough for at least two days.

- ✔ **Supplemental communications:** Tornadoes can completely knock out landline and mobile phone systems. For really critical needs, consider satellite phones that completely bypass landline and cellular systems, and VSAT network connectivity. You may also want a hand-crank or solar-powered radio to receive emergency communications.

- ✔ **Emergency power:** Generator power should keep the work location running for a few days, even if workers may be away from the facility.

- ✔ **Alternate processing facility:** You may want to set up a recovery center several miles away from your main business site if your business uses highly time-critical processes.

Tsunamis

Undersea earthquakes (and occasionally undersea volcanoes) cause *tsunamis*, great ocean waves that strike coastlines. Many parts of the world have inadequate warning systems, or they don't have any warning systems at all, which

---

Katrina, the lesson in preparation

The great Katrina hurricane of 2005 was a watershed natural disaster event in the U.S. The most pronounced effect from Katrina was widespread and persistent flooding when several levees broke during a storm surge. After more than two years, over 200,000 people were still displaced, and few of those displaced persons will probably ever return.

The scenario that took place was two-fold: First, the widespread severe flooding damaged buildings, records, and equipment. Businesses had little time to pack up assets ahead of the storm. Nearly everything they left behind at street level was destroyed. Second, public services were down for many days — transportation, electricity, and other utilities were down for many days;

the airport was closed for more than two weeks; roads were closed for many days; and authorities didn't permit people to return to some parts of New Orleans for weeks.

Businesses that relied heavily on an online presence that was served only in New Orleans had to relocate their online presence to other locations; businesses that had offsite backup tape storage (or could evacuate their backup media ahead of the storm) rebuilt their online presence with little or no advance planning.

Impaired communications was perhaps the most critical impact of Katrina. Few New Orleans businesses had satellite phones or VSAT (Internet via satellite) terminals.

---

puts millions of lives and property at risk of destruction. The 2004 tsunami in the Indian Ocean provides a vivid reminder that tsunamis are largely unpredictable and can exact a huge toll on lives and property.

Transportation considerations

With little or no advance warning, transportation systems become clogged beyond capacity before a tsunami. The tsunami itself may cause significant damage to transportation systems, especially elevated highways and railroads that are located at low elevations near coastlines. Repairs may take weeks or months.

Communication considerations

A tsunami may partially or completely destroy communications facilities at low elevations near coastlines, requiring a complete rebuild that may take weeks to months. Mobile carriers can compensate by bringing COWS (Cell sites On WheelS) into hard hit areas, permitting some mobile communications capabilities. Satellite phones are expensive, but you may be able to justify the cost.

Recovery considerations

You may want to incorporate some of these items into your DR plans if any of your business locations are at risk from a tsunami:

✔ **Emergency supplies:** Disaster response personnel may need supplies when they arrive at the business location after the tsunami. Emergency supplies should include food, water, medical supplies, blankets, and hand-crank or solar-powered radios.

✔ **Emergency power:** If public utilities are damaged, but your processing facility is otherwise workable, generator power may keep the work location running. You need to determine whether fuel trucks can work their way around damaged roadways to deliver fuel for the generator.

✔ **Supplemental communications:** Landlines and cellular networks may be congested or damaged. For really critical needs, consider satellite phones from Iridium, Inmarsat, or Globalstar, and VSAT network connectivity.

✔ **Replacement IT systems:** In the event that some IT systems (both servers and workstations) are damaged.

Landslides and avalanches

Earthquakes, erosion, ocean waves, groundwater, or heavy rain can cause *landslides* (the sudden movement of earth and rock). Several man-made causes include vibrations from machinery, construction, blasting, logging, overgrazing, and mining. *Avalanches* occur when an excessive buildup of snow leads to that snow, along with trees, rocks, and earth, rapidly cascading down steep slopes.

Damage from landslides and avalanches range from disrupted transportation and communications to direct destruction of homes and buildings, as well as loss of life. Recovery efforts to clear away material and debris can take hours, days, or longer.

You can easily avoid the risks from landslides and avalanches by not locating your business near the foot of a steep hillside. However, even if you locate your business away from these places, landslides and avalanches can still disrupt transportation and communication, which can have a devastating effect on business operations. Figure 13-1 shows the effects of a landslide in a major city.

Transportation considerations

Landslides and avalanches can cause transportation byways to be blocked for days, weeks, or longer. These blockages can make reaching affected areas time-consuming and difficult, increasing shipping rates and economic losses.

Source: L.M. Smith, Waterways Experiment Station, U.S. Army Corps of Engineers

Communications considerations

Landslides and avalanches can damage communications facilities by destroying cable systems and buildings that contain communications equipment. Landslides and avalanches can affect both landline and mobile communications because most mobile communications *backhaul* (the communications from cell towers to switching centers) that occurs over copper or fiber optic cables on overhead structures or buried in the ground may be damaged. Satellite telephones continue to function, of course, but your business may not be able to justify the cost.

Recovery considerations

You may want to incorporate some of these items into your DR plans if any of your business locations are at risk from landslides or avalanches:

- ✔ **Emergency supplies:** Emergency supplies need to include food, water, and medical supplies — enough for several days, particularly in locations with only a single route in and out. Disaster response personnel may need supplies when they arrive at the business location. Also consider including blankets and hand-crank or solar-powered radios in your emergency supplies.

- ✔ **Emergency power:** If public utilities are damaged, but a processing facility is otherwise usable, generator power may keep the work location running. You need to determine whether fuel trucks can work their way around damaged or blocked roadways to deliver generator fuel.

✔ **Supplemental communications:** Landlines and cellular networks may be congested or damaged. For really critical needs, consider satellite phones from Iridium, Inmarsat, or Globalstar, and VSAT network connectivity.

Pandemic

A global pandemic hasn't occurred for so long that, until the early 2000s, many people didn't even know the meaning of the term. The Asian SARS (Severe Acute Respiratory Syndrome) outbreak in 2002–2003 and the avian influenza threat are forcing organizations to begin contingency planning for a possible pandemic.

Pandemics in history

A *pandemic* is the outbreak of an infectious disease that spreads over a large region, even worldwide. Well-known pandemics in history include

✔ **Black Death in the 1300s:** This outbreak of the bubonic plague killed over 25 million Europeans in six years, a quarter of the entire population. Up to half of the population died in the worst-hit urban areas.

✔ **Spanish flu, 1918–1919:** This epidemic of influenza killed between 25 and 50 million people worldwide.

✔ **Asian flu, 1957–1958:** Responsible for about 70,000 deaths in the U.S.

✔ **Hong Kong flu, 1968–1969:** Influenza A caused about 34,000 deaths in the U.S.

Health experts at the World Health Organization (WHO) and the U.S. Centers for Disease Control (CDC) report that pandemics occur regularly throughout history and that we're due for another. Possible candidates include the H5N1 avian influenza that has already claimed hundreds of lives, SARS (which may re-emerge at any time), tuberculosis, Ebola, and others.

A different kind of disaster

A pandemic is a widespread disaster that seems to occur in slow motion, compared to other disasters I discuss in this chapter. If and when the next pandemic hits, it'll probably play out over several months to a few years. A pandemic is a quiet disaster: Buildings aren't destroyed nor communications systems compromised, but the effect is nonetheless profound. (See Figure 13-2.) me of the characteristics of a pandemic include

✔ **High rates of absenteeism:** More than 25 percent of workers may be absent for weeks at a time during a pandemic. Workers are either sick themselves, caring for sick family members, caring for children whose schools are closed, or fearful to venture out of their homes. This reduction in available workforce creates a general slowdown in the output of businesses across entire regions.

Unlike other types of disasters, you can't rely on contract and other outside help to supplement absent employees. All businesses in a given region have a simultaneous need, and even contracting firms experience high absenteeism in a pandemic situation.

✔ **Supplier shortages:** The availability of virtually every type of goods diminishes because the organizations producing those goods are also experiencing high absenteeism. You may have to deal with shortages of fuel, food, and other essentials for daily subsistence.

✔ **Degraded services:** Levels of service may dramatically decline when you have fewer personnel available. Repairs of public utilities take longer; fewer doctors, bus drivers, and policemen are available to assist you.

✔ **Reduced demand for non-essential goods and services:** Demand for items that aren't essential for subsistence decline, causing business downturn in many sectors.

✔ **Degraded medical care:** Hospitals may have to turn away most cases of illness, caring only for those who are the most ill but still have a chance of survival. Gymnasiums, conference centers, and other gathering places may be turned into gigantic hospital wards.

✔ **Forced quarantines of entire communities:** Hard-hit areas experience quarantines, and government health authorities don't permit workers to report to their workplaces for fear of spreading disease.

✔ **Closures of schools and public assemblies:** Schools and other public assemblies provide opportunities for disease to spread; hence, schools may be closed for days to weeks at a time.

✔ **No outside help available:** In a pandemic, large geographic regions have needs that outsiders can't meet because those outsiders are also affected by a pandemic. Communities have to survive with the resources available locally. The International Red Cross may have to spread itself extremely thin, like a single pat of butter for a thousand loaves of bread.

Transportation considerations

Aside from forced quarantines and fuel shortages, transportation isn't a major issue in a pandemic. Indeed, with many people huddled in their homes for fear of catching disease, roadways may actually be less congested.

Communication considerations

Organizations in a pandemic probably have healthy workers who are willing to work but can't report to the workplace because of quarantines, lack of transportation, or sick family members at home. Businesses need to invest in remote access and remote telecommunications capabilities long before a pandemic strikes. During a pandemic wave, organizations probably experience high rates of remote workers accessing systems from their homes, not unlike when severe storms and other phenomena keep workers away.

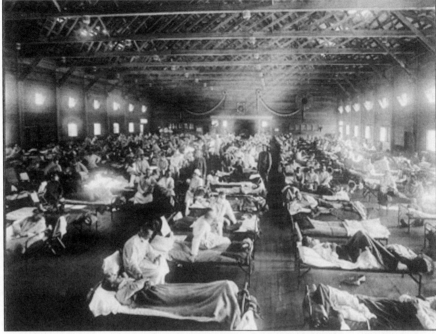

Figure 13-2:
An emergency military hospital during the influenza pandemic in 1918.

Source: National Museum of Health and Medicine, Armed Forces Institute of Pathology, Washington, D.C.

Preparation and recovery considerations

In a pandemic, no natural event inflicts damage on buildings, records, or systems. Instead, those assets suffer neglect because you don't have enough personnel available to care for them adequately. Businesses should develop contingency plans that include the following:

- ✔ **Lights-out (unmanned) processing centers:** Probably a long-term proposition that requires considerable investment, organizations need to figure out how to keep their systems running with far fewer staff members than normal.

- ✔ **Increased capacity for remote data and voice access:** With many workers able to work, but unable or unwilling to report to the business premises, organizations need to invest in additional remote data and voice capabilities. To prepare additional remote access capabilities, you need a lot of time and resources.

- ✔ **Reduced output:** Businesses need to anticipate reductions in output and also reductions in demand. But some businesses actually experience an increase in demand, depending on the goods or services those businesses produce.

- ✔ **Cross-training:** With significant staff shortages, you need to cross-train workers so available workers can carry out duties normally performed by workers who are absent.

- ✔ **Multi-sourcing critical suppliers:** Identify which of your business's suppliers are critical (without which business operations cease) and consider acquiring additional suppliers to improve the chances that you can get at least some reduced level of supplies during a pandemic outbreak.

- ✔ **Educate workers:** Some employees stay away from work simply out of fear. Educating workers on the actual risks can give them an opportunity to take appropriate precautions based on known facts.

Planning for Man-Made Disasters

Man-made disasters fall into two distinct categories: those that are deliberate, and those that are the result of an error or oversight. Each type has its special challenges and issues that planners and emergency response personnel need to keep in mind so they can avoid further damage and casualties.

Utility failures

Practically all businesses are ravenous for electricity. IT systems are especially sensitive — they don't have a tolerance for even relatively minor spikes, surges, and brownouts.

Some geopolitical locations have higher quality power generation and distribution systems than others. Quality and wealth aren't necessarily in direct proportion. In my career, I've seen consistently poor delivery of electric power in affluent areas. But to be fair, some factors are out of the control of the power system operators, such as weather and geologic conditions.

Organizations that experience more than an acceptable level of power outages (for whatever reason) need to consider the following options to assure a continuous delivery of clean power to critical systems:

- ✔ **Uninterruptible Power Supply (UPS):** Usually two systems in one. A UPS has circuitry that cleans incoming power of spikes, surges, and other noise so IT equipment receives the cleanest possible power. A UPS system also has banks of batteries that can become the primary power source for a short time — usually a fraction of an hour.

- ✔ **Electric generator:** For power outages that last more than several minutes, you need an electric generator, in addition to a UPS, to assure power availability for as long as several days.

- ✔ **Fuel storage:** For organizations that may experience power outages that last more than a few days (and if you can't easily get fresh supplies of fuel), consider building a fuel storage facility. With such a fuel storage facility, you can have continuous electric power, even during prolonged outages.

UPS and generators work together — you need both to assure continuous power. Generators take up to two minutes to come online, so you need a UPS to fill the gap between the utility outage and when the generator can come online. Similarly, a UPS can't supply power for very long, which requires a generator to provide power for up to several days.

I cover emergency power supplies more fully in Chapter 6 and Chapter 12.

Civil disturbances

Political and economic events can precipitate civil disturbances, including protests, work stoppages, strikes, vandalism, looting, and general mayhem. These disturbances can result in property damage, disruption to transportation, and temporary cessation of business operations. Law enforcement or military may block transportation routes or enforce evacuations and curfews. These events can make you want to be *anywhere* else.

Transportation considerations

During and after such periods of civil disruption, you may find transportation to and from affected areas limited by damage, barricades, closures, curfews, and fear. Workers at business locations may be stranded there for hours or days until things calm down.

Communication considerations

In more serious events, communications may be hampered or cut off, so disaster response personnel may have difficulty communicating with each other. As a result, you may have trouble getting an accurate assessment of an event's effects on business operations. You may find having a variety of landline and mobile carriers helpful; if one isn't working, perhaps another is. Workers may be able to use satellite phones if they can get to an out-of-doors location with safety.

Recovery considerations

It's difficult to say what kinds of effects a large civil disturbance might have on business operations. Here are some measures you can take to mitigate the effects of civil disturbances:

- ✔ **Emergency supplies:** Emergency supplies need to include food, water, and medical supplies — enough for several days. Disaster response personnel may need supplies when they arrive at the business location. Emergency supplies should also include blankets and hand-crank or solar-powered radios.

> ✔ **Emergency power:** If public utilities are damaged, but a processing facility is otherwise usable, generator power may keep the work location running. You need to figure out whether fuel trucks can (and will) work their way around damaged or blocked roadways to deliver generator fuel.

Terrorism and war

The extent and ferocity of terrorism and war are largely unpredictable and chaotic. All you want to do is get out of the way!

Anything can happen in a war, and you can't really know what kind of a contingency plan you'll need. No wonder insurance companies don't cover war in their policies.

The September 11, 2001 attacks on New York City and Washington, D.C. (see Figure 13-3) were unprecedented for many reasons. In the business continuity and disaster recovery professions, the attacks brought to light two scenarios that many BC and DR planners hadn't considered:

> ✔ The complete collapse of an otherwise structurally sound building
>
> ✔ The loss of a large proportion of the workers in an organization

Figure 13-3:
The New York City World Trade Center during the 9/11/2001 attack.

Source: U.S. National Park Service

9/11 forced BC and DR planners back to the drawing board, updating their contingency and emergency response plans with these new scenarios. Really, it started a multi-year effort in which organizations took the time to rethink the adequacy of their emergency plans. Personally, I think that this extra planning brought about two results:

✔ Off-site media storage centers got a boost.

✔ Businesses thought more seriously about whether they wanted to locate their processing centers in what is essentially a landmark. Many businesses instead opted for processing centers (and alternate processing centers) in low-profile, unmarked buildings.

Security incidents

Break-ins, hacking incidents, Denial of Service attacks, and large malware outbreaks are significant events and have the potential to shut down the IT systems that support critical business processes.

A security incident can reach disaster levels in a number of ways:

✔ **Data corruption:** If the incident causes data corruption, the organization may be forced to take systems offline until you can recover or rebuild the data. In large databases, this process can take several days, even on the fastest available computers.

✔ **Denial of Service (DoS):** A concentrated attack, especially when it originates from large numbers of systems, can render a server or an entire network of servers unreachable to customers and partners. Such attacks can last for hours, days, or even weeks.

✔ **Forensics:** Your organization (or law enforcement) may need to carry out forensic operations on affected systems to gather evidence for a possible prosecution. Trained personnel usually conduct forensics on *quiescent systems* (systems in which activity is halted) to provide stability, ensuring the best possible evidence gathering.

To reduce the effects of a security incident, consider these measures:

✔ **Alternate servers and storage systems:** Place alternate systems and storage systems into service while trained personnel perform forensics on affected systems. Before you place affected systems into service, however, the organization needs to be certain that they won't be compromised, too.

✔ **Distributed Denial of Service (DDoS) defense:** Some Internet service providers offer a DDoS defense service that may help to restore connectivity to customers and partners. These solutions can cost you, but so can being offline.

9/11 and Cantor Fitzgerald

Cantor Fitzgerald was a major U.S. government treasury trading firm in 2001, accounting for one quarter of all Treasury bond transactions on the open market. This multi-trillion dollar market is of primary importance for investment trading in the world economy.

Cantor Fitzgerald was located on the 101st through 105th floors of One World Trade Center, 8 to 12 floors above the point at which the plane hit the tower. Because they were located above the impact zone, virtually none of the employees in the building at the time of the attack survived. Cantor lost 658 employees, or about two-thirds of its workforce.

In 2001, Cantor was building an alternate processing facility, but that facility wasn't yet complete. The significant loss of life made recovery from this event especially difficult. Despite seemingly insurmountable odds, Cantor was back in operation out of its incomplete alternate processing facility within one week.

Business continuity and disaster recovery planners no doubt never imagined a scenario in which such a large portion of a company's workforce is killed in a single event. Prior to 9/11, no single company of any appreciable size had ever experienced such an event.

- ✔ **Alternate network locations:** If an organization is experiencing a Denial of Service or Distributed Denial of Service, you may be able to avoid disruption by relocating affected servers or networks to another logical place on the Internet. Whether this move works has a lot to do with the determination of the attackers and their ability to change their intended target.

- ✔ **Backup data:** Replication and mirroring are great technologies that can compensate for hardware failures. However, in the case of a deliberate attack, replication or mirroring may propagate the corruption to other storage systems. If this widespread corruption occurs, you may need to recover data from a recent backup — but only if analysts can determine that the attack hasn't affected a recent data backup.

- ✔ **Heterogeneous (similar) systems:** If attackers attack through known vulnerabilities in software, using heterogeneous systems may prevent an attack from reaching some systems. For instance, if an application uses both a Sun system with Oracle databases and a Windows system with SQL Server databases, an attack through the Windows system can't succeed on the Sun server. I discuss monocultures in more detail in Chapter 12.

- ✔ **Forensics training and tools:** This measure is an up-front investment of dollars and training. With better forensics preparedness, your business can respond more quickly when you need forensic activities, as well as develop alternate strategies that can minimize impact on business operations.

Part IV
The Part of Tens

"We found where the security breach in the WLAN was originating. It was coming in through another rogue robot-vac. This is the third one this month. Must have gotten away from it's owner, like all the rest."

In this part . . .

We've become a culture of top-ten lists. They're a time-honored institution in the *For Dummies* series of books. I honor that tradition in this part and give you four chapters that impart insight and wisdom that might otherwise take many years and many mistakes to figure out for yourself.

Chapter 14 describes tools that can ease the passage through a disaster recovery project. In similar fashion, Chapter 15 showcases ten Web sites that contain more DR information than I can possibly cram into this book.

Chapter 16 highlights essential DR project success factors. You *do* want your DR project to succeed, right? And Chapter 17 explains the benefits of a successful disaster recovery project — those benefits go *way* beyond disaster preparation.

Chapter 14

Ten Disaster Recovery Planning Tools

In This Chapter

▶ Using tools to develop complex disaster recovery plans

▶ Getting some quick results with template-style tools

▶ Defining your recovery operations by using Service Level Agreements

This chapter has a little bit of everything, but that doesn't include the kitchen sink. If you want to find a variety of resources, this chapter gives you complex high-end DR planning tools, template-style tools, and tools for Service Level Agreements and risk analysis.

Living Disaster Recovery Planning System (LDRPS)

www.strohlsystems.com/software/ldrps

LDRPS is a mature and highly respected DR planning product from Strohl Systems. You can choose from five versions to fit any size organization. You can also get LDRPS as a hosted Software as a Service (SaaS) solution in which Strohl Systems hosts the application in its data center so you don't need to install and maintain the software on your own premises.

Some of the features available in LDRPS include

✔ Customizable best-practices-based plan navigators

✔ Built-in standard reports

✔ Customizable reports

✔ Dependency maps

- Drag-and-drop call lists
- Location resource management
- Sample final plans
- Customizable screens
- Scheduled importing and plan publishing

LDRPS has been a successful DR planning product for more than twenty years.

BIA Professional

www.strohlsystems.com/software/biaprofessional

BIA Professional, a software product from Strohl Systems, guides you through the process of developing a Business Impact Analysis (BIA) survey, organizing the survey data, and presenting the final results. It paints a detailed picture of financial and operational vulnerabilities, disaster-related impacts, and possible recovery strategies.

A feature called BIA Professional Web Server allows your organization to post online surveys in which selected subject matter experts in your organization receive a link via e-mail that they can click to take the survey online. This survey approach allows you to easily collect data about critical business processes.

BIA Professional contains several features:

- **Audit and approval of surveys:** Support for company management review and approval of BIA surveys prior to their release.
- **Activity map:** Guides you through the steps for creating a BIA survey.
- **Question branching:** Permits the survey designer to create a survey in which users are asked only relevant questions.
- **Reporting:** Simplified report creation that includes a Report Wizard. You can create reports in Microsoft Excel, Crystal Reports, or PDF formats.

COBRA Risk Analysis

www.securitypolicy.co.uk/riskanalysis

Consultative, Objective and Bi-functional Risk Analysis (COBRA) is a set of risk analysis and security review tools that C&A Systems Security developed.

The toolset consists of a default process:

- ✔ **Questionnaire building:** The COBRA tool has a large database of questions contained in question modules that you can select from a knowledge base. Each module addresses a specific risk area, including access control, physical security, software development, and so on. You can also build and add questions manually.

- ✔ **Risk surveying:** The risk surveyor tool manages the questionnaire completion process. Users can complete the questionnaire all at once, or they can return to it later. The tool also supports *question branching,* in which the program knows which questions to ask based on the answers given to earlier questions.

- ✔ **Reporting:** The report generator produces results from completed questionnaires.

A risk analysis is a key part of a Business Impact Analysis.

BCP Generator

www.bcpgenerator.com

BCP Generator is a popular template-driven tool that you can use to create business continuity plans. Yes, this book is about disaster recovery planning, but BCP Generator makes plans that strongly resemble disaster recovery procedures.

You can use BCP Generator in one of two ways:

- ✔ **Template fill-in:** If you're familiar with your processes and want to get faster results, you can go straight to the templates and begin filling in details.

- ✔ **Interactive guide:** BCP Generator can guide you, step by step, through the entire process of creating a business continuity plan, from Business Impact Analysis to plan maintenance and everything in between.

BCP Generator gives you a highly structured Microsoft Word document that contains the entire business continuity plan, including a detailed table of contents.

DRI Professional Practices Kit

```
http://drii.org/drii/ProfessionalPractices/about_
professional_detail.aspx
```

The Disaster Recovery Institute (DRI) has developed a professional practices guide, and it has that guide freely available on its Web site. The sections in the guide are

- Introduction and Overview — How the Professional Practices Came to Exist
- Subject Area 1 — Project Initiation and Management
- Subject Area 2 — Risk Evaluation and Control
- Subject Area 3 — Business Impact Analysis
- Subject Area 4 — Developing Business Continuity Strategies
- Subject Area 5 — Emergency Response and Operations
- Subject Area 6 — Developing and Implementing Business Continuity Plans
- Subject Area 7 — Awareness and Training Programs
- Subject Area 8 — Exercising and Maintaining Business Continuity Plans
- Subject Area 9 — Public Relations and Crisis Coordination
- Subject Area 10 — Coordination with External Agencies
- Appendix A: North America — Sources and References Related to Business Continuity/Disaster Recovery

You can find a similar version of this material on the *Disaster Recovery Journal* Web site at www.drj.com/GAP.

Disaster Recovery Plan Template

```
www.e-janco.com/drp.htm
```

If you want to get on a real fast track, the DR Plan Template is a full set of DR planning template documents that you fill out. The content is broken up into the following sections:

- **Overview:** DR plan mission, scope, authorization, responsibility, and key assumptions
- **Business Impact Analysis:** Includes scope, objectives, critical time-frames, and impact statements

✔ **Backup strategy:** Includes data center systems, file servers, data at out-sourced sites, workstations, and PDAs

✔ **Disaster recovery:** Includes recovery team selection and responsibilities for damage assessment, salvage, and recovery procedures

✔ **Emergency procedures:** Actual procedures for assessment, salvage, and recovery

✔ **DR plan administration:** Lifecycle matters, including plan maintenance, training, testing, and distribution

If you use a template-centric tool such as this one, I recommend that you still create your plan by using this book and then make adjustments to that plan, as needed. By relying solely on a template solution, you may overlook critical risks and issues.

SLA Toolkit

www.service-level-agreement.net

You need Service Level Agreements (SLAs) to define service delivery in IT organizations. *Service Level Agreements* are formal service agreements between suppliers and customers that define the quantity and quality of services delivered to customers.

Disaster recovery operations are probably the most vital services that an organization performs. If your organization has complex processes and inter-dependencies, you may want to formally define recovery operations in the context of Service Level Agreements.

The sections in the SLA Toolkit are

✔ Introduction

✔ Scope of Work

✔ Performance, Tracking, and Reporting

✔ Problem Management

✔ Compensation

✔ Customer Duties and Responsibilities

✔ Warranties and Remedies

✔ Security

✔ Intellectual Property Rights and Confidential Information

✔ Legal Compliance and Resolution of Disputes

- ✔ Termination
- ✔ General
- ✔ Signatures
- ✔ Schedules

If your organization already uses SLAs extensively, you probably don't need this tool. But if you're considering SLAs, this tool may help you to better understand their structure and content.

LBL ContingencyPro Software

www.rothstein.com/data/dr743.htm

This Web-based browser software tool automates the entire business continuity plan development process and provides an effective method for maintaining the plan. The software is a knowledge-based system that certified business continuity planning experts developed.

The knowledge base in this software product contains best practices for business continuity planning, as well as hundreds of electronic tools, guides, templates, and samples. These systems are fully integrated with the Microsoft Office Suite, so you should be able to use them easily and intuitively. The software is based on a proven methodology that has successfully helped organizations recover from actual disaster events.

Emergency Management Guide for Business and Industry

www.fema.gov/pdf/business/guide/bizindst.pdf

This 67-page guide for emergency planning, response, and recovery claims to work for companies of all sizes. Produced by the U.S. Federal Emergency Management Agency (FEMA), the guide contains the following sections:

- ✔ Step 1: Establish a planning team.
- ✔ Step 2: Analyze capabilities and hazards.
- ✔ Step 3: Develop the plan.
- ✔ Step 4: Implement the plan.

✔ Emergency management considerations.

✔ Hazard-specific information. Includes fire, hazardous materials, floods, hurricanes, tornadoes, severe storms, earthquakes, and technology emergencies.

This FEMA guide is a pre-9/11 document. As I describe in Chapter 13, the September 11, 2001 attacks did change how professionals think about disaster recovery planning, but the basics in this guide are still valid.

DRJ's Toolbox

www.drj.com/new2dr/toolchest/drjtools.htm

This page is the *Disaster Recovery Journal's* own list of tools and resources. The site changes from time to time when new tools and resources become available. As I write this, the site contains the following sections:

✔ **Sample Requests for Proposal (RFP):** Several sample RFPs for planning software and DR services. *RFPs* are documents that you send to suppliers as a way of formally requesting a proposal for products or services.

✔ **Sample DR Plans:** You can download several sample plans. Seeing how someone else put a plan together can help spark ideas of your own.

✔ **Current Regulations:** Information about regulations that may influence an organization's disaster recovery planning effort.

✔ **White Papers:** Several papers on various topics, including terrorism, insurance, Business Impact Analyses, legal issues, and the impact of disasters on shareholder value.

✔ **Online Resources:** Links to other sites that contain valuable DR information.

Chapter 15

Eleven Disaster Recovery Planning Web Sites

. . . .

In This Chapter

▶ Receiving disaster recovery education and professional certification

▶ Finding resources for disaster recovery planners

▶ Networking through DR professional organizations

. . . .

*I*nformation about disaster recovery planning is updated at the speed of thought. By the time this book is in your hands, a whole new set of DR-related developments, incidents, and issues may exist.

You may also want to pursue professional certifications. Some of the organizations I talk about in this chapter offer certifications related to disaster recovery planning and business continuity planning.

DRI International

www.drii.org

DRI International was founded in 1988, and then named the Disaster Recovery Institute. DRII provides education programs and certification services to disaster recovery planning professionals. Today, over 3,500 professionals maintain professional certification through DRII.

The certifications offered by the DRII are

- ✔ Associate Business Continuity Professional (ABCP)
- ✔ Certified Business Continuity Professional (CBCP)
- ✔ Certified Functional Continuity Professional (CFCP)
- ✔ Master Business Continuity Professional (MBCP)

These four certifications represent levels of expertise and years of experience in disaster recovery and business continuity. The Web site also provides a search capability which you can use to locate DRII-certified professionals anywhere in the world.

Disaster Recovery Journal

www.drj.com

This extensive and rich Web site contains information on these topics:

- Chat boards and blogs
- Bookstore
- Vendor directory
- Events
- Tools
- Career center
- Additional resources

The *Disaster Recovery Journal* is also an in-print magazine. DRJ also organizes an annual conference called DRJ World.

This is my personal favorite Web site about DR planning.

Business Continuity Management Institute

www.bcm-institute.org

BCMI is a business continuity and disaster recovery organization that specializes in education and certification. BCMI targets individuals who don't have access to other DR planning and BC planning education where they live.

The certifications that BCMI offers are

- **Business Continuity Certified Planner (BCCP):** A foundation-level certification for practitioners who are involved in the development, implementation, and maintenance of business continuity plans.

- **Disaster Recovery Certified Specialist (DRCS):** A specialist-level certification for those who oversee specific DR planning areas in IT hardware, software, infrastructure, and applications.

- ✔ **Business Continuity Certified Specialist (BCCS):** A specialist-level certification for those who act as BC planning project coordinators.

- ✔ **Disaster Recovery Certified Expert (DRCE):** An expert-level certification for those who manage and drive organization-wide disaster recovery projects.

- ✔ **Business Continuity Certified Expert (BCCE):** An expert-level certification for those who manage and drive business continuity projects.

BCMI offers a rich curriculum of training in over a dozen topics, ranging from foundation to expert level, in business continuity, disaster recovery, crisis management, audit, and pandemic planning.

BCMI is a co-organizer of the World Continuity Congress, an annual conference dedicated to business continuity and disaster recovery planning. The annual conference is held in Singapore, and it's a replacement for the old DRI Asia conferences held there. The Web site for the conference is www.world continuitycongress.com.

Disaster Recovery World

www.disasterrecoveryworld.com

Disaster Recovery World is a small Web site that contains basic information and opportunities to purchase the following resources:

- ✔ The BCP Generator
- ✔ The SLA Toolkit
- ✔ Disaster Recovery Toolkit

It contains links to other sites with information on risk analysis and risk assessment methodologies, which are a key part of a Business Impact Analysis (BIA). Other pages contain samples and resources of interest to DR planners.

Disaster Recovery Planning.org

www.drplanning.org

Disaster Recovery Planning.org serves as a vendor-neutral clearinghouse for disaster recovery planning and business continuity planning, for both first-time planners and those with experience.

Disaster Recovery Planning.org claims that you don't need DR planning certification to add to your career portfolio. I suggest you do further research to determine what's best for your own career path.

The site includes a generic planning model and other resources for DR planners.

The Business Continuity Institute

www.thebci.org

The Business Continuity Institute (BCI) is a membership organization dedicated to the promotion of business continuity management worldwide. The BCI has over 4,000 members in more than 85 countries.

The benefits of BCI membership include

- ✔ **The prestige of membership:** They don't take just anybody's money; you have to qualify to belong to the BCI by taking an examination that assesses your skills and experience.

- ✔ **Access to other BCI members:** The Web site has Members Only pages that enable members to contact other members.

- ✔ **Access to published work:** The Web site has published articles available to its members.

- ✔ **Post and search open positions:** Whether members are seeking experts to add to their staffs or looking for employment themselves, the BCI lists open positions at no charge to members (and only members can list positions).

- ✔ **Discounts:** BCI offers discounts for training courses, conferences, seminars, books, and Professional Indemnity Insurance.

- ✔ **The *BCI Quarterly Journal:*** This quarterly journal has articles on various business continuity topics.

- ✔ **BCI Forums:** BCI holds these events in many countries throughout the world.

The BCI offers several certifications:

- ✔ **Associate of the Business Continuity Institute (ABCI):** Requires a minimum of six months of business continuity management and experience within the scope of all ten BCI certification standards.

- ✔ **Specialist of the Business Continuity Institute (SBCI):** Requires a minimum of two years full-time experience in business continuity management and a good knowledge of at least six of the ten certification standards.

✔ **Member of the Business Continuity Institute (MBCI):** Requires a minimum of two years working experience across all ten BCI certification standards.

✔ **Fellow of the Business Continuity Institute (FBCI):** Requires at least five years of full-time experience with all ten BCI certification standards and the demonstration of a thorough knowledge and understanding of the standards. You must have been a member for two years.

Disaster-Resource.com

www.disaster-resource.com

Disaster-Resource.com contains resources for executives, managers, and planners in need of basic crisis management, emergency management, and business continuity information. The site contains an online disaster resource guide that helps you find information, vendors, organizations, and other resources.

Disaster-Resource.com is operated by Emergency Lifeline Corporation, an organization that provides disaster preparedness products to corporations, government agencies, schools, and families.

It publishes the *Disaster Resource Guide,* a printed resource for organizations and government agencies that want to prepare for emergencies. The *Guide* contains articles and information from internationally recognized experts. Emergency Lifeline Corporation mails the *Guide* to qualifying subscribers free of charge.

Computerworld Disaster Recovery

www.computerworld.com

From the main page, click Knowledge Centers⇨Security⇨Disaster Recovery to get to Computerworld's main Disaster Recovery site that contains news, articles, and resources.

Computerworld has been around since computers were made from vacuum tubes and pulleys (well, almost). Their DR planning page includes a lot of news, features, and columns on disaster recovery planning. They keep the content fresh and up to date with the latest information that you need to keep your DR plans relevant and effective.

CSO Business Continuity and Disaster Recovery

www.csoonline.com/research/continuity

CSO Magazine is a great print magazine and Web site, both of which feature strategic level features, articles, columns, and interviews. Their business continuity and disaster recovery site includes many good articles from past issues of *CSO Magazine*.

You can also subscribe to online newsletters about DR planning and BC planning by visiting www.csoonline.com/newsletters. Just select the check box to the left of CSO Continuity & Recovery, enter your e-mail address in the E-Mail Address text box, and click the Subscribe button.

Federal Emergency Management Agency (FEMA)

www.fema.gov/business

A division of the U.S. Department of Homeland Security (DHS), the FEMA Business Web site has many good resources for businesses, including

- **Protect your business from disasters.** Resources for preparation from various natural disasters.

- **Emergency Management Guide For Business & Industry.** A 67-page guide to emergency planning, response, and recovery for companies of all sizes.

- **Standard Checklist Criteria For Business Recovery.** A four-section checklist that helps a business develop its own business recovery manual.

- **Flood hazard mapping.** Information to help businesses better understand the risks associated with specific locations.

- **Flood Insurance.** Information for claims adjusters, lenders, insurance agents, realtors, and so on.

Rothstein Associates Inc.

www.rothstein.com

Operated by Philip Jan Rothstein, FBCI, this Web site is dedicated to business continuity planning, disaster recovery planning, and service level management. This is one of the most extensive sites on BC planning and DR planning that I've ever seen! The Web site features

- ✔ **Articles:** A rich collection of articles on disaster recovery planning and business continuity planning.

- ✔ **The Rothstein Catalog of Disaster Recovery:** Books, CDs, and videos on disaster recovery planning. On its own, this catalog is the mother of all DR planning and BC planning resources, with more books, tools, and instructional videos than you can find anywhere else on the Internet!

- ✔ **Links:** A large collection of links to other useful sites on disaster recovery planning and business continuity planning.

- ✔ **Newsletter:** A quarterly newsletter with articles and other information.

- ✔ **Forum:** Online interactive forum.

- ✔ **Books:** A catalog of several books that the site offers for sale.

Chapter 16

Ten Essentials for Disaster Planning Success

*Y*ou need to understand many factors that lead to a successful project and disaster recovery plan before you begin a DR project. I start with executive sponsorship, which is probably the most vital factor. Then I cover other up-front formalities so your organization can understand the level of effort you need from the DR planning team to complete a successful DR project.

Executive Sponsorship

As go its leaders, so goes the organization.

An organization undertakes disaster recovery planning because company shareholders want the organization to survive through difficult times, including disasters that threaten its very existence. A DR project needs executive sponsorship in two key areas:

✔ **Prioritization of key subject matter experts:** Disaster recovery planning requires the best and brightest minds in the organization. You need the employees who are the most familiar with business operations to perform the Business Impact Analysis and risk analysis, as well as develop disaster recovery procedures. They also need to perform walkthroughs, simulations, and parallel/cutover testing.

Without executive sponsorship, these individuals are pulled in too many directions at the same time, which can threaten to stall the entire effort.

✔ **Spending priorities:** You need executive sponsorship to ensure that you can improve IT systems to support established Recovery Time Objectives (RTOs) and Recovery Point Objectives (RPOs). You may need significant investments in IT systems, infrastructure, and software.

Well-Defined Scope

Before a DR project can get under way, you need to define the precise scope of the project. Spell out exactly which business processes are in and which are out.

You can best define the scope and other key points of your DR project in a charter document. A *charter* is a formal document that defines the project as follows:

✔ **Project definition:** A statement, usually not exceeding a paragraph or two, that describes the project at a high level. A generic definition for a DR project might be something like, "Determine the priority of key business processes, including their Maximum Tolerable Downtime (MTD), Recovery Time Objective (RTO), and Recovery Point Objective (RPO). Define and fund necessary capital improvements in IT systems, and develop and test recovery procedures."

✔ **Executive sponsors:** The names of the executives who are sponsoring the project. These individuals are responsible for allocating resources (staff and budget) to support the DR project. They commit to its completion according to the key milestones that the charter defines.

✔ **Project objectives:** The desired outcomes from the project.

✔ **Project scope:** Defines which parts of the business you include in the project and which parts you don't. When you complete this project successfully, you can start new DR projects that include other parts of the business.

✔ **Key milestones:** Dates by which you want to accomplish key milestones. Here are some sample dates:

- **Sept 30, 2009:** Business Impact Analysis completed.

- **March 30, 2010:** Recovery procedures completed.

- **June 30, 2010:** Recovery procedures tested.

✔ **Key responsibilities:** Key individuals who have specific responsibilities through the entire project.

✔ **Sources of funding:** There's no such thing as a free lunch. Where do you plan to get the money for this DR project?

✔ **Signatures:** The signatures of the executive sponsors, as well as other key individuals named in the charter. Include the department heads from all departments whose resources you need for the project.

Make the charter a public document within the organization. Announce the DR project and make the charter available for reference.

Committed Resources

A DR project without people to work towards its objectives isn't a DR project at all, but only an idea. Ideas — even good ones — can't save the business if disaster strikes, and the organization can't benefit if the DR project doesn't get any resources.

Management needs to make specific commitments of specific resources and adjust certain named individuals' time and priorities. For instance, management may need to define a certain numbers of hours per week or percentage of hours worked by DR team members so the project can make the desired amount of forward progress. For instance, you could define the priorities for a system engineer's time like this:

✔ **First priority:** Critical system outages

✔ **Second priority:** Top-priority service requests

✔ **Third priority:** Disaster recovery procedure development

✔ **Fourth priority:** Medium-priority service requests

The preceding list may be a little simplistic, but these kinds of priorities — in writing — help staff members make task decisions without constant management guidance.

If staff members account for their time in weekly status reports, they should include time spent on the DR project so you can track the actual effort required to sustain the project.

The Right Experts

The ultimate success of your DR project rests in the accuracy and completeness of all the disaster recovery procedures. Those staff members and managers who are most familiar with critical business processes and the IT systems that support them need to develop and test the DR procedures.

If you place recovery procedure development in less capable hands, you end up with lower quality recovery procedures that take more time to review and improve. You'll need more time to get the project to a point at which you have adequate recovery plans.

Management needs to determine when to bring in consultants, primarily for their expertise, but also for their ability to augment the DR plan development effort.

Time to Develop the Project Plan

You need to plan any sizeable project in detail. By any measure, a DR project is a sizeable project: It requires participation from many people in different departments, and it needs to be successful.

You must identify every task required to complete the project, and identify and quantify all necessary resources — who, how much time, and how much funding you need, as well as dependencies between tasks. Only after you manage these details can you track the DR project week by week and manage it as a real project.

If you launch a DR project before you develop a plan, executive management can't put much faith in the stated milestones. Don't put a stake in the ground and declare that you'll complete the project by a specific date before you know whether that date is realistic. Your project's outcome may be compromised — it's either of poor quality or late.

Remember this saying: Good, fast, or cheap — pick any two.

Support from All Stakeholders

A DR project requires support not only from IT, but also from line managers, middle managers, and executive managers in the departments that operate critical processes. Other departments that may play a part in DR planning include

- Project Management Office (PMO), if such a department exists and manages enterprise-wide projects
- Human Resources (HR)
- Facilities
- Finance or Accounting
- Legal

> ✔ Security
>
> ✔ External Affairs, or whoever's responsible for communications to customers or shareholders

Define support from every key department in writing and include those definitions in the DR project charter described in the section "Well-Defined Scope," earlier in this chapter, and in Chapter 1. Require the department heads from every department that manages resources the DR project to sign the charter, as well.

Testing, Testing, Testing

A disaster recovery plan that you haven't tested is worth only the paper that you write it on (or the hard drive that you store it on). Until you thoroughly test all the recovery procedures, the organization shouldn't expect those procedures to save it from ruin if a disaster strikes.

You need to perform five types of testing on all disaster recovery procedures:

> ✔ **Paper:** An individual reads through a recovery procedure and makes any annotations or suggested corrections.
>
> ✔ **Walkthrough:** A recovery team reviews the recovery procedure, step by step. Issues and discussions fill the day.
>
> ✔ **Simulation:** A recovery team walks through a scripted simulation, discussing assessment and recovery procedures so they can determine whether a disaster recovery plan is reasonable.
>
> ✔ **Parallel:** A recovery team tests recovery procedures by actually building or setting up recovery systems. The team also performs test transactions on the systems to see how well the procedures work and whether team members can actually build and operate the recovery systems.
>
> ✔ **Cutover:** A recovery team performs a full *cutover,* in which recovery systems that the recovery team build or prepare on short notice support live business processes. This is the ultimate test of a DR plan.

I cover testing fully in Chapter 10.

Full Lifecycle Commitment

You aren't finished with the DR project when you successfully complete the last test. That's only the end of the first trip around the lifecycle. You must perpetually commit to the following DR plan activities:

- ✔ **Periodic testing:** Test all DR procedures regularly, according to a schedule that fits the risks associated with the individual business processes being supported. For example, life-support processes probably deserve weekly or monthly cutover testing, but you can test less critical processes less often. This testing process includes not only repeated walkthroughs, but also scheduled simulations, parallel tests, and cutover tests. You should perform a parallel or cutover test at least once per year.

- ✔ **Periodic review:** Have subject matter experts review disaster recovery procedures at least two to four times each year to ensure that those procedures are still relevant and accurate. Review emergency contact lists monthly.

- ✔ **Periodic revisions:** Periodic testing and review indicate when you need to update recovery plans and emergency contact lists.

- ✔ **Business Impact Analysis and risk analysis review:** Review the BIA and risk analysis documents at least once per year to ensure that key objectives, such as the Recovery Time Objective (RTO) and Recovery Point Objective (RPO), are still adequate.

- ✔ **Integration into business processes:** Business activities such as system upgrades, mergers and acquisitions, and new product or service launches should include routine reviews of BIA, risk analysis, and other DR documents to ensure that they remain current and relevant.

Integration into Other Processes

Don't make DR planning an island that you visit only now and again. If your organization considers disaster recovery planning a one-off or overlay, it's short-changing itself and missing opportunities to improve its DR plans. DR must become a way of life for many in the organization.

Several business processes should automatically include review of and possible revisions to the BIA (Business Impact Analysis), risk analysis, and disaster recovery procedures:

- ✔ **Major application upgrade or migration:** Any time you upgrade an IT application that supports a critical business process or migrate that application to a new platform, you should, at the very least, review and update disaster recovery procedures, as needed. During a migration to a new IT application, you may also need to revise the BIA and risk analysis. A major upgrade or migration project should include review and revisions to DR documents; otherwise, the organization may wait far too long to upgrade these documents. If a disaster occurs before you upgrade your DR documents, you drastically reduce your ability to recover those systems.

✔ **Business relocation:** If the business changes locations or adds more office space in the same or a different city, you need to revisit recovery plans to make sure they're still valid.

✔ **Merger or acquisition:** If another organization acquires your organization, or your organization acquires another organization or merges with an organization, the fundamental mission and financial profile for the organization changes considerably. You need to conduct a top-down revision to the entire DR plan, starting with the BIA and risk analysis, and continuing with revisions to all recovery procedures.

✔ **Changing market conditions:** Fundamental changes in the market, such as the entry or exit of a major competitor or a change in the structure of the market, call for a reassessment of the Business Impact Analysis and risk assessment. You may also need to make revisions to recovery procedures.

✔ **New service or product launch:** In addition to requiring disaster recovery capabilities, a new service or product launch may reposition other business processes, making some more important and others less important. You may have to deal with fundamental changes in your organization's investment in recovery capabilities.

✔ **Change in senior or executive management:** Changes in upper management sometimes lead to strategic changes in direction. Document any such changes and analyze their impact on the existing BIA and risk assessments.

Luck

Wiktionary defines luck as, "Something that happens to someone by chance, a chance occurrence."

The role of luck in disaster recovery planning deals with whether your organization experiences a disaster that threatens its survival. And your organization is pretty lucky if no disaster occurs, at least until you complete your DR plan.

Seneca, the Roman dramatist, supposedly said, "Luck is what happens when preparation meets opportunity." The preparation involves your DR planning, which gets you ready to face the opportunity of a disaster. And yes, I do mean opportunity. Disasters and other difficulties give you opportunities for greatness.

This quote from Edna Mote in the Disney film *The Incredibles* says it all: "Luck favors the prepared, darling."

Chapter 17

Ten Benefits of DR Planning

*N*ASA's work over the past forty years has supposedly led to the development of everyday products and services that millions of people enjoy today. Similarly, organizations that undertake disaster recovery planning enjoy a number of spin-off benefits that help the organization, even if a disaster never occurs.

Improved Chances of Surviving "The Big One"

No organization is immune from the effects of natural and man-made disasters. The only question is, does the organization invest in processes and systems that can assure its survival from any disaster?

Although I can't guarantee that every organization with a solid DR plan can survive any disaster, an organization with a DR plan is far more likely to survive than an organization that doesn't have such a plan. *Contingency Planning and Management Magazine* indicated that 40 percent of companies that had to shut down for three days or more failed within 36 months. This statistic should remind you that failure in your DR planning isn't an option.

A Rung or Two Up the Maturity Ladder

Carnegie Mellon University measures the maturity of business processes by using the Capability Maturity Model (CMM), developed by Carnegie Mellon's Software Engineering Institute (SEI).

The CMM has five levels. According to the SEI, "Predictability, effectiveness, and control of an organization's software processes are believed to improve as the organization moves up these five levels. While not rigorous, the empirical evidence to date supports this belief."

Here are the CMM's five levels:

- **Level 1 — Initial:** Processes are usually ad hoc. You don't even write them down, or you document them in informal ways. The organization abandons processes in times of stress. Success in the organization depends on heroics, not processes.

- **Level 2 — Repeatable:** You more formally document processes and can repeat those processes, even in times of stress. You manage projects by using project plans.

- **Level 3 — Defined:** You establish and improve processes over time. Processes drive consistency throughout the organization. Processes are only qualitatively predictable.

- **Level 4 — Quantitatively managed:** You establish, periodically improve, and measure processes. You also establish objectives for process performance. Process performance is quantitatively predictable.

- **Level 5 — Optimizing:** Incremental improvements and technology innovation improve processes. You can set process improvement objectives. You can address and measure causes of process variations, instead of simply considering those variations aberrations.

For more information about the Capability Maturity Model, check out www.sei.cmu.edu/cmmi.

Opportunities for Process Improvements

Disaster recovery planning puts the microscope to the processes and procedures that support the most critical activities in an organization. Throughout the process of analyzing and developing disaster recovery plans for a process, you may experience one or more instances of, "Hey, we can be doing *this* better!"

The activities in which you most likely find process improvements are

- ✔ **Business Impact Analysis (BIA):** Analysts take a close look at a business process to determine its participants, critical assets and systems that support the process, critical suppliers, and how you measure and manage the process. Indeed, a business process may get its closest scrutiny during a BIA. If the people performing the BIA are trained to look for improvement opportunities, they'll find them.

- ✔ **Risk analysis:** During the BIA, analysts seek and identify process risk areas, and they look for ways to reduce the risks that they find. Analysts probably identify the most significant improvements to processes and architecture during this process.

- ✔ **Recovery plan development:** When you develop the actual recovery procedures for a process, you need to take a very close look at that process and how it's performed in normal situations. If you're paying attention, you might find flaws or opportunities for improvement in the process you're working with.

- ✔ **Recovery plan walkthroughs:** Staff members who perform walkthroughs may, as they ponder and discuss individual steps in recovery procedures, discover opportunities for improving day-to-day processes and procedures. You might hear someone say, "If we do *this* in a recovery procedure, we can do *that* during normal periods and save time (or money, mistakes, and so on)."

- ✔ **Simulations, parallel tests, and cutover tests:** While performing actual recovery procedures in testing exercises, staff members may make crucial discoveries about the ways in which your organization performs processes, thus finding ways to optimize processes and reduce mistakes. One of the reasons that you need a scribe or record keeper during tests is to capture these opportunities.

Opportunities for Technology Improvements

One of the objectives of disaster recovery planning is to make systems more resilient so you can reduce disasters related to flaws in systems and architectures. When the DR planning team performs the Business Impact Analysis (BIA) and establishes key metrics, including the Maximum Tolerable Downtime (MTD), Recovery Time Objective (RTO), and Recovery Point Objective (RPO), team members can make key decisions to improve the architecture of IT systems so your organization can meet these objectives.

Higher Quality and Availability of Systems

One of the objectives of disaster recovery planning is to improve the resiliency of the IT systems that support the organization's most critical business processes. When you establish key time-related objectives, such as the Recovery Time Objective (RTO) and Recovery Point Objective (RPO), the DR project team should make improvements in the IT systems and infrastructure that support those critical business processes. Here are the changes you can make:

- Improve storage systems, including RAID, mirroring, replication, and better backups.

- Improve servers, including greater server consistency.

- Improve hardware, including redundant power supplies.

- Establish or improve the change management process to better manage changes that you make to servers and infrastructure.

- Establish or improve configuration management capabilities to better track changes that you make to systems and other components.

- Establish or improve server cluster utilization.

- Establish or improve power management systems, including Uninterruptible Power Supplies (UPSs) and generators.

Reducing Disruptive Events

One of the objectives of disaster recovery planning is to improve the resiliency of the IT systems that support critical business processes. This improved resiliency leads to fewer disruptions of those business processes when these events occur:

- **Hard drive failure:** No problem, you have one of these contingencies:

  - You have RAID technology now and will replace the hard drive during the next maintenance period.

  - You have on-site spares.

  - You can recover from backups.

  - The other server in the cluster can take over operations.

- ✔ **Power supply failure:** No problem, either

  - You have systems with redundant power supplies.

  - The other server in the cluster can take over operations.

- ✔ **Short power outage:** No problem, the UPS takes over instantaneously and can support critical systems and HVAC for up to 30 minutes.

- ✔ **Extended power outage:** No problem, the UPS takes over instantaneously, and the electric generator starts momentarily and can supply power for up to two days. After that, you can get deliveries of fuel, if needed.

- ✔ **Fire in the data center:** Quite a problem, but you have options:

  - You can recover data in your alternate processing center tomorrow.

  - Servers in the alternate processing center can take over momentarily.

  Which option you choose depends on how quickly you need those recovery servers to be on-line.

- ✔ **Earthquake:** Quite a problem, but you can set up one of two plans:

  - You can recover data in your alternate processing center tomorrow.

  - Servers in the alternate processing center can take over momentarily.

- ✔ **Your disaster scenario:** Your systems architecture provides a defined level of resilience, and your recovery procedures can guide you to a predictable recovery well within established timelines.

When these disruptive events occur, your organization can survive them because you developed response and recovery plans that get your critical systems back online in whatever timelines you establish.

Reducing Insurance Premiums

If your organization has purchased one or more policies that insure the organization against the losses associated with disasters, the insurance company that issues the premium probably offers discounts if you take certain measures to reduce the likelihood and impact of common disaster scenarios.

Having an insurance policy against disasters is an essential part of the overall plan because your organization may need the infusion of cash such a policy provides to get you through the events that unfold in a disaster. But you need the preparation and resilience that you develop during the DR project just as much.

Finding Out Who Your Leaders Are

A vital part of the disaster recovery planning lifecycle involves testing disaster response and recovery procedures. When you involve all the key personnel in testing, you may find some of the results pleasantly surprising:

- **Simulation testing:** Sequester the recovery team for a day or longer, and put them through their paces in a realistic disaster scenario. The participants perform the procedures, starting with disaster declaration and continuing with emergency communications, disaster assessment, and commencement of recovery operations. Throughout this exercise, you may witness the natural leadership abilities of one or more people as they go through the paces.

- **Parallel testing:** In this challenging endeavor, the disaster response team follows procedures to get recovery systems up and running. This test isn't easy: The team has to deal with problems and challenges that no one anticipated during walkthrough testing. Often, the entire team needs to cooperate to overcome these barriers. Stress and challenge provide opportunities for leadership: Natural leaders step up and help the entire team successfully complete its objectives.

- **Cutover testing:** This is the most stressful DR test because recovery systems actually support critical business processes. In this DR test, failure or delay isn't an option. If you have any born leaders on the team, you may see their leadership in action as the team pushes through the barriers together to get recovery systems running and supporting the business.

I cover DR testing in Chapter 10.

Complying with Standards and Regulations

Disaster recovery planning has historically been an optional endeavor for organizations that develop the will to survive a disaster. Increasingly, disaster recovery planning has progressed from being a good idea to being required by standards and regulations.

These common standards require a measure of business continuity planning and disaster recovery planning:

- **PCI DSS (Payment Card Industry Data Security Standard):** Version 1.1 of PCI states in section 12.9.1, "Create the incident response plan to be implemented in the event of system compromise. Ensure the plan addresses, at a minimum, specific incident response procedures, *business recovery and continuity procedures,* data backup processes, roles and responsibilities, and communication and contact strategies (for example, informing the Acquirers and credit card associations)." (The emphasis is mine.)

✔ **HIPAA (Health Insurance Portability and Accountability Act):** HIPAA's Security Rule contains many requirements to protect electronic patient health information (EPHI) from unauthorized access. HIPAA also requires the availability of EPHI (to health care workers when needed), including a disaster recovery plan to ensure its availability. Section 164.308(a)(7)(i) includes the following language:

> "Standard: Contingency plan. Establish (and implement as needed) policies and procedures for responding to an emergency or other occurrence (for example, fire, vandalism, system failure, and natural disaster) that damages systems that contain electronic protected health information."

Section 164.308(a)(7)(ii)(B) specifies how you must carry out this requirement:

> "Implementation specifications:
>
> (A) Data backup plan (Required). Establish and implement procedures to create and maintain retrievable exact copies of electronic protected health information.
>
> (B) Disaster recovery plan (Required). Establish (and implement as needed) procedures to restore any loss of data.
>
> (C) Emergency mode operation plan (Required). Establish (and implement as needed) procedures to enable continuation of critical business processes for protection of the security of electronic protected health information while operating in emergency mode.
>
> (D) Testing and revision procedures (Addressable). Implement procedures for periodic testing and revision of contingency plans.
>
> (E) Applications and data criticality analysis (Addressable). Assess the relative criticality of specific applications and data in support of other contingency plan components."

✔ **ISO27001:** Section A.14 of this internationally known standard for information security management contains five distinct requirements for the establishment and testing of business continuity and disaster recovery plans.

Other regulations dealing with data privacy and protection imply the need for disaster recovery planning as a means to protect information from corruption and loss. Over time, I believe national, regional, and state/provincial laws in many countries will include more requirements concerning disaster recovery planning.

You can find the PCI standard at `www.pcisecuritystandards.org`.

HIPAA is available online at `www.cms.hhs.gov/SecurityStandard/Downloads/securityfinalrule.pdf`.

You can't get ISO27001 except by purchasing it. You can buy it from the International Standards Organization at `www.iso.org`. Type `27001` into the Search text box and click Search.

Competitive Advantage

Organizations are locked in an endless competitive struggle against their peers in the marketplace. Because more organizations are going global and adopting just-in-time processes that require continuous availability and service levels, organizations need to always be available and functioning.

Even though businesses need to be more and more available, disasters continue to occur, many of which you have no control over. Organizations that become more resilient do so through disaster recovery planning and business continuity planning.

Organizations that have mature DR plans can truly say to their customers, "We will be there for you, whenever you need us, even if a disaster strikes. You can rely on us — no matter what." Thus, disaster recovery can become one more competitive differentiator. Organizations with strong DR plans can say, "We are better than our competitors because we have DR plans that will make us available in any circumstance."

Index

BUSINESS, CAREERS & PERSONAL FINANCE

0-7645-9847-3

0-7645-2431-3

Also available:
- Business Plans Kit For Dummies
  0-7645-9794-9
- Economics For Dummies
  0-7645-5726-2
- Grant Writing For Dummies
  0-7645-8416-2
- Home Buying For Dummies
  0-7645-5331-3
- Managing For Dummies
  0-7645-1771-6
- Marketing For Dummies
  0-7645-5600-2

- Personal Finance For Dummies
  0-7645-2590-5*
- Resumes For Dummies
  0-7645-5471-9
- Selling For Dummies
  0-7645-5363-1
- Six Sigma For Dummies
  0-7645-6798-5
- Small Business Kit For Dummies
  0-7645-5984-2
- Starting an eBay Business For Dummies
  0-7645-6924-4
- Your Dream Career For Dummies
  0-7645-9795-7

HOME & BUSINESS COMPUTER BASICS

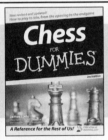

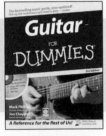

0-470-05432-8

0-471-75421-8

Also available:
- Cleaning Windows Vista For Dummies
  0-471-78293-9
- Excel 2007 For Dummies
  0-470-03737-7
- Mac OS X Tiger For Dummies
  0-7645-7675-5
- MacBook For Dummies
  0-470-04859-X
- Macs For Dummies
  0-470-04849-2
- Office 2007 For Dummies
  0-470-00923-3

- Outlook 2007 For Dummies
  0-470-03830-6
- PCs For Dummies
  0-7645-8958-X
- Salesforce.com For Dummies
  0-470-04893-X
- Upgrading & Fixing Laptops For Dummies
  0-7645-8959-8
- Word 2007 For Dummies
  0-470-03658-3
- Quicken 2007 For Dummies
  0-470-04600-7

FOOD, HOME, GARDEN, HOBBIES, MUSIC & PETS

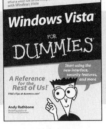

0-7645-8404-9

0-7645-9904-6

Also available:
- Candy Making For Dummies
  0-7645-9734-5
- Card Games For Dummies
  0-7645-9910-0
- Crocheting For Dummies
  0-7645-4151-X
- Dog Training For Dummies
  0-7645-8418-9
- Healthy Carb Cookbook For Dummies
  0-7645-8476-6
- Home Maintenance For Dummies
  0-7645-5215-5

- Horses For Dummies
  0-7645-9797-3
- Jewelry Making & Beading For Dummies
  0-7645-2571-9
- Orchids For Dummies
  0-7645-6759-4
- Puppies For Dummies
  0-7645-5255-4
- Rock Guitar For Dummies
  0-7645-5356-9
- Sewing For Dummies
  0-7645-6847-7
- Singing For Dummies
  0-7645-2475-5

INTERNET & DIGITAL MEDIA

0-470-04529-9

0-470-04894-8

Also available:
- Blogging For Dummies
  0-471-77084-1
- Digital Photography For Dummies
  0-7645-9802-3
- Digital Photography All-in-One Desk Reference For Dummies
  0-470-03743-1
- Digital SLR Cameras and Photography For Dummies
  0-7645-9803-1
- eBay Business All-in-One Desk Reference For Dummies
  0-7645-8438-3
- HDTV For Dummies
  0-470-09673-X

- Home Entertainment PCs For Dummies
  0-470-05523-5
- MySpace For Dummies
  0-470-09529-6
- Search Engine Optimization For Dummies
  0-471-97998-8
- Skype For Dummies
  0-470-04891-3
- The Internet For Dummies
  0-7645-8996-2
- Wiring Your Digital Home For Dummies
  0-471-91830-X

* Separate Canadian edition also available
† Separate U.K. edition also available

Available wherever books are sold. For more information or to order direct: U.S. customers visit www.dummies.com or call 1-877-762-2974.
U.K. customers visit www.wileyeurope.com or call 0800 243407. Canadian customers visit www.wiley.ca or call 1-800-567-4797.

SPORTS, FITNESS, PARENTING, RELIGION & SPIRITUALITY

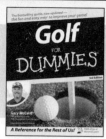

0-471-76871-5

0-7645-7841-3

Also available:
- Catholicism For Dummies
  0-7645-5391-7
- Exercise Balls For Dummies
  0-7645-5623-1
- Fitness For Dummies
  0-7645-7851-0
- Football For Dummies
  0-7645-3936-1
- Judaism For Dummies
  0-7645-5299-6
- Potty Training For Dummies
  0-7645-5417-4
- Buddhism For Dummies
  0-7645-5359-3

- Pregnancy For Dummies
  0-7645-4483-7 †
- Ten Minute Tone-Ups For Dummies
  0-7645-7207-5
- NASCAR For Dummies
  0-7645-7681-X
- Religion For Dummies
  0-7645-5264-3
- Soccer For Dummies
  0-7645-5229-5
- Women in the Bible For Dummies
  0-7645-8475-8

TRAVEL

0-7645-7749-2

0-7645-6945-7

Also available:
- Alaska For Dummies
  0-7645-7746-8
- Cruise Vacations For Dummies
  0-7645-6941-4
- England For Dummies
  0-7645-4276-1
- Europe For Dummies
  0-7645-7529-5
- Germany For Dummies
  0-7645-7823-5
- Hawaii For Dummies
  0-7645-7402-7

- Italy For Dummies
  0-7645-7386-1
- Las Vegas For Dummies
  0-7645-7382-9
- London For Dummies
  0-7645-4277-X
- Paris For Dummies
  0-7645-7630-5
- RV Vacations For Dummies
  0-7645-4442-X
- Walt Disney World & Orlando
  For Dummies
  0-7645-9660-8

GRAPHICS, DESIGN & WEB DEVELOPMENT

0-7645-8815-X

0-7645-9571-7

Also available:
- 3D Game Animation For Dummies
  0-7645-8789-7
- AutoCAD 2006 For Dummies
  0-7645-8925-3
- Building a Web Site For Dummies
  0-7645-7144-3
- Creating Web Pages For Dummies
  0-470-08030-2
- Creating Web Pages All-in-One Desk
  Reference For Dummies
  0-7645-4345-8
- Dreamweaver 8 For Dummies
  0-7645-9649-7

- InDesign CS2 For Dummies
  0-7645-9572-5
- Macromedia Flash 8 For Dummies
  0-7645-9691-8
- Photoshop CS2 and Digital
  Photography For Dummies
  0-7645-9580-6
- Photoshop Elements 4 For Dummies
  0-471-77483-9
- Syndicating Web Sites with RSS Feeds
  For Dummies
  0-7645-8848-6
- Yahoo! SiteBuilder For Dummies
  0-7645-9800-7

NETWORKING, SECURITY, PROGRAMMING & DATABASES

0-7645-7728-X

0-471-74940-0

Also available:
- Access 2007 For Dummies
  0-470-04612-0
- ASP.NET 2 For Dummies
  0-7645-7907-X
- C# 2005 For Dummies
  0-7645-9704-3
- Hacking For Dummies
  0-470-05235-X
- Hacking Wireless Networks
  For Dummies
  0-7645-9730-2
- Java For Dummies
  0-470-08716-1

- Microsoft SQL Server 2005 For Dummies
  0-7645-7755-7
- Networking All-in-One Desk Reference
  For Dummies
  0-7645-9939-9
- Preventing Identity Theft For Dummies
  0-7645-7336-5
- Telecom For Dummies
  0-471-77085-X
- Visual Studio 2005 All-in-One Desk
  Reference For Dummies
  0-7645-9775-2
- XML For Dummies
  0-7645-8845-1

HEALTH & SELF-HELP

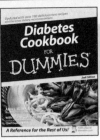

0-7645-8450-2

0-7645-4149-8

Also available:

- Bipolar Disorder For Dummies
  0-7645-8451-0
- Chemotherapy and Radiation
  For Dummies
  0-7645-7832-4
- Controlling Cholesterol For Dummies
  0-7645-5440-9
- Diabetes For Dummies
  0-7645-6820-5* †
- Divorce For Dummies
  0-7645-8417-0 †

- Fibromyalgia For Dummies
  0-7645-5441-7
- Low-Calorie Dieting For Dummies
  0-7645-9905-4
- Meditation For Dummies
  0-471-77774-9
- Osteoporosis For Dummies
  0-7645-7621-6
- Overcoming Anxiety For Dummies
  0-7645-5447-6
- Reiki For Dummies
  0-7645-9907-0
- Stress Management For Dummies
  0-7645-5144-2

EDUCATION, HISTORY, REFERENCE & TEST PREPARATION

0-7645-8381-6

0-7645-9554-7

Also available:

- The ACT For Dummies
  0-7645-9652-7
- Algebra For Dummies
  0-7645-5325-9
- Algebra Workbook For Dummies
  0-7645-8467-7
- Astronomy For Dummies
  0-7645-8465-0
- Calculus For Dummies
  0-7645-2498-4
- Chemistry For Dummies
  0-7645-5430-1
- Forensics For Dummies
  0-7645-5580-4

- Freemasons For Dummies
  0-7645-9796-5
- French For Dummies
  0-7645-5193-0
- Geometry For Dummies
  0-7645-5324-0
- Organic Chemistry I For Dummies
  0-7645-6902-3
- The SAT I For Dummies
  0-7645-7193-1
- Spanish For Dummies
  0-7645-5194-9
- Statistics For Dummies
  0-7645-5423-9

Get smart @ dummies.com®

- **Find a full list of Dummies titles**
- **Look into loads of FREE on-site articles**
- **Sign up for FREE eTips e-mailed to you weekly**
- **See what other products carry the Dummies name**
- **Shop directly from the Dummies bookstore**
- **Enter to win new prizes every month!**

* Separate Canadian edition also available
† Separate U.K. edition also available

Available wherever books are sold. For more information or to order direct: U.S. customers visit www.dummies.com or call 1-877-762-2974.
U.K. customers visit www.wileyeurope.com or call 0800 243407. Canadian customers visit www.wiley.ca or call 1-800-567-4797.